MANAGING THE UNTHINKABLE

MANAGING THE UNTHINKABLE

Crisis Preparation and Response for Campus Leaders

EDITED BY
Gretchen M. Bataille
and Diana I. Cordova

Foreword by John G. Peters,
President Emeritus, Northern Illinois University

STERLING, VIRGINIA

Published by Stylus Publishing, LLC.
22883 Quicksilver Drive
Sterling, Virginia 20166-2102

Library of Congress Cataloging-in-Publication Data
Managing the unthinkable : crisis preparation and response for campus leaders / edited by Gretchen M. Bataille and Diana I. Cordova; foreword by John G. Peters, President Emeritus, Northern Illinois University.—First Edition.
pages cm
ISBN 978-1-62036-071-2 (cloth : alk. paper)
ISBN 978-1-62036-072-9 (pbk. : alk. paper)
ISBN 978-1-62036-073-6 (library networkable e-edition)
ISBN 978-1-62036-074-3 (consumer e-edition)
1. Universities and colleges—Security measures—United States.
2. Universities and colleges—United States—Safety measures.
3. Universities and colleges—United States—Administration.
4. Crisis management—United States. 5. School crisis management—United States. I. Bataille, Gretchen M., 1944– editor of compilation. II. Cordova, Diana I., editor of compilation.
LB2866.M36 2014
371.7'82—dc23

2013047785

13-digit ISBN: 978-1-62036-071-2 (cloth)
13-digit ISBN: 978-1-62036-072-9 (paper)
13-digit ISBN: 978-1-62036-073-6 (library networkable e-edition)
13-digit ISBN 978-1-62036-074-3 (consumer e-edition)

Printed in the United States of America

All first editions printed on acid-free paper that meets the American National Standards Institute Z39-48 Standard.

First Edition, 2014

10 9 8 7 6 5 4 3 2

To the exemplary leaders in higher education who commit themselves to ensuring safe campuses for students and to sharing their wisdom with a new generation of campus leaders.

CONTENTS

FOREWORD

On February 14, 2008, Valentine's Day, I was sitting in my office looking forward to dinner that evening with my spouse and a few close friends. I received a phone call from Northern Illinois University's (NIU) chief operating officer, informing me that there was a confirmed report of a shooting on campus and that our crisis management response plan should be activated. A lone shooter broke into a large lecture hall where 160 students were attending a general education geography class. He opened fire and killed 5 students, 4 women and 1 man, and wounded about 30 others, some severely. He turned the gun on himself as our security force was about to enter the classroom.

The unthinkable had happened. In the span of a few brief minutes, a single, unanticipated, horrific event drastically altered the focus of our academic community and challenged the leadership, governance, and reputation of our university. I was stunned and devastated, as were the members of the senior leadership team, the entire university, our alumni, and the greater DeKalb community.

Immediately, we were faced with myriad decisions and considerations that have become all too familiar with such episodes: tending to the needs of the victims and their families; securing the safety and counseling needs of the campus; dealing with the onslaught of media coverage and the requests from public officials for information; planning vigils, a memorial ceremony, and a permanent memorial for our fallen students; communicating transparently and often with the university's internal and external stakeholders about the status of the tragedy; and commencing the long and arduous process of grieving, healing, and recovery.

On February 14, 2013, NIU held a remembrance ceremony, marking the fifth anniversary of the darkest day in our history. The campus has moved forward with a sense of caring for one another, and although much has returned to normal, the healing and recovery continues, and will for some time. As I reflect on that day and its aftermath, I am thankful to all those who provided valuable insights and recommendations on how to prepare and respond to such episodes. Without the lessons learned from the Virginia Tech tragedy, my campus would not have engaged in a review and update of our campus emergency plan, or assembled a senior crisis management team, or practiced our response by simulating a range of incidents. When the unthinkable occurred on February 14, 2008, we had anticipated and planned for many of the major decisions that would confront us.

Crisis management has become an important aspect of leading higher education institutions. Although we wish it were otherwise, natural disasters, accidents, and deliberate incidents such as shootings can and do occur on college campuses. Although difficult and painful, these events can be mitigated with serious planning, preparation, and practice. It is essential for all leaders in higher education, especially presidents, to think deeply about these issues and to ready their campuses to respond.

The editors of this volume have assembled an important and comprehensive array of case studies that provide practical and useful information for campus leaders as they prepare and deal with crises. The authors have shared from personal experience thoughtful insights and helpful recommendations, covering many significant aspects of crisis management. In the chapters of this volume, you will find compelling and heartfelt firsthand accounts of the importance of presidential leadership in a crisis and information about how to build an effective crisis leadership team, how to deal with the media and develop a sound communications strategy, as well as how campuses can move forward with recovery and healing even after the most devastating events. In short, this edited volume is a primer on how to prepare your campus for a crisis.

Effective leadership is the single most important factor in a successful response and recovery from a campus crisis event. To be effective, campus leaders must develop a crisis management plan, practice for emergencies regularly, and develop a sense of shared responsibility in dealing with a crisis among members of the academic community. Although this is not the most stimulating or exciting work we do in the academy, it may be the most important. Reflecting on the lessons learned from the authors of this volume is a good start for those who will be called upon to provide leadership on their campus in a time of crisis. I am thankful for the authors' contributions to the growing body of knowledge on crisis management.

John G. Peters
President Emeritus
Northern Illinois University

PREFACE

In June 2012, the American Council on Education (ACE) convened 16 presidents along with media experts and attorneys for a Presidential Roundtable on "Leading in Times of Crises." There was overwhelming interest in the topic, even though most presidents readily agreed that crisis planning wasn't always at the top of their "to-do" list. The resulting monograph by Bataille, Billings, and Nellum (2012), titled *Leadership in Times of Crisis: "Cool Head, Warm Heart,"* generated widespread interest, prompting us to expand the inquiry and invite presidents and other senior administrators to contribute to this book. We began by looking at some of the earliest crises that generated widespread interest, such as the collapse of the bonfire at Texas A&M University, and realized that the crises that embroil campus leaders today are as likely to arise from governance issues as from natural disasters, such as hurricanes and floods. Often, as the world saw after the Boston Marathon bombing, campuses become inadvertent victims of crises when their students are killed or injured or when the perpetrators are college students.

The overwhelming mandate is that all senior administrators need to be prepared to address any threat to the campus—whether that threat is one that endangers students and employees or is a situation that will affect the long-term reputation of the campus. We are grateful to Stephanie Bell-Rose and the TIAA-CREF Institute, for sponsoring the initial Presidential Roundtable, and to ACE, for encouraging us to expand this project and allowing us to use portions of the ACE publication to introduce our readers to these new essays. Susan Slesinger at Stylus encouraged us to collect these essays and was with us from beginning to end; we appreciate her guidance. Throughout the process, we had the able assistance of Hadja Bangura and Afiya Catlin, at ACE, and Rebecca Robinson, English PhD student at Arizona State University. But it is the contributors, who took the time to respond to our request and to provide guidance to their colleagues, to whom we are most grateful. When we talked with them, we asked them to focus on how their own campus crisis can be instructive to their colleagues. As a result, some of them provided details of events, and others used an event on campus to provide advice that they wished they had received earlier in their careers. In every case, these essays illustrate the incredible resiliency of campuses when faced with what some have called "the unthinkable."

Gretchen M. Bataille and Diana I. Cordova

INTRODUCTION

Campus events require that presidential leadership is strong and unwavering in the best of times, but the qualities of leadership are tested during a crisis. Presidents and chancellors, along with their leadership teams, have had to respond to natural disasters, such as floods and tornadoes, as well as to human-made crises, such as riots, accidents, challenges to academic freedom, data security breaches, and illegal activities. The national news has documented mass shootings, dormitory fires that have claimed lives, and athletic scandals that have severely challenged leaders in higher education. In recent years, higher education has been rocked by accusations related to staff in athletics at the Pennsylvania State University, University of Arkansas, and Syracuse University. After a 10-month investigation, *Sports Illustrated* (Dohrmann & Evans, 2013) exposed potential infractions at Oklahoma State University from 1999 to 2011 that included payments to student athletes, academic dishonesty, and sexual favors to lure recruits. The death of a band member at Florida A&M University prompted every campus to review potential hazing within campus organizations and to ensure that their policies address the situation and promise serious consequences. It appears that 100-year floods are attracted to college campuses. In January 1995, the University of California, Santa Barbara, closed when rains deluged the coastal area, causing floods and mudslides. In this volume, President Sally Mason documents the devastation of the flooding of the Iowa River on the University of Iowa campus. In September 2013, President Philip DiStefano found himself closing the University of Colorado at Boulder campus, postponing a football game, and facing the high waters of Boulder Creek. The use of pepper spray on students at the University of California, Davis, compelled the chancellor to speak out publicly about the situation and caused staffing changes in the police department. Student deaths, rapes on campus, cheating scandals, and natural disasters all focus attention on a campus—sometimes only for a short time and in other cases for months and sometimes years. In some cases, such as St. Mary's College of Maryland, unorthodox decisions, such as using a cruise ship for a residence hall, prove to be an ingenious and positive way to address the mold issues in traditional residence halls, yet the president who weathered that crisis found himself in a crisis of a different sort when enrollment declined in subsequent years.

Any crisis event requires that leaders are savvy in their relationships with the media and that they work effectively with their own public affairs staff. The campus is a microcosm of a small town—with faculty, staff, students, alumni, and the surrounding community all potentially affected by the actions—or inactions—of the campus leader. Colleges and universities have experienced a significant number of what pundits call "career-ending events." Although not all presidents and chancellors leave their posts, many find themselves questioning their own responses or being questioned by boards, legislators, and the public. The challenges presidents and chancellors must confront increase as new technologies dominate campus communications and federal and state regulations call for increased and more complex reporting. There is often little time to thoughtfully plan a course of action; instead, presidents are called upon to make rapid decisions—whether to use the campus alert system, contact the media, schedule a press conference, or retreat behind closed doors. Each action has a reaction, and campus leaders need to anticipate the results of their decisions.

There are frameworks for crisis management that are well documented, and campus leaders should know about state and federal regulations and policies, the Incident Command System (ICS), the National Incident Management System (NIMS), the Campus Security Act of 1990, and the Jeanne Clery Disclosure of Campus Security Policy and Campus Crime Statistics Act (Clery Act). Similarly, in many crises, relationships with other agencies are critical. The leadership team must be aware of the American Red Cross in a hurricane, Centers for Disease Control and Prevention (CDC) for an epidemic, the FBI and CIA for terrorist activity, Homeland Security for student credentials, the Federal Emergency Management Agency (FEMA) for earthquakes and floods, and local or state police for investigations beyond the campus.

What is always important is who and what is guiding leadership decisions. Many campuses have well-established crisis communication or risk management teams. Some presidents assume that the vice president for administration or the public affairs officer knows how to manage a crisis, but it has become clear that this is a team sport. Only those campuses with well-defined policies and processes can begin to address the newest crisis, and even then, there will be variables that were never encountered before or new twists that change everyone's perception of what to do. Considering what expertise is needed on the team is critical—and sometimes the team members need to be interchangeable and fluid. For example, a situation that affects facilities needs more participation from that side of campus, whereas a cheating scandal needs full participation from the academic team.

Even in a crisis, the day-to-day work continues. But some incidents change the campus routine—do you have graduation ceremonies when there has been a human tragedy on campus? Are finals canceled when storms impede travel and knock out power? Who decides when and how to alter the usual patterns? How does the campus deal with a racial incident that occurred off campus? Should it be clear that the president has made the tough decisions, or is it better to say the crisis team has made this recommendation? Does the answer depend on the circumstances?

In the end, presidents may build a reputation—good or bad—or they may leave a legacy that marks their tenure forever. Often during the crisis, the long-term result of decisions will not be clear. Sometimes an excellent leader can make one mistake and wipe out years of successful leadership. One event can change the course of a campus, alter the reputation of a leader, and forever change the external perception of the institution.

The following essays are instructive in that the authors demonstrate that responses to a crisis depend on the circumstances and, in the end, may be the result of luck as much as careful planning. As some have said, the more planning the campus does, the more likely that the outcomes will seem like fortuitous results. What all these authors communicate is the importance of recognizing that every campus leader must be prepared to respond and willing to do so even in the face of uncertainty.

Reference

Dohrmann, G., & Evans, T. (2013). How you go from very bad to very good very fast. *Sports Illustrated, 119*(11), 30–41.

PART ONE

PREPARING FOR AND MANAGING A CRISIS

The most important element in crisis management is planning—tabletop exercises, mock disasters, and continuous or nearly continuous policy revisions. This may lead to the prevention of the worst consequences of a disaster, but nothing can be done to avoid disasters altogether. The authors of the chapters in this section have all experienced crises and have used their experiences to document "best practices" for the future.

After 13 years as president of the University of South Florida, Judy Genshaft has experienced many crises, but the common denominator has been her stalwart belief that ethics and "doing the right thing" are at the heart of decisions made during and after a crisis. Transparency, accountability, and ethical behavior must be the expectations for all campus leaders.

Recognizing that Oklahoma State University is in the unfortunate position of being in a location prone to weather conditions such as tornadoes and storms, Burns Hargis and his coauthors did not expect that the defining crisis for the campus would be the deaths of athletes in two plane crashes ten years apart. The authors dissect the responses to both natural disasters and the crashes by looking at the literature on crisis management. In the end, they, too, conclude that it is the empathy and caring of the campus leaders that ultimately matter. They outline what a campus must do to be prepared.

The Texas A&M University bonfire has been described, analyzed, and used as a case study since it occurred in 1999. In her chapter, Cynthia Lawson places this event in the context of how one incident can be instructive in helping campuses manage many different kinds of crises. What is clear in her essay is the power of a strong leader who supports and values the contributions of every team member.

Dolores Stafford managed many crises during her years as chief of police at The George Washington University, and she addresses crises from the perspective of the police, who must establish trust on the campus and beyond before any crisis occurs. She reviews the federal laws, such as Title IX and the Clery Act, that require campuses be responsive or face the consequences of fines or, more important, loss of lives or reputation because the laws were ignored.

What is clear from these chapters is that management of a crisis is made easier when campuses have engaged in careful planning. Although organizing tabletop exercises, appointing multiple crisis teams, finding off-site locations for the teams to meet, and establishing solid relationships with local authorities takes time, it is time well spent.

I

IT'S NOT THE CRIME, IT'S THE COVER-UP (AND THE FOLLOW-UP)

Judy Genshaft

University and college campuses are privileged places, seemingly immune from the turmoil of the outside world. They are places where everybody is smart, mature, and well-behaved—except when they are not.

Despite our insular world teeming with bright minds and endless potential, our campuses inhabit the same hazardous world as everyone else. As much as we like to build physical or metaphorical walls around ourselves, we can't stop real life from intruding. In many ways, we might be more vulnerable; no one expects something awful to happen on a university campus.

This chapter looks specifically at managing an institution's reputation in the face of serious adversity. But before we go further, let me emphatically say this: Reputations are important to protect, but not more important than lives. None of the insight, analysis, and guidance should be construed as protecting reputation first. I make this disclaimer for good reason: Some people really do think universities put institutional reputations above all else, and at times the conduct of institutional officials in the face of present danger or blatant wrongdoing reinforces the notion that we protect our institutional "brand" at all costs.

There's a better way: Build and protect the brand by doing the right thing in the face of a crisis. Facing the crisis with a clear head and a reasoned approach, and then doing your best to fix any systemic breakdowns that contributed to the crisis, won't just protect the institutional reputation; it can *become* the institutional reputation.

We live in a fragile bargain with those who make up our campus. Our institutions are strengthened by their intellect, work ethic, and leadership skills and equally dependent on their good behavior, level-headed decision making, and good conduct. We have to have a lot of faith in human beings to be at their best as leaders of large institutions. We also must have a plan for what to do when people are at their worst.

To see smart, committed people in action in a moment of need is one of the great rewards of being a chief executive. And as the president of a university that has had its share of rocky episodes, I can tell you that managing your reputation amid scandal is when you will learn more about the strengths and weaknesses of your organization than you could ever imagine. You'll probably learn something about yourself, too—or at least you should, if you want to outlast the next crisis to come along.

I should warn you: There will always be another crisis. But there doesn't always have to be another scandal. There is a difference between a crisis and a scandal. Bad things happen, and bad decisions are made every day—how you handle them determines whether it becomes an isolated event or something larger that rocks your institutional foundation.

The Tone at the Top

They say there is no second chance to make a first impression. After 13 years at the helm of the nation's ninth-largest university, I can also tell you there is no second chance for campus leaders who completely bungle a crisis. In this day and age, everything we do is dissected, tweeted, and filed away for future reference. You will be judged not just on what you did in the heat of battle, but by what lessons your institution learned, what mechanisms you corrected, and the follow-up that demonstrates institutions should be continually evolving and perfecting how they manage the complicated human terrain.

A poorly managed campus crisis will change the narrative of your institution. It will change how people feel about it, whether they want their students to attend, or, if they are professors, whether they want to teach and conduct research there. Donors can pick anywhere to send their money; the vast majority of them prefer to invest resources in institutions they feel good about. The public expects us to be aware of the warning signals of an impending crisis, but we don't always see the crisis coming. Whether you own up to the responsibility or not will say much about what kind of reputation your institution will have in the future.

Forward-thinking leaders will look for existing weaknesses and create management systems that minimize risk. They should be sensitive to the culture that exists in their institution, whether it predates them or not. The "tone at the top" cited in Judge Louis Freeh's investigation of the Pennsylvania State University (Penn State) scandal serves as a cautionary note for all institutional leadership. Although some are still debating whether the Freeh report is fair and accurate, reports that Penn State became a place where people at many levels either were fearful or unsure how to report what they saw to the proper authorities tells us something was fundamentally wrong in the organization. The atmosphere clouded people's thinking and stifled individual ability to put the safety of children first.

As much as we'd all like to pretend that is not happening at our school, some version of that culture is pervasive throughout all institutions. Too much is at stake—power, money, fame, glory—and ethical behavior is not something routinely reinforced in our society. That's why institutions need clear protocols on how all employees should handle problematic issues as well as mechanisms that allow them to report problems without fear of retribution. Creating an atmosphere of transparency, accountability, and ethical behavior isn't something you do when a scandal strikes to protect your reputation; it's what you do to reinforce your good name every day.

You can't build a perfect organization, but you can build one that is resilient and open to meaningful follow-up in the aftermath of an event. The Boy Scouts' motto is "Be Prepared"; a more modern version could be "Be prepared and be prepared to follow-up." Crisis preparation and communication is an ongoing task that starts the first day you take office, as you begin building your credibility as a leader and foster the community's trust in you and your decision-making abilities. If a system fails, fixing what is broken—the follow-up—is essential to the institution's reputational recovery. It's the constant attitude of "we can and will do better" that builds self-introspection and resilience into an institution.

The follow-up will be what helps regain public trust, supports or restores good reputation, and keeps the institution true to its ideals. The only thing worse than having a crisis is having the same crisis a second time.

The Science on the Subject

Management and communications researchers in recent decades have produced a rich body of knowledge that dissects and explains how crisis events develop into reputational hazards. The academic literature is quite helpful in exploring how organizations rebound from a crisis because these scholars have taken a dispassionate and analytical approach. Of course, that's not exactly how the real world will work when your campus is in crisis. I know—I've been there, and it's a gut-wrenching experience. That's why I prefer to look at crisis and reputation management as a two-part, interlocking strategy: one built out of a cool-headed analysis based on knowledge of how organizations work and the other based on experience of what I've seen in the trenches. Every crisis will call for a combination of detached decision making and good old-fashioned gut instinct honed by years of experience. If you are a leader in touch with your institution, you will know the right balance between the two as the circumstances warrant.

You don't have to look far to find solid underpinnings to the institutional traditions and habits that make for such a painful and public learning curve in crisis response, management, and communications. Some of the leading thinkers on crisis management even argue that institutions predominantly have two modes: precrisis and crisis. I am a very optimistic person by nature, but they aren't wrong. If you aren't in the throes of managing a crisis right now, you might want to be perfecting your crisis response, because surely in that vast institution you manage, somebody is doing something that could erupt into a crisis. W. Timothy Coombs has produced an excellent body of work on crisis management, communication, and reputation management. Coombs's research informs us to expect not only how and why people will react to or blame us for a crisis on campus, but how we will be judged in handling the aftermath. Not surprisingly, failing to properly handle smaller events or past crises will play a major role in how your institutional reputation is constructed and how it fares in the long run (Coombs, 2004, 2007a, 2007b).

Some communication scholars even argue that higher education is particularly primed for poor handling of crises, in part because we're successful at our primary mission of educating students and creating new knowledge. We are so preoccupied with achievement we can't see a crisis until it is upon us (Boin, 2005). The more prestigious and accomplished the institution, the bigger blind spots we have to something being amiss (Tompkins, 2005). Arrogance and hubris, the scholars agree, breed vulnerability to crisis (Weick & Sutcliffe, 2001).

Research has shown that the experience of repeated success creates screens that are particularly blinding in an organization (Tompkins, 2005). The Learning Barrier Model depicts reliance on success as a separate barrier because of the additional influence the experience has in limiting the potential to see and share warning signals and failures (Veil, 2010). An organizational culture that focuses solely on past success can hinder future success by blinding the organization to potential failure. Because a crisis can build slowly, organizations can be oblivious to warning signs. Others who have taken a wider look at the landscape of crises and crisis management have also sought to understand why institutions repeatedly stumble over the same issues time and time again. Not only do we not do a very good job learning from each other's experiences, but we don't see the patterns in our own houses particularly well. In the book *The Politics of Crisis Management: Public Leadership Under Pressure*, the authors asked the question: "Why do leaders fail to see crises coming and act to avert them?" In their analysis, the researchers likened a crisis to a disease. It begins with a vulnerable state of the body, which may be induced by hereditary factors or result from unhealthy behavior. The incubation phase sets in when pathogens proliferate and make themselves at home. When they reach a certain threshold, the pathogens overtake the body's defense system and make the patient feel sick. The disease is now manifest, and the battle for recovery, or survival, can begin. A crisis follows a similar pattern of development (Boin, 't Hart, Stern, & Sundelius, 2006).

As campus leaders, it's our responsibility to create systems with early warning mechanisms so that no single person can wreak havoc. Most crises have early warnings that aren't detected (Mitroff & Anagnos, 2001). Some of the monitoring is routine: We do audits of how money is spent; we require annual reports so we generally know what divisions are doing and if they have accomplished their goals. Our campus police departments review incident reports to spot troubling patterns, and in the wake of the Virginia Tech shooting, our campus mental health services have new tools to deal with potentially dangerous individuals. Our athletic departments have a whole host of National Collegiate Athletic Association (NCAA) compliance procedures to follow, and our staff members undergo training to make sure they understand the rules and how to follow procedures. Our student affairs offices do anti-hazing classes and offer preventive workshops on such topics as sexual violence and substance abuse.

But the reality is that few, if any, institutions have the resources necessary to establish anything more than routine checks and balances, and frankly we run the risk of becoming giant bureaucracies with an oppressive management structure—or even a higher education version of the dreaded "nanny state"—if we go too far. The key, it seems to me, is that attention at the top must be paid to that information generated in reasonable monitoring systems.

Organizations build their reputations over decades or generations. They build them by delivering on expectations (stellar ratings, institutional growth or success on the football field or basketball court are just a few ways to build reputation). But invariably when there is a crisis, the questions of why it happened will be asked. If the answers come up as a lack of oversight, misplaced values, or unchecked arrogance, that's a reputation killer. You still might be graduating excellent students, winning athletic matches, and making great discoveries, but people won't feel good about you. And every time another controversy arises, what you will hear is how the newest event is the latest in a string of controversies. A poorly managed crisis will cast a long shadow.

Communications scholars often discuss the notion of "reputational capital" (Alsop, 2004; Dowling, 2002) as what will sustain you through and after a crisis. Once you draw down that capital, you have to replenish it, and therein lies the importance of follow-up. Writing eloquently in the 2011 book *Institutional Failures: Duke Lacrosse, Universities, the News Media, and the Legal System*, Howard M. Wasserman notes:

> Of course, an institution is its people. An institution does nothing (for good or ill) unless the people within the institution do something. . . . We cannot evaluate or understand how any individual acted without understanding the institutional structures within which he acted and the incentives that motivate and explain individual and macro-level action. Moreover, we cannot evaluate an institution's success or failure or its ability to improve its performance in the future without considering those incentives and whether and how they must change. (p. 5)

What I've Learned So Far

Early in my presidency at the University of South Florida (USF), I was called upon to manage several controversial situations. One of the most troubling episodes came just one month after I arrived on campus, when several members of the USF women's basketball team, as well as current and former employees, went public with allegations of racism against the team's coach. As you can imagine, the allegations were shocking, tragic, and greatly disappointing to those of us who value diversity, equality, and—what I consider to be our most important responsibility—the protection and nurturing of our students.

I was so new as president that the larger Tampa Bay community had not had a chance to get to know me. I had very little reputational capital to spend, yet here was a problem that hit at the heart of one of our society's most persistently difficult and emotional conflicts. The barrage of headlines was steady, as lawsuits and official complaints came in; I was limited in what I could say publicly to manage the situation and assure the public that a thorough and independent investigation would be completed. I called on retired Judge Joseph Hatchett, a former Florida Supreme Court judge and also a former chief judge for the U.S. 11th Circuit Court of Appeals, to conduct an independent investigation that would establish the facts and uncover where our internal system for properly handling discrimination complaints broke down. It turns out we didn't have a credible system in place at that time.

Judge Hatchett's careful review work took time—and throughout the investigation, the headlines kept coming. There's nothing you can do about that, other than reinforce the message that you are working diligently to uncover the facts and reiterate your values. You have to be deliberative and careful in your process because you only have one chance to get it right.

When Judge Hatchett's report was completed, our institution's own lack of proper policy for handling complaints of racism was faulted. We moved quickly to institute a new policy that requires supervisors to report allegations of racism to an independent office empowered to review such complaints. We then worked to find out what our students, faculty, and staff really felt about the climate on campus. I sought and received the resignation of the athletic director, whose judgment in handling the initial allegations did not meet my expectations. USF was fortunate it could then turn to Lee Roy Selmon, a community icon known for his strong ethics and deep personal convictions, to lead that athletic department.

A newspaper reporter later would ask me about the decision to ask for the resignation of the athletic director. I answered, "It got to the point where there was a lack of confidence in the judgment of the athletic director. You have to be able to trust the leaders around you. And I think at that point in time, the confidence in some of the judgment calls and the responsiveness to the community was at risk." I still believe that today, and that's still the standard to which I hold my leadership team.

Fast-forward to this year: We have had our share of crises, but not another case similar to the one previously described. That's good news, but just because more than a decade has passed, it does not mean we should consider our work done. USF is working on the next evolution of how it handles diversity issues on campus, this time not because of embarrassing headlines, but because it's the right thing to do.

We recently appointed a new chief diversity officer on campus who will lead a system that not only responds to complaints but works proactively to educate, inform, and build bridges amid our diverse campus community. My goal is to create a positive campus environment where people of all different walks of life learn to live and work with each other. That's a value I intend this institution to live on a daily basis and a value I hope continues to bolster the university's reputation as an inclusive environment.

The old saying goes, "Character is what you do when no one is looking"; to me, principled leadership is what you do before there is a crisis that forces you to act. A reputable administration must have three bedrock principles:

integrity, accountability, and fairness. These are standards that must be communicated throughout the leadership team and enforced when the situation arises. Just as the institution's reputation was built piece by piece over years, that reputation is protected by building the core values of leadership the day you take office. That guidepost will be the difference between bad events (which are inevitable) and an outright destruction of your reputation (which is preventable).

Keeping good lines of communication open with the governing board is essential, but it is also important to do so with the surrounding community and other leaders. When something serious goes awry, this will allow you to quickly reach out and keep key stakeholders in the loop, while also involving them in what is seen as a community institution. Universities and colleges that develop a siege mentality when things go wrong are often left to sink on their own. Students, faculty, and alumni also are key constituencies that often are overlooked as a crisis (emergency communications aside) begins to unfold. They are a powerful voice and will be willing to speak up for their institution, but once you've lost credibility with them, it will be very difficult to regain your footing.

What you say as an event unfolds will set the tone for how your institution weathers the storm. You don't have the luxury of waiting too long to speak, nor do you have the luxury of misspeaking. Higher education needs to look no further than Duke University's lacrosse incident to know how treacherous it can be to issue statements in the early days of a high-profile, volatile incident when you don't have all the facts at your disposal. The telephones in our communication office light up quickly when something happens, and every reporter and news producer is demanding a statement from the university. Your students and faculty, who are certainly free to do so, will be on social media eagerly offering their opinions. We've established that saying nothing is not an option if you want to preserve your credibility and reputation. The challenge then is to strike a balance between addressing concerns quickly and not saying something that isn't supported by the facts.

If you don't know all the facts, there is no shame in saying so. What you can say emphatically is that your institution is taking the matter seriously, that you have built mechanisms into your institutional structure to deal with such problems, and that you have the utmost concern for the well-being of your campus community. It's an opportunity to restate those core principles you started building on your first day on the job. The unequivocal support of campus officials for their accused colleagues at Penn State, with no mention of victims, led the public to view the institution as dismissive, uncaring, and insensitive in the face of a horrific crime.

You can seriously undermine your institution's credibility by saying nothing or saying the wrong thing, so here's a checklist to think about before a crisis is at hand:

- Assure your campus and the general public that you are addressing the situation.
- If there are obvious victims, acknowledge them and embrace them. If your campus truly is a "family" and members of that family are harmed, you will be troubled and grieving with them. If the true victim of the situation is not apparent, there are graceful and genuine ways of extending your concern without presupposing the facts.
- Assure your campus and the public that you are seeking the facts of what occurred and how it might have occurred, and are doing so in a prompt, impartial, and credible manner.
- Reiterate that your administration stands for transparency and accountability. This is an opportunity to make clear your bedrock principles.
- If you need an independent investigation to get to the bottom of what happened, be the first to ask for one. You will do your administration and your campus a great disservice if you let a situation deteriorate to the point where someone else is calling for an independent investigation. Then you will look like you are only reacting to outside pressure; that builds confidence in no one.
- Communicate, communicate, and communicate—all along and with everyone who has a stake in the situation. If you need to bring in outside help to keep up with the media calls and public relations, there are many skilled and reputable crisis communication firms around the country that can help. They will be expensive, but not as expensive as trying to repair your reputation after it is trashed. Make sure your governing board is as fully informed as they can be; remember they are community leaders who are getting telephone calls from their own constituencies demanding answers. Don't leave them out in the cold. Hold town hall–style meetings, so your community can express their fears/frustration/disappointment. In the absence of solid information, rumor and innuendo will fill the void.
- Use the Internet to your advantage. Post whatever documents you can on your website for all to see; if you are a public institution, you will probably have to release the documents anyway, and if you are a private institution, your forthrightness will be commended. Use social media to be an inclusive communicator.

Institutions have long felt this level of openness would leave them vulnerable to liability; we have found it actually minimizes liability because those who have been harmed do not feel as if the situation is being swept under the rug. Penn State has endured a difficult time, but they have used their university website to clearly communicate reform measures and then track progress. It's easy to find, and it's written without jargon or pretense. Likewise, Duke University continues to maintain an easily accessible portal to the full library of documents related to the lacrosse incident and the resulting internal examination and reports. The refreshing candor of both these institutions conveys a genuine intent to fix what went wrong. Universities are centers for higher learning and such post-incident transparency enables other institutions to learn and improve. Moreover, anyone who wants to read the actual source documents—rather than media reports of what they said, which often do not fully reflect nuances—can do so.

Reputation management requires some soul-searching, both before and after an event. Sometimes that involves confronting beloved campus institutions or long-held traditions. Maybe it's something easy to rectify, like making sure people in a position of responsibility are properly trained and have the tools they need to carry out their responsibilities. Or it could be a much tougher scenario, such as an atmosphere in which people are afraid to do what's right. At times, the events will go beyond the campus walls. For educational institutions, these scenarios are all potential hazards but also incredible opportunities to address long-standing issues that bring a community together holistically.

In the end, you are only human. You cannot stop people from being at their worst, but as an institutional leader, you can strive for people—yourself included—to be at their best. Even in this "gotcha" culture, in which toppling esteemed institutions is almost sport, people do recognize leadership that is genuinely principled. Creating a management style and culture that is transparent, forthright, and credible from the beginning will save your institution's reputation and allow you one day to hand over that very precious asset to the next leader.

References

Alsop, R. J. (2004). *The 18 immutable laws of corporate reputation: Creating, protecting, and repairing your most valuable asset.* London: Kogan Page.

Boin, A. (2005). Disaster research and future crises: Broadening the research agenda. *International Journal of Mass Emergencies and Disasters, 3*(3), 199–214.

Boin, A., 't Hart, P., Stern, E., & Sundelius, B. (2006). *The politics of crisis management: Public leadership under pressure.* Cambridge: Cambridge University Press, 2006.

Coombs, W. T. (2004). Impact of past crises on current crisis communication. *Journal of Business Communication, 41*(3), 265–289. doi: 10.1177/0021943604265607

Coombs, W. T. (2007a). *Ongoing crisis communication: Planning, managing, and responding* (2nd ed.). Thousand Oaks, CA: Sage.

Coombs, W. T. (2007b). Protecting organization reputations during a crisis: The development and application of situational crisis communication. *Corporate Reputation Review, 10*(3), 163–176. doi: 10.1057/palgrave.crr.1550049

Dowling, G. (2002). *Creating corporate reputations: Identity, image, and performance.* New York: Oxford University Press.

Mitroff, I. I., & Anagnos, G. (2001). *Managing crises before they happen: What every executive and manager needs to know about crisis management.* New York: AMACOM/American Management Association.

Tompkins, P. K. (2005). *Apollo, Challenger, Columbia: The decline of the space program.* Los Angeles, CA: Roxbury.

Veil, S. R. (2010). Mindful learning in crisis management. *Journal of Business Communication, 48*(2), 116–147. doi: 10.1177/0021943610382294

Wasserman, H. M. (2011). *Institutional failures: Duke lacrosse, universities, the news media, and the legal system.* Farnham, Surrey, UK: Ashgate.

Weick, K. E., & Sutcliffe, K. M. (2001). *Managing the unexpected: Assuring high performance in an age of complexity.* San Francisco, CA: Jossey-Bass.

2

BUILDING RESILIENCE TO NATURAL DISASTERS ACROSS THE CAMPUS ECOSYSTEM

Burns Hargis, Lee E. Bird, and Brenda D. Phillips

A variety of potential disasters seem to lie in wait for schools and universities today. Regardless of the source—intruders, accidents, hazardous material spills, or natural disasters—campus leadership must be in place and ready to act. Not surprising to many of us, our degrees generally fail to prepare those in leadership positions for unexpected events and the human, economic, infrastructure, construction, and environmental consequences. Further, our academic environments train us to collect and analyze data over time, waiting to draw a conclusion. However, disasters do not wait for data analysis to unfold; they require rapid decisions in a context of uncertainty.

We frame our understanding of those at risk, and the possibilities of assisting them, within an ecosystem framework (Bronfenbrenner, 1979; Garbarino, 1982). In short, an ecosystem consists of four levels: micro-level, meso-level, exo-level, and macro-level. At the micro-level, people live their daily lives working in offices, attending classes, and studying in the library. They interact in a face-to-face manner as they produce research, learn theories, and prepare for careers. Their efforts, experiences, and safety are influenced by meso-level actions that occur between agencies or organizations, including student associations, academic units, and administrative offices. Meso-level organizations connect campus leadership, environmental departments, emergency and risk managers, police, and fire departments in efforts to reduce threat impacts. Exo-level actions, usually seen in the form of policies, influence meso-level actors as they address the risks experienced at the micro-level. Each of the prior levels exists within and is subject to macro-level conditions, such as organizational culture and political economy. These latter two conditions emerge as particularly important in a safety context. Organizational culture can embrace or eschew safety concerns. Institutions can also succeed or fail based on their own economic conditions and budgetary choices, often as influenced by the broader state and national economic realities.

Making the ecosystem of Oklahoma State University (OSU) even more complex is the existence of a widespread campus system dispersed 106 miles across the state. The main campus of OSU is in Stillwater, about halfway between OSU campuses in Tulsa and Oklahoma City. Tulsa is also home to the OSU Center for the Health Sciences. The OSU Institute for Technology offers additional educational opportunities in Okmulgee. Across our campuses and facilities, we have a variety of locations subject to specific concerns. It is possible for high winds and power outages to disrupt laboratory and research facilities, the veterinary teaching hospital, or outbuildings that house animals.

Within any of our campus settings, we find a diverse population that must be recognized and addressed. International students make up a significant proportion of our campus population, with 1,700–1,800 on the Stillwater campus every semester. The Oklahoma disaster context is new to students from Sri Lanka, Brazil, or Romania. Many bring family members who may speak little or no English with them. With warnings issued mostly in English across the state, they remain at risk. Actions to protect, prepare, and warn students emerge as a continuous task. We offer weather and safety information during a mandatory two-day orientation upon arrival. International students also receive e-mail and in-person briefing from our emergency manager, housing staff, and student affairs personnel.

Visitors are usually unfamiliar with the locations of safe buildings or the procedure they need to follow in an emergency. Living and learning in tornado alley means that when weather threatens, many families take protective action by coming to campus basements. We shoulder responsibility for not only our students, but for faculty, staff, visitors, and even the surrounding community and state. Whether the problem is an intruder, bomb threat, or sudden hailstorm does not matter—but ensuring that everyone leaves our campus safely does.

Indeed, varieties of emergencies and disasters happen daily, from slips and falls to medical crises, microwaves that cause small fires, influenza outbreaks, hail and ice storms, and sudden tragedy that envelops us all. The scale, magnitude, and scope of each event vary, but the knowledge, skills, and abilities needed to respond remain the same. Clearly, safety is a core function of any academic institution. Students cannot learn in an environment where they do not feel safe. Whether severe weather or potential intruders threaten, it is the responsibility of the campus leadership team to assess information, determine the appropriate response, and implement decisions to keep everyone as safe as possible.

OSU has built a campus leadership team for disasters. Our story addresses the core aspect of emergency preparedness and response: building relationships based on trust and knowledge. Though we will not know which event may challenge us next, we do know that we will be called upon again. Our story begins in 2001, with the tragedy of a plane crash; follows us through various natural disasters that have affected campus; and wraps up with consideration of biological, viral, technological, and hazardous materials.

A Starting Point

On Saturday, January 27, 2001, at 5:37 p.m., tragedy struck our OSU family. A plane carrying 10 members of the OSU men's basketball team (athletes, trainers, and staff) as well as local media and pilots, crashed near Strasburg, Colorado, east of Denver. Then-president James Halligan organized the OSU leadership team using a concentric crisis circle model (Bird, Burks, & Bowers, 2002). At the heart of the model, the team moved to surround the immediate family (parents, siblings, children, intimates) of those who died; it then moved out to associates (other team members, fraternity brothers) and the larger community. The core leadership team included the president, director of athletics, and the vice presidents for business/external relations and student affairs, along with public information staff. Additionally, numerous personnel provided crucial care, including office support staff, action teams from athletics, student affairs (counseling, campus life/volunteer coordination, and residential life/dining services), and business/external affairs (public information, campus police and parking, human resources, and the physical plant). An associate vice president established an on-site team for the Colorado crash site.

Our first efforts took campus leaders into meetings with the team and coaches and then into residence halls, where friends and roommates needed support. From 7:00 p.m. to 11:00 p.m. that evening, the leadership team helped the campus family through the worst day of their lives. Coach Eddie Sutton called the families during this time, as shock spread quickly through the larger OSU family. President Halligan went to the airport to address the media. We determined to do everything we could and to always err on the side of compassion. A balancing effort ensued, between structuring an appropriate response and mourning deeply ourselves.

We met continuously, 24 hours a day, for the families and friends. The first formal planning meeting occurred from 2:00 a.m. to 4:00 a.m. on Sunday and involved designating responsibilities for the on-site team, family and campus visits to those in the concentric circle, and a campus memorial service. Visits to families commenced on Sunday at 10:00 a.m. and continued through 10:00 p.m., with additional contacts through Wednesday. Meanwhile, university personnel began to organize a memorial service. The university assisted families and friends from around the country in making travel arrangements. We also counseled athletes who feared flying to impending games and matches. On Monday, the coaches, team, counseling staff, and others did a walk-through of the memorial service. Logistical needs included accommodating 1,000 guests. Families gathered on Wednesday, January 31, for the memorial. Following a meal, families received teddy bears that they carried into the service inside Gallagher-Iba Basketball Arena. The 14,000 in attendance rose without prompting, in a silent and powerful embrace. Impromptu memorials sprang up as well, including flowers placed at the "Spirit Rider" statue, depicting our cowboy mascot carrying an OSU flag astride a galloping horse. Funerals continued through Tuesday, February 6. OSU staff attended all but one of the funerals. The experience of "closure," however, does not occur with burial, and we continued to support those affected (including ourselves) for months and even years to come.

On March 18, families came to campus for a dinner that included a preview of a planned Colorado Memorial at the crash site. President Halligan continued to visit families through May, as other campus leaders coordinated the return of personal effects and provided counseling. In August, families went to the Colorado site to establish a permanent memorial. The day before the memorial, staff working to organize the event faced sweltering heat, prompting concern over possible effects for family members the next day. Accordingly, a helicopter stood by, hidden behind a ridge, should a mourner be overcome and require medical transportation. Large containers of iced drinks were provided.

The next day arrived cold and drizzly. Families left hotels on buses, as local officers blocked highway exits so the caravan vehicles could arrive together. At the site, officers and victim advocates lined up two abreast to allow mourners privacy from media as they walked to their seats. In a chill wind, these same officers called their own families to bring blankets out to those assembled. As the memorial service completed, the wind subsided and the sun came out, with beams of light reaching down to the turf. Families could then take an escorted walk to the crash site; National Transportation Safety Board (NTSB) officials came along for family members who wanted to ask questions. Music played with a dual purpose: to provide comfort and to block media microphones from overhearing private family conversations. We provided CDs of the music to families and OSU personnel. From the day of the crash to the memorial service, Colorado communities reached out to total strangers and provided steadfast support. The city of Strasburg offered lunch for families and memorial personnel at a nearby elementary school following the ceremony (www.okstate.com/trads/ten-colorado.html). We remain indebted to their kindness.

We learned a great deal from our campus tragedy. We learned anew that we must always try to do the right thing in a timely manner. Up close and personal is the way to manage unexpected pain and heartache. We sent out small, intimate groups of campus leaders to speak with families. Initial visits with families involved learning the names of family members, including family pets. We found counselors to help those bereaved to tell their own family members, especially children, of the deceased. We also gathered the names of family friends and gave them our contact information so they could support their loved ones. The university assigned a counselor, an athletic department member, and a human relations representative to each family. Cost was never a primary consideration, and the university covered air and ground transportation and hotel costs in Stillwater and Colorado. We bought land in Colorado for a memorial site. Money was raised for a campus memorial called "The Praying Cowboy." As the on-campus memorial developed, we brought families in for a meal and gave them granite disks bearing the image of our "Spirit Rider" on a base that displayed the memorial image (www.okstate.com/trads/ten-campus.html).

Our attitude became "you need this, you got it." And we found student and staff volunteers, food, and drivers—for anything they needed, OSU found a way to get it done. And we remember. Every year, on January 27, an OSU vice president travels to Colorado to lay a wreath in remembrance (http://memorial.okstate.edu). Every year we hold a moment of silence during a basketball game close to the date of the crash. Every April, thousands of people turn out for 5k and 10k events that raise money for the counseling center (www.remembertheten.com).

Natural Disasters

Natural disasters represent a more common experience for OSU. The Federal Emergency Management Agency (FEMA) lists Oklahoma third nationally in dealing with natural disasters. Only Texas (332) and California (211) surpass

Oklahoma's 167 Presidential Disaster Declarations. Certainly severe storms (tornadoes, high winds, hail, ice, and blizzards) represent our most pressing concern, but our campus has suffered damage from other events, such as floods and fires (structural and wild land). Indeed, a variety of "unexpected events" have arisen over the past several years, requiring campus leadership attention, including addressing significant economic impacts (see Table 2.1).

TABLE 2.1
Disasters and Hazards at Oklahoma State University, 2008–2012

Date	Type of Event	Total Loss Estimation	Actual or Anticipated Insurance Reimbursement (Deductible $500,000)
Nov. 2008	Water leak; failed cap on a hot water system floods rooms in campus hotel.	$82,504.32	None
Feb. 2009	Hail storm; 19 buildings damaged.	$411,233.19	None
June 2009	Hail storm; 153 buildings damaged; 133 insured buildings.	$2,860,097.53	Reimbursed for total costs of 133 insured buildings minus deductible of $500,000. 20 buildings were bonded and insured on a separate insurance policy with a deductible of $100,000; total $821,734.37.
Nov. 2009	Sewer backup; Multi Modal Transit Facility; damage to furniture.	$256,885.66	None
Feb. 2011	Freeze, sleet, snow; 40 buildings affected; sprinkler pipes freeze damaging arena escalators, elevators, and decor; power plant cooling tower collapses.	$781,240.83	$442,081.23 (actual reimbursement)

(*Continues*)

TABLE 2.1 (*Cont.*)

Date	**Type of Event**	**Total Loss Estimation**	**Actual or Anticipated Insurance Reimbursement (Deductible $500,000)**
Mar. 2011	Vehicle fire in automotive building, Okmulgee campus.	$915,208.98	$415,208.98 (from State Risk Management)
Aug. 2011	Wind, heavy rain, fire destroys poultry building; winds destroy roof on football stadium.	$2,439,236.38	Expecting reimbursement of $1,900,000 once finalized.
Late 2011	Sewer leak at stadium; pipe damage.	Estimated replacement $1,635,000	Loss currently in judicial system.
Nov. 2011	Earthquake; 4 buildings damaged.	$200,000	None
Nov. 2011	Tornado through Tipton Irrigation Research area destroys 2 buildings, equipment, and irrigator.	$323,154.51	None
April 2012	Lightning storm; damages alarm system, one structure, and antenna system.	Estimated $77,332.32	None
May 2012	Hail; 2 greenhouses damaged.	$60,344.86	None
TOTALS		$8,404,238.58–$10,039,238.58	$1,679,024.58–$3,579,024.58

We do not mess with tornadoes in Oklahoma, and we have identified shelter locations and resources to protect our OSU family (www.osuokc.edu/weather/shelters.aspx).

Beyond the expected storms, other natural disasters present planning and preparedness challenges. A catastrophic drought (D4 Level, the worst) for the past few years has meant that students have faced continuing challenges to fund their education. Parents have had to sell off livestock and have fought hard to save generations-old family farms. Drought conditions generated major wildfires in 2012, with faculty, staff, and students overcome by rapid-onset losses of homes, vehicles, pets, livestock, and personal possessions. Within our system, several faculty and staff lost everything. For households lacking sufficient insurance, wildfire and drought losses left those affected struggling to maintain family, work, school, and recovery. And even unexpected, low probability natural hazards occur here, too. Just a few minutes after the November 6, 2011, football game (which we won), a historic magnitude 5.6 earthquake rattled the area. A nearby institution, St. Gregory's University, sustained damage to historic buildings that cost $2.8 million to repair.

In recent years, we have experienced many such natural disasters, fortunately with minimal damage, but that could change quickly for us or for any educational institution. Consider, for example, the effects of Hurricane Katrina on higher education institutions in Louisiana and Mississippi or the more recent impacts of Hurricane Sandy in New York, New Jersey, and other affected areas. Research projects stopped, funding disappeared, and degree progress ceased. Some universities suffered losses significant enough to create financial exigency, resulting in faculty and staff downsizing. Students, displaced sometimes for years, failed to return to many affected institutions.

Other Types of Disasters

Natural disasters do not represent the full range of possible crises. Campus laboratories contain a variety of hazardous materials. Occasionally, we experience minor incidents that require our environmental health and safety team to clean up. The nature of our research facilities also requires quarterly, mandated training with personnel, including a dynamic student population. Damage to research facilities would mean disruptions of critical work vital to sustaining external funding and producing socially beneficial results.

Research facilities, classroom instruction, and business continuity in general rely on computational infrastructure. Daily, frequent assaults on our cyber-capacities require dedicated staff to avoid attacks ranging from e-mail phishing to capture of confidential data. Those potentially affected must be continually educated about risks, with staff prepared to quarantine viruses and restore damaged capacities.

People living and working together routinely spread human viruses as well. Pandemic planning at OSU has spanned the campus, involving a wide array of offices. Reducing widespread illness has meant developing a health care pandemic plan, preparing for a quarantine, being ready to move courses onto distance education platforms, offering flu shots, and installing hand gel dispensers. Even the president's office passes out hand sanitizers, labeled in "America's brightest orange" of course!

Insights and Advice

From a variety of events, our campus leadership team has gelled in a way that sometimes only crisis can create. Based on our experiences, we offer critical advice.

- *Teamwork.* Relationships, particularly knowing who can do what and with whom, truly matter. Knowing who you can rely on means that you can move forward, trusting that those around you will shoulder necessary tasks ably and responsibly.
- *Preparedness and Planning.* Campus leaders cannot afford to sit back blissfully and hope that it will not happen here. Preparedness includes developing plans and procedures, ensuring that everyone understands their role and that those who might be affected have been prepared as well. Planning helps to reduce losses (Burby et al., 1999).
- *Resources.* Campuses must find needed resources. Expenditures will be required, but if it makes sense to purchase it, campus leadership must find a way to get it done. The type of resource will vary over time, from stockpiling pandemic supplies to erecting new firewalls, so resource management must be dynamic.
- *Flexibility.* Planning is critical because it enables people to understand their roles, responsibilities, resources, and operational procedures. However, disasters routinely challenge established plans. Key personnel may be out of town when the tornado arrives, and others may need to step in. Flexibility thus serves as a key principle guiding overall management approaches (Dynes, 1994).
- *Mitigating Risk.* A campus must be a safe place, which means determining which hazards exist and how we can build a more resilient place to live, work, and learn (National Academies, 2012; Meo, Ziebro, & Patton, 2004).

Teamwork

Developing a strong leadership team is a single, important first step among many that must be taken. Experience matters when disaster strikes. Campus leaders derive experience from myriad events—smaller, individual circumstances, such as a student experiencing a seizure, to storms that produce flash flooding down a main campus avenue to jolting tragedies that bring us together in grief. We must draw from these experiences to develop capable leaders from within our institutions—people willing to not only lead in times of calm but also in times of crisis. Emergency management demands involvement from all of us—campus leaders, faculty, and staff, and even our students.

The Campus Leadership Team

A strong and effective business model relies on surrounding the top decision maker with informed, capable personnel. Though the president of any campus ultimately makes the call to cancel classes, review policies, or spend money, he or she relies on key personnel to review options. Their expertise feeds into the overall energy and focus of the leadership team, providing strategies for public information, policy making, operational decision making, and more. Although we provide training and regular interaction among our campus leadership team, it is also true that events may drive how a team gels.

After September 11, 2001, all of our campuses realized the importance of having a strong leader at the helm. We ensured that high-level administrators were visible, to offer a sense of safety as events unfolded. We conducted threat assessments of potential targets (primarily stadium-focused) and designed new operational planning around a terrorist attack. Everyone felt affected by the events personally through the loss of loved ones or psychologically by the viciousness of the attacks. We realized early on that we would need to do two things: provide for psychological safety/healing and assess our campus for potential risks.

We answered queries regarding campus safety from the public, including those who assumed that international students might be a threat. Out of concern, area clergy volunteered to ride on campus buses as added safety for international students. Along with other campuses, we organized a memorial service, which continues annually. September 11 was not anticipated, but our previous experience mattered, and we drew from that to inform the current management challenge. As a result of September 11 and other events, we have pre-identified campus and community counselors and therapists who could help in an emergency.

Staff Expertise

Any campus setting requires people skilled in a wide range of physical and human management capabilities. A few years ago, we hired a professional, experienced emergency manager. OSU also maintains an office of environmental health and safety to oversee laboratory inspections and manage hazardous materials events. Our risk manager focuses on events that might be of concern in an effort to reduce potential impacts from physical harm to individuals to financial harm to the university. A behavioral consultation team conducts threat assessments and provides support not only to those at risk personally but to those who might become involved in managing such threats. All campuses must maintain a police or security presence, and in our case, we do so through a strong campus police department and good relationships (including joint training) with city police.

Faculty Expertise

Campuses can also draw from faculty expertise. OSU hosts the longest-established Fire Protection and Safety Technology Program in the nation. We also offer a unique PhD and MS in Fire and Emergency Management and support a Center for the Study of Disasters and Extreme Events. Individual faculty members across the campus offer additional depth on wildland fires, blast resistance, viral infections, pathogenic diseases, terrorism, and psychological trauma. We have tapped into this core of knowledge by asking faculty members to serve on safety committees and task forces and to assist with emergency planning.

Students

Without doubt, students contain a ready reserve of energy that campus leaders can leverage for internal and external good (Sundeen & Raskoff, 1994). College students represent an incredible work force, with many skills in place or under development. Campus-sponsored activities like the "Big Event," in which students conduct community-based service, allow them to develop organizational and leadership skills as well as service orientations.

Other community organizations can provide frameworks for learning as well, such as Habitat for Humanity or local efforts to feed the hungry. The more a campus initiates such efforts, the more they are ready for an event like Hurricane Sandy. For example, after the 2011 tornado destroyed so much of Joplin, Missouri (183 miles from OSU), student groups provided disaster relief. They picked up debris, worked on home repairs, and listened as survivors talked. Such service also helps volunteers who benefit from a need to help and an increased sense of personal well-being (Lowe & Fothergill, 2003; Thoits & Hewitt, 2001).

Indeed, student associations, fraternities, sororities, Reserve Officers' Training Corps (ROTC) classes, and more form a body of students whose organizational mission directs them to serve. Though campus leaders may be concerned about liabilities associated with students involved in disasters on and off campus, steps can be taken to mitigate risks. Further, training is essential to avoid the "SUV," or spontaneous unplanned volunteer, problem that can lead to massive management challenges (Phillips, Mwarumba, & Wagner, 2012). The U.S.-based Citizen Corps (www.citizencorps.com) provides organizing frameworks and training in many locations (Flint & Stevenson, 2010; Franke & Simpson, 2004). On our campus, the student-based Community Emergency Response Team (CERT) has been in place for some time. CERT puts students through a range of emergency training protocols so that students make informed choices during a disaster event. To date, the bulk of campus CERT has addressed basic first aid, evacuation, and triage. However, providing opportunities for CERT students to continue to participate, remain motivated, and maintain training has proved challenging. Inviting student CERTs to support campus and community events, such as athletic events, can keep up their skills and interests.

Nationwide, Citizen Corps includes Fire Corps, Neighborhood Watch, Volunteers in Police Service, and Medical Reserve Corps (MRC) (Hoard & Middleton, 2007). Here in Oklahoma, the state offers legislative-based protection to volunteers who become trained and credentialed through MRC. Oklahoma MRC volunteers have conducted triage during mass emergencies, such as Hurricane Katrina, staffed related shelters, and assisted with pandemic prevention. The Oklahoma MRC is currently developing county animal response teams (CARTs). With a veterinary school, agricultural college, and extension background as part of OSU, connecting with an organization like MRC-CART makes good sense, especially given the rural surroundings of our multiple campus locations. Remembering the wildfires of 2012, we realize the importance of aiding our broader community, including the pets and livestock of staff and students.

Emergency Operations Planning

We established an emergency operations center (EOC) working group around 2006 that led efforts to create an EOC and hire an emergency manager. Four years ago, through the EOC working group, we finished the emergency operations plan (EOP), which is designed as a local, stakeholder-driven process. Structurally, the EOP relies on a functional approach consistent with most emergency planning recommended at the local level for all-hazards planning

(FEMA, 2010). The plan also addresses specific hazards (e.g., snow or hail protocol) through annexes. Plans must be dynamic, though, and to ensure its relevance, we update the plan annually. Most important, people who use the plans must know the plans. Accordingly, we engage our campus leadership team in tabletop exercises, including real-time messaging to test knowledge, decision-making capabilities, and role enactment (Lindell & Perry, 2003).

Large Venue Event Planning

Football games bring visitors to campus who are unfamiliar with emergency procedures. Efforts to enhance their safety include an EOC in the stadium. Mutual aid agreements exist with many agencies. In addition, we often include state- or federal-level law enforcement in the EOC. Campus Environmental Health and Safety stands ready to manage safety incidents. Game day event personnel receive training on security and safety procedures. Extensive emergency planning, training, and exercising has taken place as well.

On game day, our emergency manager monitors weather conditions inside the stadium EOC. The OSU Police Department takes calls from fans inside the stadium, directing event staff and police in response. Student Conduct and Student Disability Services also provide staff members in the stadium to help address concerns.

Build Resources

University safety requires an investment, which can return significant gains: People survive disasters and attacks, buildings resist blasts and storms, and people know how and when to act. Building resources at OSU has involved numerous efforts. We highlight three here, including developing a traditional EOC, establishing a campus-wide alert system, and providing handy reference materials for departmental use.

Emergency Operations Center

Emergency managers, professionals well trained in disaster management, coordinate efforts to prepare and plan for, respond to, recover from, and reduce (mitigate) disasters within an EOC. An EOC is a location where emergency managers gather campus leaders to monitor situations, communicate, and make decisions (Neal, 2003, 2005). University president Burns Hargis secured funding for building the EOC, which contains a main meeting room and large table, television monitors, computers, and several surrounding rooms for press and small meetings.

In nonemergencies, the general EOC may be used for drills and tabletop exercises. If a sufficiently large storm bears down on the university, response team members specific to a university context (e.g., dining, housing, physical plant, road clearing, police, and others) meet in the EOC. After examining weather models, televised reports, and other intelligence, team members talk about needs and concerns specific to their respective areas. OSU does not activate or open the EOC during small-scale incidents. Instead, an emergency manager activates the EOC in various stages, which may lead up to calling in the full team tasked with specific emergency support functions (ESFs) as organized in the EOP.

Campus Alert System

We spent two years assessing vendors for emergency alert. After the study, we chose an enhanced system that permits simultaneous text, e-mail, and phone messaging coupled with automatic posts to social media (Facebook, Twitter) and the university safety web page. This type of system fits well with research that recommends a robust and redundant warning messaging system (Sutton, Palen, & Shklovski, 2008; Lindell & Perry, 1992; Mileti & Sorensen, 1990). Alert capabilities extend to all five campuses, with an option to specify alerts for a particular campus. As a further stage in delivering warnings, we will soon install desktop alerts that will interface with the vendor system. To increase warning information even further, we have converted 25 buildings to deliver voice messages throughout the building. We will continue to update approximately two buildings per year.

Flip Charts With Emergency Procedures

A few years ago, we created flip charts with various emergency procedures. Though ideally we wanted to place them in every classroom, costs prohibited doing so. The easy-to-use reference materials were distributed one per department and to administrative personnel. Content included information on a range of possible emergencies from fires or tornadoes to explosions or intruders. Flip charts guided readers to specific steps that could be taken should an adverse event arise.

Flexibility

Two contrasting approaches characterize debate over emergency management: either a command-and-control approach or a more flexible, adaptive approach (Tierney, Lindell, & Perry, 2001; Dynes, 1994). Today, campus leaders tasked with university safety must know and be able to use both approaches. Nationally, the United States has adopted the National Incident Management System (NIMS, see www.fema.gov/national-incident-management-system), which requires knowledge of the Incident Command System (ICS). Planning tends to follow recommended protocol for developing procedures. The National Response Framework, for example, organizes emergency responsibilities into functional areas managed by primary and secondary agencies (see www.fema.gov/national-response-framework). Local planners use similar efforts as we have done at OSU. Further, disasters do not respect jurisdictional boundaries. Events spill over into the broader community and vice versa. University campus leaders need to know how emergency managers organize and operate in order to generate smooth coordination with the broader community. We have trained personnel to understand and use NIMS, ICS, and functional planning.

In addition to understanding emergency management jargon and protocol, we have learned that a flexible, adaptive approach is also needed. Disasters are much like being in the army. We train soldiers and expect them to follow command and execute the plan. The problem is that the enemy—or the tornado, the intruder, the unexpected hazardous materials spill—did not read the plan. All disasters require some degree of creativity to respond, which emanates from the adaptive capabilities of the campus leadership team. EOPs can anticipate many—but not all—events. In 2012, a client to the veterinary teaching hospital backed into a gas meter, disrupting hospital operations for a while. EOPs do not usually include such unusual events. Accordingly, we must exercise creativity at times to respond to unanticipated events. We have since mitigated a repeat accident with the simple installation of a braced, steel frame in front of the meter.

Mitigate Risk

Mitigation involves efforts to reduce potential risks. Structural mitigation measures include strengthening the built environment (blast-resistant doors and windows or earthquake retrofitting). Nonstructural mitigation measures involve planning, securing insurance, and policy making, coupled with an internally driven and collaborative effort (Kiefer, Farris, & Durel, 2006).

Our main campus lies embedded in the City of Stillwater, a community of about 45,000 people. A few years ago, Stillwater conducted a mitigation planning effort. Such work requires that all stakeholders participate in identifying hazards, assessing risks, and prioritizing actions (Godschalk, Brody, & Burby, 2003; Pearce, 2003; Burby, 2001; Fordham, 1998).

Stillwater invited OSU's active participation, and both faculty and administrators attended monthly planning sessions. The city's efforts inspired additional campus mitigation planning for a range of potential hazards, an unusual type of planning for most universities (Comerio, 2000). After conducting the hazards assessment, we outlined an extensive list of mitigation activities and made assignments for implementation (www.ehs.okstate.edu/mit_activities.pdf).

Disaster-Resistant Buildings

From a systems approach, we need to not only prepare people to face risk but also consider the built environment (Mileti, 1999). In the summer of 2011, a significant storm rolled over Stillwater, causing damage to buildings housing animals, people, and important research experiments as well as the stadium roof. Though no animals were harmed, one construction worker required rescue. The financial impact of the physical damage reached $2,500,000. Campuses must do what they can to design disaster-resistant buildings. Given the aging nature of many campuses, this means both actively designing new buildings with the latest materials and technology for blast resistance (for explosions, severe weather), intruders (external barricades), and seismic resistance (e.g., adding appropriate shelving in laboratories). Though some may cringe at the potential financial impact, the true value of mitigation lies in future loss reduction. Mitigation benefit-cost analysis shows a 4:1 overall savings down the road—this is a good investment (Rose et al., 2007).

Insurance

Given predictions that losses will continue to mount across the United States (Quarantelli, 1996, 2006), prudent action requires investing in insurance. Insurance coverage requires financial commitment but the payoff is clear: reduced overall losses from unexpected events. Disaster-specific insurance premiums may be required and, depending on what a hazards identification has revealed, absolutely necessary (Kunreuther, 2006; Kunreuther & Roth, 1998). Our own experience (see Table 2.1) clearly demonstrates the financial impact and the value of insurance.

Policy Making

Any event requires honest debriefing. Often called a "hot wash," there must be a gathering of those involved to openly discuss what happened, how it went, and what can be done differently. Our hearts broke again on November 17, 2011. A plane carrying two OSU women's basketball team coaches and two alumni crashed during a recruiting trip to Arkansas. In the aftermath, OSU moved to increase safety regulations for coaches and staff, similar to actions taken after the plane crash in 2001, impacting student athlete travel. Regent-approved modifications to our travel policy included increasing regulations on air travel, particularly the use of small planes, and outlining specifications for pilot licensing.

Conclusion

Oklahoma State University, an extension-centered, land-grant university, embraces scholarship for use-inspired research (Stokes, 1997). Leveraging our intellectual capital to safeguard students, faculty, staff, visitors to campus, the families of international students, fans who attend games, conference and event attendees—and so many more—is at the heart of who we are. More than 100 similar extension institutions exist across the United States, along with colleges and universities dedicated to the production and dissemination of knowledge into our communities. Our common core—teaching, research, and service—makes us collectively a powerful repository that is harnessed for greater good. Toward that end, it is incumbent upon us to develop campus leadership internally to assist not only our own people and places, but also our communities and our nation. We serve as role models not just within our campuses, but as symbols of informed and capable action. Our own campus leadership extends into the places where we live, work, play, worship, serve, raise families, form bonds, and dedicate our time, and it may be needed at a moment's notice. Disasters do not respect campus boundaries, with tornadoes crossing rapidly from campus housing areas into residential neighborhoods. We need to be ready.

References

Bird, L. E., Burks, S., & Bowers, P. (2002). Rising to the challenge of campus tragedy: From crisis to community. Presented at NASPA, Boston, MA.

Bronfenbrenner, U. (1979). *The ecology of human development: Experiments by nature and design*. Cambridge, MA: Harvard University Press.

Burby, R. J. (2001). Involving citizens in hazard mitigation planning. *Australian Journal of Emergency Management, 16*(3), 45–51.

Burby, R. J., Beatley, T., Berke, P. R., Deyle, R. E., French, S. P., Godschalk, D. R., . . ., & Platt, R. H. (1999). Unleashing the power of planning to create disaster resistant communities. *American Planning Association Journal, 65*(3), 247–258.

Comerio, M. C. (2000). *The economic benefits of a disaster resistant university*. Berkeley: Institute of Urban and Regional Development, University of California, Berkeley.

Dynes, R. R. (1994). Community emergency planning: False assumptions and inappropriate analogies. *International Journal of Mass Emergencies and Disasters, 12*(2), 141–158.

Federal Emergency Management Agency. (2010). *CPG 101-Developing and maintaining emergency operations planning*. Washington, DC: Author.

Flint, C., & Stevenson, J. (2010). Building community disaster preparedness with volunteers: Community emergency response teams in Illinois. *Natural Hazards Review, 11*(3), 118–124.

Fordham, M. (1998). Participatory planning for flood mitigation: Models and approaches. *Australian Journal of Emergency Management, 13*(4), 27–34.

Franke, M., & Simpson, D. (2004). Community response to Hurricane Isabel: An examination of CERT organizations in Virginia. *Quick Response Research Report 170*. Boulder: Natural Hazards Center, University of Colorado. Retrieved from http://www.colorado.edu/hazards/research/qr/qr170/qr170.pdf

Garbarino, J. (1982). *Children and families in the social environment* (2nd ed.). New York: Transaction.

Godschalk, D., Brody, S., & Burby, R. (2003). Public participation in natural hazard mitigation policy formation. *Journal of Environmental Planning and Management, 46*(5), 733–754.

Hoard M., & Middleton, G. (2007). Medical Reserve Corps: Lessons learned in supporting community health and emergency response. *Journal of Business Continuity and Emergency Planning, 2*, 172–178.

Kiefer, J. J., Farris, M., & Durel, N. (2006). Building internal capacity for community disaster resiliency by using a collaborative approach: A case study of the University of New Orleans disaster resistant university project. *Journal of Emergency Management, 4*(2), 24–28.

Kunreuther, H. (2006). Disaster mitigation and insurance: Learning from Katrina. *ANNALS, AAPSS, 604*(1), 208–227.

Kunreuther, H., & Roth, R. J. (1998). *Paying the price: The status and role of insurance against natural disasters in the United States*. Washington, DC: Joseph Henry Press/National Academies.

Lindell, M. K., & Perry, R. W. (1992). *Behavioral foundations of community emergency planning*. Washington, DC: Hempshire.

Lindell, M., & Perry, R. W. (2003). Preparedness for emergency response: Guidelines for the emergency planning process. *Disasters, 27*(4), 336–350.

Lowe, S., & Fothergill, A. (2003). A need to help: Emergent volunteer behavior after September 11th. In J. Monday (Ed.), *Beyond September 11th: An account of post-disaster research* (pp. 293–314). Boulder, CO: Natural Hazards Research and Applications Information Center.

Meo, M., Ziebro, B., & Patton, A. (2004). The Tulsa turnaround: From disaster to sustainability. *Natural Hazards Review, 5*(1), 1–9.

Mileti, D. (1999). *Disasters by design*. Washington, DC: Joseph Henry Press, National Academies.

Mileti, D., & Sorensen, J. (1990). *Communication of emergency public warnings: A social science perspective and state-of-the-art assessment*. ORNL-6609. Oak Ridge, TN: Oak Ridge National Laboratory. Retrieved from http://emc.ed.ornl.gov/publications/PDF/CommunicationFinal.pdf

National Academies. (2012). *Disaster resilience*. Washington, DC: National Academies Press.

Neal, D. M. (2003). Design characteristics of emergency operating centers. *Journal of Emergency Management, 1*(2), 35–38.

Neal, D. M. (2005). Case studies of four emergency operating centers. *Journal of Emergency Management, 3*(1), 29–32.

Pearce, L. (2003). Disaster management and community planning, and public participation: How to achieve sustainable hazard mitigation. *Natural Hazards, 28*, 211–228.

Phillips, B., Mwarumba, N., & Wagner, D. M. (2012). The role of the trained volunteer. In L. Cole & N. Connell (Eds.), *Local planning for terror and disaster: From bioterrorism to earthquakes* (pp. 177–188). New York: Wiley-Blackwell.

Quarantelli, E. L. (1996). Emergent behaviors and groups in the crisis time of disasters. In K. Kwan (Ed.), *Individuality and Social Control: Essays in Honor of Tamotsu Shibutani* (pp. 47–68). Greenwich, CT: JAI Press.

Quarantelli, E. L. (2006 online, originally published 1996). The future is not the past repeated: Projecting disasters in the 21st century from current trends. *Journal of Contingencies and Crisis Management, 4*(4), 228–240. doi: 10.1111/j.1468-5973.1996.tb00097.x

Rose, A., Porter, K., Dash, N., Bouabid, J., Huyck, C., Whitehead, J., . . . , & West, C. T. (2007). Benefit-cost analysis of FEMA hazard mitigation grants. *Natural Hazards Review, 8*(4), 97–111. doi: 10.1061/(ASCE)1527-6988(2007)8:4(97)

Stokes, D. E. (1997). *Pasteur's quadrant: Basic science and technological innovation*. Washington, DC: Brookings Institution.

Sundeen, R., & Raskoff, S. (1994). Volunteering among teenagers in the United States. *Nonprofit and Voluntary Sector Quarterly, 23*(4), 383–403. doi: 10.1177/089976409402300407

Sutton, J., Palen, L., & Shklovski, I. (2008). Backchannels on the front lines: Emergent uses of social media in the 2007 Southern California wildfires. In F. Fiedrich & B. Van de Walle (Eds.), *Proceedings of the 5th International ISCRAM Conference* (pp. 624–632). Washington, DC. Retrieved from http://www.iscramlive.org/dmdocuments/ISCRAM2008/papers/ISCRAM2008_Sutton_etal.pdf

Thoits, P., & Hewitt, L. (2001). Volunteer work and well-being. *Journal of Health and Social Behavior, 42*, 115–131.

Tierney, K. J., Lindell, M. K., & Perry, R. W. (2001). *Facing the unexpected*. Washington, DC: Joseph Henry Press.

3

THE POWER OF LEADERSHIP AT A TIME OF TRAGEDY

Cynthia Lawson

Throughout my long career in public relations at a Fortune 500 company and at five different higher education institutions, I have faced a number of crises, including a teaching assistant who exposed hundreds of students to tuberculosis before dying from the disease en route on a cross-continental airplane trip, a chemical explosion, fires, electrocutions, kidnapping, active shooters, bomb scares, rapes, plane crashes, multiple deaths resulting from car crashes, tropical storms and hurricanes, drownings, suicides, and murders. With each crisis came a new lesson not only for me but, more often than not, for the entire leadership team at the university where the event occurred.

The most notable crisis, however, was the Texas A&M University bonfire collapse that occurred in November 1999—an accident that killed 12 students and injured another 27. Since then, a variety of articles and chapters in books have been written about various aspects of the Texas A&M bonfire collapse. These publications range from textbooks to personal accounts by victims' family members to critiques by crisis communication experts and public relations professionals. In recent years, Harvard University has used the bonfire accident as part of its Crisis Leadership in Higher Education, a joint offering of the Harvard Kennedy School and the Harvard Graduate School of Education. The program draws on the complementary expertise, knowledge, and experience of the Harvard Kennedy School in crisis management and the Harvard Graduate School of Education in higher education.

It's a powerful opportunity for presidents, chancellors, and other senior leaders to engage this important topic, as well as other crises, in a way that no other institution can by learning from, in their words, "one of the best managed crises in higher education."

As executive director of university relations at Texas A&M at the time of the bonfire collapse, I managed the communications surrounding that horrific accident. Although the actual rescue and recovery lasted 24 hours, a commission investigated the accident for another 6 months, the university planned and constructed a memorial over the next 5 years, and the ensuing lawsuits pended several more years beyond that. To say it was a life-changing experience for all of us—victims and their families, students, faculty, administrators, and alumni—is an understatement. More than a decade later, not a week passes that I don't think about that fateful night in some way, because a student from a university somewhere in the United States has called to interview me about the bonfire crisis, or a reporter has called to get my thoughts on the latest higher education crisis du jour, or some memory of that tragic night is triggered for some unknown reason.

To give an idea of the magnitude of the bonfire stack when it collapsed, some estimated that the logs collectively weighed the equivalent of two 747 jumbo jets, fully loaded with fuel, luggage, and passengers. One of my most vivid memories of that night was of Texas A&M president Ray Bowen as he stood in front of the collapsed stack. Dust still hovered in the air from the extraordinarily large logs that had tumbled into an enormous pile. The site was backlit with generators because the stack of logs had been erected in a field at considerable distance from a source of electricity. That light, refracting from the dust particles, cast an eerie glow on the scene. I looked over at President Bowen, who was standing in the distance, his shoulders slumped, and wondered what was going through his mind at that very moment. I thought, "Ray must have the weight of the world on his shoulders right now." Years later, I broached the subject with him during a conversation about our most vivid memories of that horrific night. He remembered that moment very well, and he recalled exactly what he was thinking, but it was not what I had expected. He was thinking that the head of facilities was working with first responders to focus on the rescue and recovery operations; the vice president of finance was making sure that everyone had the resources they needed to address the many challenges that arose; the vice president for governmental affairs was communicating regularly with legislators at the state and national levels; the vice president of student affairs was mobilizing his staff to respond to the needs of students and their parents; and I was focusing on the more than 300 media who had come to the site to cover the story, as well as the hundreds of other media outlets that were contacting the university relations office by phone and e-mail, asking relentless questions and requesting interviews. But for President Bowen, in his mind, he had no specific role. He told me he felt useless at that moment.

Nothing could have been further from the truth, of course. He had a very specific role—that of leader. There was no doubt that his leadership role was invaluable during the immediacy of this tragedy and over the next several years. Knowing that he always was available for a briefing, consultation, or assistance with a particular decision was something that his leadership team often talked about in the aftermath of the tragedy. For me personally, he attended every press conference and most of our press briefings. His sense of calm amid the swirling crisis reassured the campus community and tens of thousands of Aggies around the world who were watching. He reassured all of us that everything was being done to rescue the students still trapped within the stack and to care for those who had been rushed to local area hospitals.

Perhaps his leadership was best seen in his relentless effort to develop and implement an investigatory process to determine the cause of the collapse—one that was beyond reproach. He identified the CEO of one of the best-run construction and engineering companies in Texas, Leo Linbeck, who had no association with the university and who agreed to chair the investigation pro bono. President Bowen also directed that there be full-scale cooperation from faculty, staff, students, and alumni. He asked anyone and everyone to provide any knowledge whatsoever of the accident—whether in the form of history, pictures, video footage, facts, or rumors—to the investigatory team. Nothing was to be held back. Every document that had anything to do with the bonfire throughout its entire 90-year history went to the university library for cataloging and archiving, so that the investigatory team could complete its task with thoroughness. Media outlets also had access to this same information. Transparency was paramount, much to the chagrin of university lawyers, but that transparency went a long way in restoring confidence in the institution, its leadership, and ultimately, the future of Texas A&M University. Donations increased, as did enrollments.

President Bowen also empowered his senior leadership team to make whatever decisions were necessary, even without his approval, because he realized that the pace of the crisis was faster than university procedures would support. Decisions had to be made "right then, right now." Over the years, public relations colleagues have often asked me, "How did you know for certain that you really had his support?" At some point within the first hour of the collapse, I remember asking President Bowen, whom I barely knew (I had been at Texas A&M for only four months when the stack collapsed), "How do you want to handle the crisis communications response?" I was deferring to him because I had just left a university where the chancellor always wanted to micromanage everything, especially the media. I wasn't sure what role President Bowen really wanted, or even expected, to play when it came to media relations. "That's what I hired you for," he said. And then, looking me directly in the eyes, he added, "Just do the right thing, Cindy."

It was such a simple directive, but it was an empowering one. I knew that if I let the "right thing" govern my decision making, I would have his total support. The others on his leadership team felt likewise. Clearly, because the decision-making process during a crisis is often one that requires quick assessments and decisions, chancellors and presidents need to let their subordinates do what they do best. And they need to support them in whatever ways they can. Crisis circumstances should not be met with protocol paralysis.

President Bowen also provided emotional support. Sometimes it was an acknowledgment that he understood the challenges—emotional and otherwise—we were facing. Sometimes, it was just a small word of encouragement. But mostly, it was simply that he was our rock—an anchor—someone who was steadfast for all of us. He personally provided encouragement to the many rescue workers and first responders and comfort to the thousands of students surrounding the stack, who were on their knees praying for the victims. In an unprecedented move, President Bowen even provided for the needs of victims' families—funeral expenses, travel expenses, food, and hotel accommodations.

I asked President Bowen what advice he would give other presidents and chancellors in a crisis based on his experience with the bonfire crisis. His advice (Ray Bowen, personal communication, January 22, 2013):

- Speak with one voice. The president does not need to compete with system chancellors and board members who may want to be on TV, or with other people who may want to speak on behalf of the university.
- Surround yourself with people who have a huge amount of common sense and take advice from them.
- Take advice from lawyers, but do not allow them to make decisions for you. Doing the right thing is far more important than worrying about preempting any legal fallout that may ensue as a result of the crisis.

University of North Carolina, Wilmington (UNCW), chancellor emerita Rosemary DePaolo, for whom I worked from 2006 until 2011, weighed in on this last point when I asked her a similar question about "lessons learned" from some crises she experienced. "Don't listen to any single, particular constituency. Every voice needs to be heard, because each individual is viewing the crisis from his or her unique perspective—whether that's a lawyer, a police officer, your PR person, or a system president," she said. "Doing so allows you to forge a much better response—one that is multifaceted and addresses many of the issues that likely will surface among various constituent groups" (Rosemary DePaolo, personal communication, February 10, 2013).

As mentioned previously, the bonfire was not the only crisis I have experienced. At another time in my career, I was called once again in the middle of the night to facilitate crisis communications when a natural gas explosion killed two international students and seriously injured another. At the time, the university president was on vacation, and the provost was out of the country. Next in line in terms of crisis leadership was the new vice president of student affairs, who had little knowledge of the university, let alone its crisis response protocols. Crisis management then fell to the associate provost. Although he had been at the university for more than 20 years, he never had familiarized himself with the university's crisis response plan; it never occurred to him that both the president and the provost would be absent during a crisis. Because there wasn't time to teach him, the chief of staff for the vice president of student affairs and I had no choice but to step up to the leadership plate. Fortunately, both of us had had considerable crisis management experience. At that moment, however, I realized how very important it is for an entire senior leadership team to be knowledgeable about an institution's crisis response plan and their respective roles in that response.

Having made a similar observation years before, during a crisis situation at another institution where she had been dean, UNCW chancellor DePaolo once asked her administrative assistant to pull her away from an externally reviewed practice drill 10 minutes after it began. She wanted to see how well her senior leadership team would perform in her absence. In her words, "The team floundered considerably" (Rosemary DePaolo, personal communication, February 10, 2013). She used that experience as a "teachable moment" for her senior team. She subsequently not only required each person to become familiar with the university's emergency response protocols, but also insisted that everyone on the senior leadership team participate in all future drills and exercises that were scheduled several times each year.

As someone who has participated in, or evaluated, more than 100 drills at universities as well as corporations, cities, municipalities, and counties, I have come to realize that the absence of senior leadership at drills and exercises is rampant. Indeed, this is the single greatest complaint I hear from my public relations colleagues at universities across the country. Managing a crisis situation, without knowing the plan or the role senior leaders will play during any given crisis situation, can create a crisis itself—a management crisis or even a void of leadership altogether. It's the last thing you want, or need.

I confess that early in my career I, too, was one of those individuals who resisted involvement in practice drills. My first public relations job was managing educational programs at Detroit Edison, a Fortune 500 electric utility, where I worked for the vice president of public affairs, Saul Waldman. Before joining Detroit Edison, Waldman had been a public relations executive for Chase Manhattan Bank in New York City. On November 11, 1969, that bank was bombed; it was one of eight corporate bombings to hit New York City that year. His experience with that particular crisis became the impetus for his efforts to develop a crisis communications plan at Detroit Edison in the mid-1970s—a time when many utilities were being assaulted by antinuclear demonstrators. Waldman asked me to read the plan and then asked that I assume the role of managing the Joint Public Information Center. In that role, I would have to advise senior managers and vice presidents about what they should or should not say while simultaneously managing the joint communications efforts of community agencies and the Nuclear Regulatory Commission.

"What if I messed up?" I thought. "I don't want to be embarrassed in front of these vice presidents." As a young employee who was new to the PR field, I didn't want to put myself in this position, and the easiest way out seemed to be to avoid the drills altogether. I came up with every excuse in the book, but Waldman laughed at me and gave me a direct order. I remember he added, "You never know when you might need this someday." At the age of 30 and with limited experience, I couldn't possibly think of any future scenario outside a nuclear accident that would require my needing this skill. For almost a decade, I begrudgingly participated in those semiannual drills. The training was grueling; they lasted a couple of days each time.

The night the bonfire collapsed, that someday arrived. Those years of training were tested in ways I never would have imagined. How grateful I was, and still am, that Waldman not only provided me with all that crisis communications training, but also critiqued my performance along the way so that I could acquire the necessary skills to do it well. Moreover, because Texas A&M had no crisis communications plan at the time of the collapse, I resorted to implementing the only crisis communications plan I knew—Detroit Edison's plan for a nuclear accident. It worked exceedingly well. I tracked Waldman down later that November morning to thank him. Apparently, he had been watching television like millions of other Americans, because his wise response was, "Get back to work, Cindy; call me in a month" (Saul Waldman, personal communication, November 18, 1999). He hung up.

As the old adage says, "Practice makes perfect." With practice, the crisis response becomes automatic. Drills and exercises also provide an opportunity for assessing the university's response plan under a variety of crisis scenarios. They help in identifying vulnerabilities in those response plans and provide the impetus for making changes to those plans. Moreover, because crises often involve other local, state, and federal agencies outside the university community, such as the fire department, police department, FBI, health departments, and various United Way entities, it is critically important that senior leaders get to know the individuals with whom they will interact in a crisis, learn how they operate and what to expect from these organizations, as well as how to work effectively with them during crisis scenarios.

Drills also provide an opportunity to assess how particular individuals may operate under stressful circumstances. At one institution where I worked, an employee came to me the day following a full-scale drill. She was in tears and hysterical. The drill made her realize that she would not be able to psychologically cope during a real crisis situation. Her presence likely would have added unnecessary stress for our communications department in a crisis. I subsequently removed her from any role in our crisis communications plan, suggesting instead that she consider "going home" in the event a major crisis erupted on our campus. Without that practice drill, however, I would have never known that she would react this way.

I would be remiss if I failed to mention how important it is to conduct a practice drill without the use of electricity. Today, many of our communication tools, from alert systems and loudspeakers to blast e-mails, and from writing to disseminating press releases, are useless without a source of electricity. Years ago, Robert Gates, who followed Bowen as president of Texas A&M University and who later became U.S. secretary of defense, applauded me during a cabinet meeting for "having the best crisis communications plan he had ever seen." Given the fact that he had been CIA director under President George H. W. Bush, I beamed with pride. He quickly deflated my ego, however, by adding, "I just have one question: How are you going to manage this phenomenal communication response if you have no electricity?" I was speechless. He was right. Over the next several weeks, I challenged my staff to help me answer this perplexing question.

- We purchased manual typewriters to write press releases, as well as a plentiful supply of carbon paper.
- We identified the radio and television stations in the city and surrounding communities that had backup generators for nonstop broadcasting. In the event of a crisis, our plan was to drive copies of press releases to each of those media outlets.

- Because Texas A&M was extremely large, the university had its own bus system for transporting students across campus. The dispatch area was one of the few places at the university supplied with a backup generator. To communicate to the campus community, we planned to use the dispatchers to spread key messages to the bus drivers, who, in turn, would communicate messages to the students as they embarked onto or disembarked from the buses.
- Because physical plant and landscape workers used walkie-talkies, our plan called for dispatchers to alert these workers so that they could disseminate messages to faculty and staff, building by building, classroom by classroom, and office by office.
- We learned that most university offices had analog phone lines that were dependent on electricity. A list of digital phone lines was developed for each department, so that some interdepartmental communications could continue during an emergency.

The university also began purchasing cell phones for mid-level employees as opposed to senior-level administrators alone. I shared my plan with President Gates; he was satisfied. And I was truly grateful that he had asked, even though I have to admit I was quite embarrassed that I had never thought of that question, especially given the fact that I had worked for more than 14 years at an electric utility company.

Strange but true, many months later, the electrical grid in Texas, from Dallas to Corpus Christi, failed. The majority of the state was blacked out, and power was not expected to be restored for the rest of the day. After a decision was made to cancel classes, we quickly deployed our alternate communications plan. It worked like a charm—for the most part. Students wanted to know what was happening, and without cell phones, transistor radios, and today's social media tools, the only way they could get information was to hop into their vehicles and listen to the car radio. As you might predict, the students became bored; they didn't remain in their parking spaces for long. They traveled around the town, but without electricity to operate the traffic lights, the roads quickly became congested. There were traffic jams everywhere. In the aftermath, we modified our plans once again. The university began to encourage students to purchase transistor radios, and it supplied residence hall directors with several of them. Although I teased him repeatedly, President Gates swore to me that he had not enlisted his CIA friends to test our new crisis response plans sans electricity.

Because universities often must interact with outside entities, it also is imperative that university leaders ensure that their institution's emergency response plan, including the crisis communications component, is compatible with the Incident Command System (ICS). Emergency responders throughout the United States use the ICS, and a federal mandate for protocol consistency arose in the aftermath of September 11, 2001. When response plans are based on the same operating system, rescue and recovery among numerous agencies become relatively seamless. Processes and protocols are automatically integrated. Everyone has a clear understanding of their roles and responsibilities. Documentation is consistently applied as well. An emergency plan not based on the ICS is equivalent to trying to have a meaningful conversation with individuals who each speak a different language. In a crisis situation, there is little time for interpretations and explanations.

In experiencing so many different crises over the years, it has become quite clear to me that in many of these situations, the university could have taken action toward preventing the crisis from happening in the first place. I find myself continually questioning, "When will we ever learn?" But many university leaders are slow in asking that question and slower in answering it or doing something about it. Unless state or federal legislation requires that changes be made in the aftermath of some horrific tragedy somewhere, far too few universities engage in disciplined proactive crisis mitigation.

In the aftermath of their horrific crisis experiences, both President Bowen and Chancellor DePaolo created a task force charged with identifying the university's vulnerabilities and risks—in protocols, processes, and procedures; overseas exchange or academic programs; facilities; infrastructure; and so on. The teams also were tasked with identifying action steps to address each of these vulnerabilities and risks. As budgets allowed, each university began to address their vulnerabilities and potential safety issues. In subsequent years, each task force identified and addressed new vulnerabilities, thereby developing a process for continuous improvement in terms of crisis mitigation and enhanced safety measures.

Chancellor DePaolo shared some additional lessons she learned from her own crisis experiences, which included two stalking/murder/suicides that occurred within a month of one another (Rosemary DePaolo, personal communication, February 10, 2013):

- Consider having an outside expert evaluate your crisis response plan. Too often university leaders either put their heads in the sand, denying that anything could possibly happen at their institutions, or they become defensive, rebutting individuals who dare question existing practices. Campus safety is paramount, and that includes having the best possible crisis response protocols in place.
- Don't let a crisis divert your attention so much that you forget your primary role of providing leadership for the ongoing "business of the

campus." The job of president/chancellor goes on; you must focus on the rest of your job as well as the crisis itself.
- All crises are monumental at the time they are occurring. It's important to have someone around you who is able to put what's happening in perspective.
- If you can, hire a PR person who has experience in crisis communications. A well-managed crisis may not be perceived as being well managed if communication efforts are poor. Similarly, a crisis that is not well managed may be perceived as being well managed if your crisis communications are well executed.

I couldn't agree more.

4

WHAT CAN YOU DO TO KEEP YOUR CAMPUS FROM HAVING TO REBUILD IN THE FIRST PLACE?

Dolores Stafford

I spent 26 years in law enforcement and public safety and 20 of those years as chief of police. When I assumed the role of chief at the George Washington University (GW), I was 27 years old and one of the youngest chiefs in the country. This is important as I discuss my perspectives on rebuilding trust and reputation because I spent the early part of my career as a leader doing just that, in a department that had seen its share of difficult times. I had not been responsible for the poor reputation that the GW Police Department had when I walked in the door, but I was asked to retool the department and rebuild a reputation that had been tarnished in the 1980s. When I left GW in 2010, the police department enjoyed a stellar reputation at the university and in its surrounding communities. Over the years, we became a progressive law enforcement agency that was recognized by our peers in the industry as a top-notch campus public safety department.

As we examine crises that institutions of higher education face, we often fail to ask if the campus had a strong reputation and a high level of trust before the critical incident. Campuses must build trust with their communities prior to a critical incident and then make sure not to lose the trust they have built once a critical incident occurs.

Institutions of higher education that enjoy a strong reputation and have a high level of trust from their constituents and the community at large can respond to and deal effectively with emergencies on campus; they typically have developed that reputation because the key departments and staff within the institution have built trust with community members, one person at a time. A solid reputation follows close behind. Presidents need to look at this from a departmental level first. The level of trust for and reputation of an institution as a whole is derived from the level of trust for and reputation of the individual departments and their staff members, including the campus police/public safety agency, given its role as a first responder in a crisis situation, and the media affairs or external relations department, as the "face" of the institution during and following a crisis. The president of an institution may be the face of the institution, but in many of these critical incidents, the long-term face of the institution often will transition to the media specialist on the campus. Key departments that are intimately involved with the institutional response to a crisis must build the necessary level of trust with the campus community; their local counterparts in the town, city, or county where the campus is located; and the local media. Sometimes administrators on campuses get so caught up in the day-to-day responsibilities that come with their jobs that they don't make sufficient time to build strong relationships with their external partners. Campus leaders should make a list of everyone they want to meet and/or maintain a strong relationship with in the city or town where the campus is located. They should subsequently carve out one hour of each week to go to lunch or have coffee with someone on the list. In this manner, campus leaders can create a much broader and stronger group of allies that the institution can turn to in a time of crisis. This seems so basic, yet most campus leaders don't prioritize building and strengthening relationships with their external partners.

Some colleges and universities have survived tragedies and media firestorms, and some have become stronger institutions in the aftermath of the crisis. Some of these incidents were caused by significant crimes on campus, some were caused by natural disasters, and others were caused by the failure to comply with federal laws or regulations (such as the Clery Act and Title IX) that govern the institutional response to crimes and other emergencies on campus.

GW is an urban institution located six blocks west of the White House. The GW campus keeps growing, but when I was there, the campus consisted of 46 acres, or 20 square blocks, with approximately 130 buildings on the Foggy Bottom campus. Those buildings included a new state-of-the-art hospital, a medical school with research facilities, a large medical faculty office building, several large science buildings, and many other facilities.

There were approximately 25,000 students enrolled at GW and 8,000 students living on the campus in 28 residence halls. GW has more than 3,000 international students from more than 30 countries. The World Bank Headquarters building borders the east side of the campus, the Department of State is directly south of the campus, and the Watergate complex borders the west side of the campus. The northern boundary is Pennsylvania Avenue.

I always viewed building relationships as one of my key priorities as the chief of a 185-person sworn campus police agency. I led the Consortium of Universities Chiefs' Council for 15 years, which provided me with the opportunity to periodically meet with the leaders of the key agencies and governmental officials in the District of Columbia. Although DC can be bureaucratic, building relationships with the key leaders and even with the federal agencies in DC and, more important, building relationships among our organizations were critical to our success in responding to and recovering from critical incidents over the years. We dealt with many critical incidents during my tenure, including but not limited to 9/11 (the initial reports were that the Department of State on our southern border had been hit), several International Monetary Fund/World Bank protests literally on our campus, a hostage situation, major fires, anthrax threats, lab explosions, and major oil and gas leaks.

There are three categories of critical incidents: natural disaster or accidental incident, crimes and other incidents purposely perpetrated by humans, and failure to handle an incident according to accepted practices or state/federal mandates. All three types of incidents can cause a media firestorm, but only the third one will be viewed as the institution being at "fault" or responsible for the incident. However, if you are not prepared to respond to the first two types of incidents, you will be highly criticized for a flawed response to any incident.

Several large-scale natural disasters have been so devastating that the campuses were not initially able to continue operations. One example is Hurricane Katrina and its effect on colleges and universities in New Orleans, which have been well documented and used as a case study for the report published by the International Association of Campus Law Enforcement Administrators (IACLEA, 2006).

Years before Hurricane Katrina, Gustavus Adolphus College in Minnesota experienced an incident that was not as well documented or studied on a national level. The college was hit by a tornado on March 29, 1998, and sustained $60 million worth of damage as a result. At that time, there had never been another institution of higher education in the United States that had sustained as much physical damage in a single incident. Immediately following the tornado, a local TV news reporter quoting the director of public safety said, "Gustavus Adolphus College will never be able to recover from the tornado," and soon after that evening news report, the president of Gustavus Adolphus College reported that the college was going to reopen in three weeks.

The president put his reputation on the line with that statement, but this bold move kept all of the students and employees invested in the institution. Students and staff saw that the place they went to school or work had been physically damaged beyond the point where people thought it could recover in a reasonable amount of time. If you are a student, do you start to look to transfer to another school? If so, do your tuition dollars go with you? If you are an employee, do you start to look for another job? If you allow your students and staff to believe that they don't have a place to go, they will start to disengage, and then your problems grow exponentially.

Gustavus Adolphus College had an enrollment of 2,650 students at that time. The incident occurred during spring break, which thankfully limited the number of injuries on campus (there were about 60 students on campus). The tornado was 1.5 miles wide, and it was on the ground for 62 miles. There were materials from the library found 60 miles away in the Twin Cities. The leadership had to close the entire campus initially to conduct an assessment of the structural integrity of every building on campus. Eighty percent of the glass windows on campus had exploded because of flying debris. The leadership limited access to the campus to critical employees for several days, until the structures were deemed to be safe.

This incident is a textbook example of "rebuilding" a campus after a major incident. The president of the college was right; they did reopen three weeks after the tornado hit. How did they get the campus ready to resume classes?

- They brought in portable Federal Emergency Management Agency (FEMA) structures to use as classrooms and put them in their parking lots.
- They brought in special portable kitchens in large trailers to provide food service.
- They prioritized repair, cleanup, and renovation of the residence halls to ensure that the students had safe places to live on campus (replacing windows, repairing floors, etc.).

It wasn't a perfect plan from an aesthetic perspective, but the main concern needed to be functionality. They had a plan to get the key facilities and operational units functional so they could get back to the business of educating students. It took some time to clean up and renovate the other facilities to get them back into full operational mode, but the temporary solution got the students back on campus, and they remained committed to Gustavus Adolphus College. The plan got the employees back to work, but more important, the faculty and staff were committed to Gustavus Adolphus College because they continued to be paid while the college was closed, which maintained and even increased the loyalty of those employees to the institution.

Campuses need to implement certain plans and procedures to prepare for and recover from a natural disaster or incident that damages some or all of the facilities and potentially the ability to continue operating at 100 percent capacity.

Campuses must develop or continue to update and refine an emergency response plan. It never ceases to amaze me that so many institutions of higher learning do not have an all-hazards emergency response plan. Some of the institutions that do have one have not opened them in years. It is simply a notebook on the shelf that allows them to say that they have a "plan" if there is an emergency on campus. After 9/11, Hurricane Katrina, Virginia Tech, and all of the other major incidents on campuses in the past 10 years, it is clear to me that institutions of higher education must have a thorough and relevant response plan.

Along with the emergency response plan, campuses need to develop or continue to update a continuity of operations plan. It is critical that each institution looks at all of the major incidents that have occurred and affected campuses around the world and use the lessons learned to develop a thorough plan to ensure continuity of operations if some or all of the facilities are damaged or unusable. If a college can't hold classes, it is out of business. Tulane University faced this problem following Hurricane Katrina, and it could have been catastrophic for the institution because they were unable to hold classes for the remainder of the semester, owing to the amount of physical damage to the campus. They were able to develop an incredibly creative plan of action by working with various colleges and universities across the country to quickly enroll their students at those institutions for a semester. The students received credit at Tulane for all of the courses they completed at the other institutions, so the students didn't miss a beat in terms of continuing classes and earning the credits they needed to pursue their degrees. The other side of the spectrum was implemented by Gustavus Adolphus College, with the use of the temporary classrooms. The bottom line here is that each institution should develop a plan for various options in the event that some or all of the facilities on a campus cannot be used for some extended period of time. Campuses refer to tabletop exercises and practices, but many of them do not actually exercise the emergency response plan.

This has always been important, but it has not necessarily been a priority at many colleges and universities. In 2008, the Higher Education Opportunity Act (HEOA) added a requirement under the Clery Act that mandated that each institution must conduct at least one exercise of its plan each calendar year. It is imperative to exercise the plan so that all leaders on campus understand their role during an emergency, and the campus can continue to enhance the plan as participants learn what has not been addressed in an exercise environment, rather than when the real emergency happens on the campus. Campuses must make sure that the emergency response and continuity of operations plans are not just "good in theory" but that they work in practice.

In every exercise or actual event, communication is critical. Gustavus Adolphus College did a great job of communicating immediately following the incident and during the recovery phase of the incident. For example, the president immediately communicated that the campus would reopen in three weeks, so everyone knew the goal. They held weekly meetings for employees to update them on the plan of action and the progress that was being made to reopen.

Campus leaders set up a phone bank and called every student to tell them what happened, not to come back to campus the following week, and the plan for reopening. In fact, they made several calls to each student during the recovery phase. Not every institution could implement a plan to call *every* student, but it is clear that this kind of one-on-one communication enhances an institution's effort to keep people informed and engaged in the process. They used the best of both worlds by communicating globally to the campus and larger community using the media, e-mail, website, and other means of communication, and they communicated individually with students and employees because they were deemed critical to the long-term recovery of the institution.

Campus leaders must be prepared with backup communication systems and duplicate documentation. The tornado at Gustavus Adolphus College made it clear that plans, records, and files could literally be up in the air. Can the campus respond effectively if offices are destroyed and staff members have no access to what was in these offices? Are essential files and documents backed up off-site? The campus needs contact information for students and employees because without it recovery efforts will be hampered. Does the information technology (IT) department currently have an off-site location backing up the computer files for the institution? These are lessons that every institution should have learned from campuses that have had to recover from disasters like Katrina. Gustavus Adolphus College moved their computer systems to another nearby university to maintain communication during the recovery phase of the incident. They now have a memorandum of understanding (MOU) for those types of continuity of operations plans. During Katrina, one of the biggest challenges was the fact that all of the emergency generators were damaged in the flood. The lack of power would obviously hamper the recovery efforts at any institution. Does the institution maintain enough supplies on hand for post-emergency needs? These are just some of the issues that need to be assessed as part of the emergency planning process.

Establishing relationships externally must be done prior to needing to use those relationships. Institutional personnel needed to have excellent relationships with local first responders, the media, vendors, and other institutions of higher education. The need for some of these relationships is more obvious than the need for others. For example, the campus should have contracts in place with various vendors that require them to prioritize a response to the campus in an emergency over other routine work that they have scheduled. The level of damage at Gustavus Adolphus College required them to have hundreds of tradesmen working on campus to meet their goal of reopening in three weeks. Campuses should have MOUs with other institutions of higher education, including those that are nearby and those outside the region, in the event that an emergency affects multiple colleges and universities in the region. Gustavus Adolphus College had tradesmen, public safety staff, and other assistance from around Minnesota and surrounding states working on campus to assist with the recovery efforts. Campus leaders must focus on building strong relationships with the local media. If they trust the leaders on the campus, they will often work with the campus to make sure the story they tell is accurate.

Campuses will have a good chance at maintaining reputation and trust with the community following an emergency on campus by adhering to the following: (a) have effective and well-thought-out emergency response and continuity of operations plans; (b) test those plans so people understand their roles and the roles of everyone else on the team and use the results of those exercises to enhance and improve plans; (c) communicate honestly and effectively with the campus community, the media, and the larger community; (d) pay attention to systems, equipment, and supplies and plan accordingly; and (e) build effective relationships and partnerships with key external constituencies.

Institutions must also review insurance policies with a hurricane or tornado in mind. At Gustavus Adolphus College, the vice president for finance and the risk manager had conducted a thorough review with a disaster management team from the insurance company prior to the tornado. They were insured by a third party, and the level of coverage they chose fully protected the institution following the tornado. The insurance covered everything except the trees and grass. That was an insurance review that was well worth the time and effort!

More serious for a campus is the failure to handle an incident according to accepted practices or state/federal mandates. I am a nationally recognized expert in the Clery Act and Title IX. I started consulting with campuses in 1997 on their efforts to comply with the Clery Act. One of the most challenging aspects of the Clery Act is the ongoing disclosure requirements requiring timely warning notices and emergency (immediate) notification to the campus community. Many of the campuses that have been audited about their Clery compliance efforts have failed to appropriately "warn" the campus community, as mandated by one of these two requirements of the law.

Many campuses over the past several years have faced a significant amount of media scrutiny for not warning the campus community following a crime or an emergency in a manner that is deemed timely by the U.S. Department of Education. Virginia Tech is the most obvious campus that did not meet the requirements of being timely in their communication about the shooting in West Ambler Johnston Hall, according to the department, and they sent an e-mail to the campus community in just over two hours (which was much quicker than most campuses were doing it prior to 2007). But there are other campuses as well that have been challenged for not assessing specific crimes for a potential timely warning notice, such as LaSalle University, Penn State, and the University of Alabama in Huntsville. It appears that every time a sexual assault is reported on a campus and there is media attention around the issue, the Department of Education is looking at whether or not the campus counted the crime statistic and whether or not they assessed the crime for a potential timely warning notice.

The basic requirements are as follows: A timely warning notice should be issued for any Clery crime category that is "considered by the institution to represent a serious or continuing threat to students and employees" (U.S. Department of Education, 2011, p. 112). An emergency (immediate) notification should be issued for any incident or emergency that poses "an immediate threat to the health and safety of students or employees occurring on campus," and this includes crimes, natural disasters, and other emergencies (U.S. Department of Education, 2011, p. 98).

Many campuses have not pulled together the leadership team to discuss these requirements or to develop institutional operating procedures to implement these two requirements. This means that following an actual crime or emergency incident, administrators are often spending time debating the requirements of timely warning and immediate notification notices, and if they agree to send a message under the auspices of one of these requirements, they spend time "crafting the perfect message"—all of which takes time. When there is a potential ongoing or serious threat or an immediate threat to health and safety, the Department of Education expects that these messages will be distributed as soon as pertinent information is available, so time is of the essence. If an institution distributes a notice but does not do so in a timely manner, the institution will likely face public scrutiny from the campus community, the media, and the Department of Education for failure to comply with the Clery Act.

My advice to institutional leaders is simple: Following a timely report of one of the Clery crimes (particularly crimes against people, i.e., homicide, aggravated assault, robbery, and sexual assault), ask yourself one question: Am I certain that there is no further danger to anyone else on campus? If you cannot answer "yes" to that question, issue a timely warning notice to the community to tell them about the reported crime and provide them with guidance or prevention information so they can try to protect themselves from becoming the victim of a similar crime.

In order to avoid having to rebuild campus reputation and trust around ongoing disclosure issues, institutions should do the following:

1. Develop a policy/procedure that outlines the standard practices of the institution with regard to issuing timely warning notices and emergency (immediate) notifications.
2. Train key administrators in the specific requirements around issuing timely warning notices and emergency (immediate) notifications (there are different requirements for each of these).
3. Review the Campus Public Safety incident reports to understand the types of incidents occurring on and around the campus and discuss likely scenarios in advance of them occurring to determine the parameters that should be set in the policy/procedure.
4. Develop periodic tabletop exercises with scenarios for the leadership team to discuss and review.
5. Develop templates for various potential timely warning notices and emergency (immediate) notifications to speed up the process of distributing a notice to the campus community when it is deemed necessary.

If the campus does not issue the correct warning, it will receive notice that it will be audited by the Department of Education, and it will likely receive significant media attention as a result of the failure to warn the community and the impending audit. There are several steps the institution can take, under these circumstances, to begin to rebuild trust with the community, including but not limited to (a) directly and publicly acknowledging the communication failure, (b) announcing a review of the current practices for issuing warnings/notifications to the community, and (c) hiring a consultant to conduct an independent review of Clery Act compliance (to get ahead of the Department of Education).

Finally, the reality is that most campus public safety agencies have a practice in place and typically issue a timely warning notice in the event of a homicide, aggravated assault, or robbery that occurs on campus unless they are in conflict with the senior administration about whether or not it is necessary (which happens sometimes when campuses have not completed the five-step process discussed previously). The crime that has caused the most challenges for campuses about issuing warnings to the community is sexual assault. There are people who are of the mind-set that a timely warning notice is not necessary or required if the perpetrator and the victim are acquainted (non-stranger sexual assault). This thinking is based on a faulty premise of believing that because they knew each other that the perpetrator is not a danger to anyone else in the community. Looking back at the key question following any crime report, campus leaders must be certain that there is no further danger to anyone else on campus. If the perpetrator has not been arrested or the institution has not taken some other action to mitigate an ongoing threat, the perpetrator may assault another victim on campus. Thus, if a sexual assault has been reported to the institution officials in a timely manner and the threat has not been mitigated, the institution should issue a timely warning notice.

Institutions now also face scrutiny for these types of cases under the auspices of Title IX. I recently completed a Freedom of Information Act request to the Department of Education Office of Civil Rights (OCR), and I requested all audit reports involving discrimination cases for the past six months. OCR sent me close to 70 audit reports that met those criteria, which means that OCR is conducting a significant number of audits of harassment and discrimination cases (including alleged sexual misconduct). Recent examples of campuses being audited for potential Clery Act violations and Title IX violations include Amherst College and the University of North Carolina, Chapel Hill. Both of these cases have received a significant amount of media attention. In order to avoid having to rebuild reputation and trust as a result of potential Title IX violations, institutions should do the following:

- Identify and train Title IX coordinator(s) to oversee and or conduct a civil rights investigation into any report of sexual misconduct received by responsible authorities on the campus.
- Identify the "responsible employees" in institutional policies to clarify to whom sexual misconduct should be reported on campus for purposes of Title IX oversight.
- Train the "responsible employees" on their responsibilities under Title IX.
- Develop and publish institutional policies that contain all of the required elements outlined in the April 2011 Dear Colleague Letter. There are at least 15 requirements that must be addressed in a sexual misconduct policy.

Campuses that are being audited by the OCR, like those campuses that have already faced this issue, will likely have to hire an expert to review the policies and procedures and assist with rebuilding trust with the administration. As history has shown, rebuilding trust around an allegation of mishandling a sexual misconduct case is typically a difficult task for any administration without outside assistance. This issue typically engenders a strong reaction by the campus constituents, and there is typically a significant amount of mistrust for the "administration" of a campus following this type of allegation. As an example, Amherst College, in conjunction with a consultant, has started the process of changing the culture. That will take time, but Amherst president Carolyn A. Martin took a bold step by immediately addressing the issue head-on by praising the complainant's courage and stating that "all of this has created an opening . . . for which I am very grateful" (as quoted in Lipka, 2012, p. A22). According to a *Chronicle of Higher Education* article,

> It's an unusual response for the president of a campus in crisis. "Many universities, when news breaks, tend to dismiss it or make token efforts," says Laura Dunn, a survivor of sexual assault and advocate of security in higher education. (Lipka, 2012, p. A22)

Dunn's observation is correct and something that presidents should avoid because people are fairly adept at recognizing a token effort to resolve an issue when they see one. Amherst College took some other bold steps to rebuild its reputation and trust among students, including holding a series of open meetings for students and parents to voice concerns, developing a web page dedicated to "sexual respect" that details actions taken and planned, adding students to the institution's Title IX committee, and creating a new sexual respect task force. Amherst is clearly working diligently to change the campus culture, and for that, they have been earning back the trust of the campus community. They developed a substantive plan of action, and that is what is necessary when this type of situation erupts on a campus.

All of this leads me back to one of the questions I posed in the beginning of this chapter: What can you do to make sure you don't lose the trust you've built once a critical incident occurs? Campuses must review response plans and make sure they are prepared to respond quickly and effectively to any kind of emergency or critical incident on campus. Campuses must review compliance efforts with regard to the Clery Act and Title IX. Campuses must have proper policies, procedures, and practices in place to be above reproach when the U.S. Department of Education or the Office for Civil Rights contacts the institution following an incident to question the response and determine if the actions complied with these complex federal laws. In short, every campus must be prepared before a crisis occurs to be able to address all aspects of the situation immediately and to be able to meet the expectations of an often unforgiving public.

References

IACLEA. (2006). *Campus public safety preparedness for catastrophic events: Lessons learned from hurricanes and explosives.* West Hartford, CT: International Association of Campus Law Enforcement Administrators.

Jeanne Clery Disclosure of Campus Security Policy and Campus Crime Statistics Act, 20 USC § 1092(f). (1990). Retrieved from http://www.law.cornell.edu/uscode/text/20/1092f

Lipka, S. (2012, November 9). Despite rape crisis, campus isn't looking to move on. *Chronicle of Higher Education,* p. A22.

Title IX, 20 USC § 1681–1688. (1972). Retrieved from http://www.dol.gov/oasam/regs/statutes/titleix.htm

U.S. Department of Education, Office of Postsecondary Education. (2011). *The handbook for campus safety and security reporting.* Washington, DC: Author.

PART TWO

ACCIDENTS, CATASTROPHES, AND NATURAL DISASTERS

No campus leader knows when a hurricane, flood, or other natural disaster may hit a campus, but geography often provides some warning for the campus. Those campuses in "hurricane alley" or near a natural waterway are aware that they must be constantly vigilant, and often the crisis preparation is geared toward the expected disaster. Campuses in California prepare for earthquakes, and those in the Midwest prepare for tornados and floods, but what happens when either a natural disaster or accident disrupts the campus in ways never anticipated? The contributors to this section all knew of the potential for disaster, but even the best preparation doesn't mitigate the effects on a campus. In the chapters that follow, the authors share their candid accounts of how they dealt with the crisis confronting their campus and discuss lessons learned as well as best practices resulting from their experiences.

Less than a year into her presidency, Sally Mason faced an unprecedented test of leadership as she led the University of Iowa through one of the top-10 worst natural disasters in U.S. history, "the Great Flood of 2008." Months of anticipation and weeks of preparation were not enough to prevent over $1 billion in damages to campus facilities and infrastructure. President Mason's chapter details how the campus and local community banded together to prepare for a crisis of unprecedented proportions and engage in a massive recovery and renewal process—one that continues to this day.

On April 27, 2011, an exceptionally large and destructive EF-4 tornado ripped through the heart of the city of Tuscaloosa, Alabama. Although the campus of the University of Alabama did not suffer structural damage as a result of the tornado, many of the residential areas where faculty, staff, and students lived were completely decimated by the massive storm, calling for a coordinated effort on the part of the university and the city of Tuscaloosa. In his chapter, Mark D. Nelson analyzes the impact of the storm, the strategies and principles guiding the decisions made by the university's Emergency

Preparedness and Response Planning Team, as well as the many lessons learned through the long recovery process. This account demonstrates the importance of good relationships between the campus and the community when disaster strikes.

Sometimes ingenuity and sheer luck can play a critical role in recovering from a campus crisis, as Joseph Urgo deftly conveys in his chapter. When confronted with a severe "mold crisis" affecting two main residence halls at St. Mary's College of Maryland that resulted in the displacement of more than 350 first-year students, the leadership team did not blink when presented with the ingenious yet unorthodox solution of renting a cruise liner and docking it right on campus to provide temporary housing for the displaced students. The solution to the crisis was so emblematic of the institution's core values and mission that it galvanized the will of the campus community and resulted in extensive local and national media coverage for the institution.

Often, little attention is paid to those institutions that work selflessly behind the scenes to support other colleges and universities, their local communities, states, or regions during a time of crisis. Bonita J. Brown's chapter explores both the internal as well as the external considerations that came into play as the senior leadership team of the University of North Texas (UNT) carefully weighed the decision and managed the complicated logistics inherent in providing shelter to more than 350 evacuees of all ages, including 80 students from a nearby university, when two back-to-back hurricanes wreaked havoc on the Gulf Coast region during the summer of 2008.

One important lesson derived from the chapters in this section is the fact that campuses need to generate detailed crisis and communications plans covering a wide range of emergency scenarios. However, it is not enough to create these plans and only refer to them during the crisis. These documents need to be tested at least once a year (if not more frequently) to find and address any pitfalls in the current strategies and procedures. Campus crisis teams and their backups need to participate in tabletop exercises to become familiar with each other and anticipate how they will respond during a crisis. In addition, crises on other campuses are teachable moments and can be used as case studies for the leadership team to reflect on how they would handle the situation on their campus. Although it is impossible to anticipate every potential crisis scenario, it is of critical importance to have a preliminary plan in place that can serve as a departure point for the crisis team, were the unthinkable to occur.

5

RISING WATERS AND CAMPUS RENEWAL

Leading the University of Iowa Through and Beyond the Flood of 2008

Sally Mason

At 4:00 a.m., on June 16, 2008, I awoke from a fitful sleep and quietly made my way to the west porch of the University of Iowa's President's Residence, dreading what I might see as I looked down and across the swollen Iowa River. After months of extraordinary weather that included a near-record 60 inches of snow that was slow to melt and two weeks of unrelenting spring rains, the Iowa River had overflowed its banks, the sandbag walls that we had spent days building were breached, and floodwaters were pouring into our music building and our much-loved and storied performing arts center, Hancher Auditorium. After months of anticipation and weeks of preparation, the Great Flood of 2008 had fully arrived, altering the course and the face of the university forever. I had assumed my role as president of the University of Iowa only 10 months earlier, and it appeared that whatever brief honeymoon I might have enjoyed was over. As I watched the muddy waters of the river lap against the limestone edifice of Hancher Auditorium, I knew that this day would be one of many long ones to follow and that the flood would be an unprecedented test of leadership—one that my leadership team and I would live with and recount for years to come.

I recalled having asked campus leaders and regents during my interview for the job the previous June, "Does that river ever flood?" Having lived in the Midwest for more than three decades, I had seen the Wabash, the Kansas, the Missouri, and the Mississippi Rivers flood frequently in the spring following snowmelt and rain. I was assured that indeed the Iowa River had experienced flooding periodically, with the most recent, and surely the worst, being a 100-year flood event in 1993, when nearly all of the tributaries to the Mississippi River flooded. Little did we know that that 100-year event was a minor prelude to what was about to happen in 2008.

In February 2008, I had a conversation with senior vice president and chief financial officer, Doug True. Because of the heavy winter snowfall, he was assembling a small group to consider what we might have to do in the event of a flood. I was startled when he mentioned this, and I questioned him at length. He persuaded me that this was simply anticipatory and that it would involve our lead risk manager and some facilities people.

The planning had begun, and prophetically none too soon. Sporadic meetings turned abruptly to weekly meetings by May, and the group began to grow. Donna Pearcy, our chief risk manager, who was not previously accustomed to a large-scope leadership role, very ably and capably stepped up and led operations throughout the entire event and beyond. By June, flood meetings had become daily events held in our police department's conference room (our "war room"), and I insisted on attending—not to lead, because I was not the most knowledgeable or best qualified person to lead in this case, but to listen, assess our options, and intervene in decisions that would ultimately require my input.

To place this disaster in perspective, the flooding and tornadoes in eastern Iowa in 2008 still rank as one of the top-10 worst natural disasters in U.S. history that the Federal Emergency Management Agency (FEMA) has been involved with, and it is certainly the worst in the university's long history. In fact, the University of Iowa at the time was the largest single-entity disaster that FEMA had ever dealt with, having sustained nearly $1 billion in damage to campus infrastructure and facilities.

To fully understand what was happening in Iowa City requires a brief history. To the north of Iowa City lies the Coralville Dam on the Iowa River, a 100-foot-high earthen dam that was built as a flood control project by the U.S. Army Corps of Engineers, completed in 1958 and forming the Coralville Reservoir, one of our area's most popular recreation areas. In 2008, by June 11 the water level had reached one foot above the reservoir's spillway (712 feet above sea level). The reservoir gates were fully open, and by June 13, inflows to the reservoir peaked at an estimated 50,000 cubic feet per second. By comparison, normal river inflows are at least 100-fold less than what we experienced during this unprecedented event.

By this point, all nonessential travel in Iowa City had been discouraged. Several east–west bridges across the Iowa River had been closed. We had been monitoring the situation on campus for many days, but disaster was imminent, and I needed to make some decisions. Following vigorous discussions in the war room, we asked all nonessential university personnel to leave campus for at least the coming week. I insisted that all employees remain in pay status and be encouraged to volunteer to help save homes, the campus, or other entities in jeopardy of flooding. The sandbagging and salvage efforts all up and down the eastern Iowa corridor were monumental, and volunteers were needed everywhere.

Communications became a critical component of daily activities—with our governing board and the governor, with our internal and external constituents, and with the world at large. The national and international press descended on Iowa City, from the BBC to the Weather Channel, providing ample opportunity for the world to see what was happening and to react. We held daily press briefings, and I personally volunteered to do interviews and be available to the press, mostly to keep the media from distracting those who were feverishly working to save parts of the campus.

On the evening of June 14, the Coralville Reservoir crested almost five feet over the spillway, at a level that exceeded the record 1993 level when Iowa and much of the Midwest had also experienced historic flooding. Our community and campus had been sandbagging for a number of days, but on June 15, those efforts were suspended, and many streets and neighborhoods were closed and evacuated. It was too dangerous to remain near the river, and we simply had to hope that our efforts would be enough. The peak flood stage of the Iowa River in Iowa City was reached on June 16, and the river did not go below flood stage until July 7, 30 days after it had risen above that mark, and only 7 weeks before the start of our fall semester.

The damage to our campus was devastating. More than 2 million square feet of building spaces were flooded. Many were damaged because utility tunnels leading to our power plant flooded, causing water to back up into buildings along the river, buildings that ironically would have been protected by the sandbag walls that we had built. Hardest hit was our arts campus, where sandbag walls proved ineffective. Only two years prior, we had opened the new Art Building West, an internationally recognized architectural treasure designed by Steven Holl. This building had won three major architectural awards prior to the flood and has earned two more since then. Four to five feet of water entered the first floor, seriously damaging offices, classrooms, gallery space, and studios.

Luckily we had enough advance warning of the flood to remove 99 percent of the value of the collection in our Museum of Art (housed in another building just across from Art Building West), including the world-renowned Jackson Pollock "Mural." Thanks to the efforts of students and staff, nearly all of the collection was saved. Less than two days before this building was filled with floodwater, several large trucks were backed into the loading dock, and most of the collection, including "Mural," was loaded and moved to a storage facility in Chicago. We had no one to spare for security purposes, so the move was done quickly and quietly by our own students and staff.

Hancher Auditorium, our performing arts center, built in 1972 and designed by Max Abramovitz, was home to such historic performances as the Joffrey Ballet's premiere of *The Nutcracker*. Water reached Row R of the auditorium and was one foot above the stage.

Our research enterprise was also impacted by the flood. The Iowa Advanced Technology Laboratories (IATL), located in a building designed by Frank Gehry, included important interdisciplinary research labs for our departments of chemistry and physics and multiple departments from our College of Engineering, as well as such research entities as the Center for Global and Regional Environmental Research, the Optical Science and Technology Center, and a portion of the Center for Computer-Aided Design. Although the damage to the physical structure of this building was significant, more than $30 million in equipment located in nanotechnology labs was lost as well.

The University of Iowa is also world-renowned for its research in hydraulics. The C. Maxwell Stanley Hydraulics Laboratory houses IIHR—Hydroscience & Engineering, formerly known as the Iowa Institute of Hydraulic Research, one of the world's premier—and the oldest U.S. university-based—fluids research and engineering laboratories. The American Water Works Association designated the Stanley Hydraulics Laboratory Building an American Water Landmark because of IIHR's current and past impact on the way water is studied and used locally and around the world. Not surprisingly, the building sits immediately adjacent to the river, and although the upper floors remained undamaged, the subbasement, where computer and server rooms were located, was flooded, necessitating the removal of this delicate, critical equipment.

In all, nearly two dozen University of Iowa buildings—2 million square feet—were impacted by floodwaters, also including our student union, several liberal arts buildings, a residence hall, and our main library. Campus infrastructure was also significantly impacted; because of the flooding of the old and fragile underground utility tunnels, our main power plant had to be taken offline. All told, the nearly $1 billion in damage that we suffered far exceeded the $6 million suffered during the previous record 1993 floods.

Although some buildings were not affected directly by flooding, all were affected in some way once our power plant was disabled. We had to act quickly to ensure that steam and power were available to academic facilities and, even more important, to our hospital. Our facilities staff, in anticipation of the worst, had located temporary boilers that could be rapidly assembled if we could get them to Iowa City. It was amazing to see the pieces of two large temporary boilers hauled in on large trucks within days after the floodwaters took down our power plant. These boilers were quickly assembled on both sides of the river and made functional, thanks to 24/7 efforts by a number of our facilities managers.

Even buildings that were not serviced by our power plant were affected. The Levitt Center, home to our alumni association and our fund-raisers, was not flooded or even in danger of flooding. However, because floodwaters were nearby, power had to be temporarily turned off in this building. This was difficult because we were being contacted by hundreds of friends and well-wishers asking how they could help. I volunteered the President's Residence public spaces so that our senior fund-raisers could set up phones and temporary work spaces to continue receiving flood relief gifts that were coming in from all parts of the country and around the world. In all, we received just over $1 million in contributions, which were put to good use, especially to help our displaced art and music faculty, staff, and students. My husband and I had houseguests for about a week until power could safely be restored to the Levitt Center.

Although the flood devastated much of our campus and community, it became abundantly clear to me how much this disaster brought out the remarkable solidarity of our community and its generosity in extending mutual aid and support—in essence, its own collective leadership. As the floodwaters rose, we pulled together to protect homes and businesses as well as the university. People from every conceivable background were on the front lines sandbagging, providing meals and aid to volunteers, and moving valuable items, from computers and pianos to library books, to safe ground—students, professors, staff members, administrators, construction workers, Amish farmers, bankers, and business owners. We formed a line of unity against the flood, and many even sacrificed time protecting their own homes in order to help us. More than 1 million sandbags were filled on our campus alone, 250,000 of which were sent to communities downstream after the flooding had receded in Iowa City.

We could not have accomplished what we did with thousands of individuals running around doing things independently. At the same time, even as the floodwaters overran the riverbanks, we would never have been able to coordinate our efforts with just one person—say, the president of the university—deciding what to do and trying to tell those thousands of people what to do.

There were many aspects to the flood that required leadership decisions and action. The physical aspect was obvious. We needed people to evacuate precious resources from our buildings and build sandbag walls. My husband and I spent the better part of a day filling sandbags near our student union. We quickly realized we were neither skilled nor strong enough to be quick and effective at this task—and time was of the essence. Our facilities management team was crucial to our leadership in battling the flood. Just as I had deferred to Chief Risk Manager Donna Pearcy as she led the day-to-day planning of operations, I also knew I had to defer to Don Guckert, associate vice president and director of facilities management, to direct and coordinate the activities on the ground. And he and his team members did a spectacular job.

In the meantime, I was in daily contact with David Miles, president of the Iowa Board of Regents. As our efforts became more frantic, I shared my growing concerns with President Miles, and a short while later, I received a phone call from Iowa governor Chet Culver. Within hours, the National Guard was with us on the banks of the river. Because nearly all of our Guard members had been previously deployed to the Middle East, they were experts in building effective sand-filled floodwalls, which they did quickly and with little fanfare. I coordinated our work with them through Lieutenant Colonel Anthony Wolf, who joined us daily in our war room and became an important member of the leadership team as National Guard liaison.

Even as we battled the flood itself, dozens of decisions had to be made. Some I made quickly because of the urgency of the situation, and I relied on experience and instinct to "do the right thing." But this is an academic institution, and there were dozens of questions to be answered in those immediate days afterward and in the weeks and months to come. Do we cancel the summer session? What happens to students who were planning to graduate that summer? Do we cancel all the other activities on campus—the Iowa Summer Writing Festival, the youth camps, the arts events, and so forth? How do we handle our new student orientation sessions? And once the flood was over, if we resume classes, where would those classes be held? Could we offer all the classes we had scheduled? Where would displaced faculty find office space?

My major partner in these areas was Lola Lopes, our interim executive vice president and provost. Provost Lopes, who came out of retirement to serve in this interim position, certainly did not anticipate this kind of "temporary" job. But she was masterful in the way she handled the academic decisions and in her advice to me. And as the summer went on, we realized that all our decisions were interrelated—what to do about building repair had a lot to do with academic decisions, for example. None of these decisions could be made in isolation from each other, and teamwork was essential to continue in our recovery. When our new executive vice president and provost, Wallace Loh, came on board on August 1, I kept Dr. Lopes on as a special advisor because of her clear leadership skills, her deep knowledge of our campus, and the experience she already had had with the flood.

We were determined to forge ahead undaunted—and it is amazing to think back now on how we did it—but we were open for business for our summer session beginning June 23, and we held most of our significant summer campus activities, such as our Iowa Summer Writing Festival workshops. We then successfully opened our fall semester on time with enough of our infrastructure restored to offer all the classes we promised and to provide housing to all students who wanted it. More than 1,600 classes had to be relocated over the summer and fall through departmental space shuffling and leased space. I never once wavered in my commitment to the campus and the public—I was determined to stay the course, to finish the summer session, and to begin a new fall semester on time. And we accomplished all of those things.

In the end, our efforts were so successful that we had an all-time record enrollment in the fall, and only two students—out of 30,000—were reported to have canceled their registrations because of the flood. In fact, many new students and their families had their confidence in the University of Iowa affirmed because of the way we handled the flood. And many became part of our team and our Hawkeye family right away because, even as the floodwaters threatened in June, it was not unusual to see parents sandbagging down by the river while their son or daughter was at orientation sessions.

To this day, I remain touched by the outpouring of concern we received throughout the summer and the donations to our flood relief fund from all over the state of Iowa, the country, and even the world. We heard from every state in the nation and 15 foreign countries. I received e-mails from alumni living as far away as Japan and China asking, "What can I do to help?" One incoming international student from Taiwan wrote me to ask if she should come to campus early to help with our flood recovery. This was all the more touching because she noted that she had just recently helped her own family through a devastating earthquake.

Partnership and teamwork have been cornerstones of my leadership philosophy ever since I began working in higher education administration. I have practiced those principles consistently, but their importance was brought home to me more dramatically during the flood of 2008 than perhaps at any other time in my life. And since those dark days of June 2008, the importance of partnership and teamwork has remained paramount in our recovery process.

Our recovery process continues even as I write this in the early months of 2013, nearly five years after the flood. At the moment, the major milestones of our recovery, which will be marked by the opening of three entirely rebuilt facilities, are scheduled to occur in 2016. As we all realized during the summer of 2008, all of our decisions are interrelated. As well, the city of Iowa City, surrounding communities, the state of Iowa, and even the federal government are involved in how we proceed.

Even as the flood unfolded, we very quickly realized that our recovery would be a long, arduous process. One of the first things I did once the flood itself was over was appoint an internal campus task force to advise the administration on our recovery, including experts on flooding and hydraulics in our own backyard from our globally recognized hydroscience and engineering program. We also continued to work—and still do, in some cases—with our city, state, and federal officials; the Iowa Department of Natural Resources; Iowa Homeland Security; FEMA; and the Army Corps of Engineers. The university's governing body, the state Board of Regents, as well as our governor, state legislature, and federal delegation, of course remain critical—and fortunately highly supportive—partners in our campus recovery.

We realized, especially early on, that we needed to extend our team to people beyond the campus and governmental agencies. We had to learn how to live with the Iowa River and how best to protect and use the significant investments we have along the river—some of our most important buildings. Even during previous flood events, we had never faced the kinds of daily and ongoing decisions that have now become standard operations for us. No one here had been trained for the specific tasks of long-term flood mitigation, but we are now. We knew we needed help from experts and turned externally to Ayers Associates, a firm that has considerable expertise and experience in flood mitigation. We also extended the services of our campus master planning consultant, Sasaki Associates. Both of these organizations have provided essential perspective and assistance to our own excellent facilities management staff in coming up with creative solutions to the challenges of protecting our buildings and critical infrastructure.

I have also needed to practice one other leadership quality more than I ever have before—patience. The scale of our disaster was bad enough; it takes a long time to repair, restore, or rebuild 2 million square feet of university facilities. But working with FEMA gives new meaning to moving forward at the most deliberate pace possible. I am not casting aspersions on FEMA—the agency has been an important partner, and we are eternally grateful for the generous support that we are receiving from them. But the structure and procedures of this federal bureaucracy—much in the interest of due diligence with the taxpayers' money—are slow, to say the least. One of the idiosyncrasies of FEMA is that each time we entered a new round of application or negotiation, about every three months, we encountered a new team, necessitating a perpetual reeducation process. When an academic community, a local community, and an entire state are anxious to have their university campus back to full function, I as the institutional leader must not only advocate patience but set the example through my own practice.

One major glitch with the FEMA process that we did encounter was an unexpected Department of Homeland Security Office of Inspector General (OIG) audit of FEMA Region VII in the summer of 2012. The audit questioned FEMA's decision to replace rather than repair three of our most significant flood-damaged buildings—Hancher Auditorium, the Voxman Music Building and Clapp Recital Hall, and Art Building East. The OIG determined that FEMA's decision was in error and recommended reversal of that decision more than three years after these facilities had been abandoned, at FEMA's direction. Almost immediately, some amazing collective Iowa leadership came to the fore. Our Board of Regents president, the governor, the state's entire federal delegation (not just our district's), and Iowa's Homeland Security and Emergency Management administrator—in a truly bipartisan effort—stepped forward to support the University of Iowa and urged FEMA to abide by its original decisions. Although this unfortunate development stalled the decision-making process at the federal level, we knew that we could not afford delay "on the ground," so I insisted—and assured our university and larger communities—that planning for our new facilities continue uninterrupted. A final decision from FEMA and the secretary of the Department of Homeland Security did require unrelenting prompting by me and many others, as well as direct help from the governor and a key senator, but in the end we were grateful to receive the final sign-off by the secretary affirming FEMA's original funding decisions, allowing us to continue with our forward momentum.

Our flood recovery has not been about simply restoring the campus to the point it was before the flood hit. Leadership is also about vision. As a research university, our job is not only to educate and conduct groundbreaking research, but also to discover and inspire. Our ultimate goal—whether we are teaching our undergraduates, seeking medical cures in our labs, creating great art in our studios, writing the next Pulitzer Prize–winning novel, or bringing advanced technology to public use—is to make life better for all. To do so, we must be the best at envisioning possibilities and seeing where we have the opportunity to make the most significant impact.

Many leaders over the years have expressed the idea that in tragedy and crisis can come opportunity. A good leader takes negative circumstances and not only turns them positive, but I believe pushes recovery to heights and achievements not imagined before. To rise above the storm has taken on new (and literal) meaning for all of us in eastern Iowa. In that spirit, we now refer to our flood recovery as "campus renewal." We have an opportunity to improve—even reimagine—our campus in ways that never would have been possible before the flood.

The centerpiece of this campus renewal is a new arts campus. Our arts campus facilities—visual arts, theater, and music—were all in the floodplain along the river and were thus all damaged, many of them beyond repair. The University of Iowa has a long, storied history in the arts. Grant Wood, Mauricio Lasansky, and Elizabeth Catlett were among our prominent art teachers and students. Our music building was named after world-renowned woodwind educator Himie Voxman. Playwrights such as Tennessee Williams and actors such as Gene Wilder are University of Iowa alumni. Our university was the first in the country to offer academic credit for creative work; to encourage young artists, musicians, and writers; and to grow our world-renowned Writers' Workshop. We pioneered the Master of Fine Arts degree in the 1920s. More than 80 years after the first academic degree for creative work (in music) was awarded, the University of Iowa is ready to redefine creativity in the university once again.

One of the biggest challenges facing the university immediately after the flood was accommodating our music and studio arts students and faculty, who have very specific facilities needs and whose buildings were now completely unavailable. Since 2008, our studio arts programs have been housed in an empty home improvement big box store on the edge of town, and our music students have been scattered around different buildings, many in the downtown Iowa City area. Although these situations have constrained our programs significantly, two important realizations arose from these circumstances that we are capitalizing on in our plans for new facilities.

Our studio arts students were originally housed in a 1930s facility—built with funding, in part, from the Works Progress Administration and the Carnegie Corporation—that had had several additions attached to it over the years. Although this building had historical value (e.g., Grant Wood taught here), the facilities for modern art students and faculty were inadequate and divided up in a rather disorganized way. Despite the distance from our main campus, the large, open space of the big box building created new synergies and interactions that our studio arts students and faculty had not been able to foster before. Our new studio arts building will capitalize on and incorporate some of the advantages realized and lessons learned as a result of this forced relocation.

The opposite situation happened to our music program, which was taken from a single building and scattered throughout campus and the near-downtown area. But our music faculty and students grew to realize how advantageous it was to be near downtown and the main campus and a lot of the creative energy that happens there. And our city, as well, was looking for opportunities to enhance the cultural life of Iowa City's vibrant downtown even more. As a result, our state-of-the-art new music building will also become part of our community's dynamic central business and cultural district.

We have an extraordinary opportunity now to provide the best and most visionary facilities that will bring our storied arts programs into the twenty-first century. The arts empower us. They fuel human progress. They unite us in wonder, awe, and appreciation. They stretch the limits of possibility and imagination, and they urge us forward, together. Our vision for the arts at Iowa extends far beyond our campus or even this state. The arts can connect us across borders and boundaries. In the decades ahead, we want the world to turn to the University of Iowa for artistic innovations that challenge, inspire, and ultimately unite us in our common future.

To accomplish this grand plan, we are fortunate to have brought well-known and visionary architects onto our arts campus renewal team. The world-renowned Pelli Clarke Pelli firm has designed our new performing arts center. César Pelli and his associates have built spectacular performing arts centers throughout the world and are perhaps best known for the Petronas Towers in Malaysia and New York's World Financial Center, which surrounds the area where the World Trade Center twin towers stood. Likewise, we are thrilled to have as our new School of Music building and recital hall designer LMN Architects of Seattle, another firm highly experienced in innovative performing arts venues. LMN is known for Benaroya Hall, home of the Seattle Symphony, and the Conrad Prebys Music Center at the University of California, San Diego. We were also very excited to bring Steven Holl back on board as architect for the new studio arts building, which will be built adjacent to his award-winning Art Building West. Mr. Holl was the 2012 winner of the American Institute of Architects' Gold Medal, the highest honor that an individual architect can receive from the AIA, putting him in such renowned company as I. M. Pei and Frank Lloyd Wright.

An important part of leadership is capitalizing on strengths. Just as we are moving forward with a visionary new arts campus that is founded on the achievements of the past century, we are also combining our expertise in hydraulics and fluid dynamics with the experience of the flood, all in the service of not just knowledge, but even more important, application for communities across our state and throughout the world. Another one of the major, positive results of the Great Flood of 2008 is the creation of the Iowa Flood Center, under the direction of Professor Witold Krajewski.

One of the individuals who reached out to me during the flood was then National Science Foundation (NSF) director Arden Bement. He visited our campus and toured damaged facilities shortly after the floodwaters had begun to recede. Even during the flood, our researchers were conducting experiments designed to provide understanding of flood-related phenomena, including an NSF-sponsored airborne laser mapping initiative of the flooded Iowa River. We were all grateful to Director Bement for his visit during the flood and the many helpful suggestions he made to our researchers regarding possible NSF-sponsored grant opportunities.

As a result, in our flood center we have been studying how decision makers deployed resources among Iowa communities during the flood in order to better guide future decision-making processes during extreme events. The Iowa Flood Center is already playing a key role in flood frequency and forecasting studies in our state, developing new flood inundation maps, establishing community-based programs in Iowa to improve flood monitoring, and training a new generation of experts in flood research, prediction, and mitigation.

The research, discovery, teaching, and learning we are now doing in the wake of the flood is not and cannot be limited only to the Iowa Flood Center, however. As a new leader in the area of floods, we are now looking at broad questions from multi- and interdisciplinary perspectives. For example, in the area of biology, we are asking about the impacts of flooding on plant and animal communities. In the area of aquatic ecology, we are asking about floods' natural roles in ecosystems and how we can mitigate damage to human society as we respect natural processes. In the area of cyberinfrastructure, we are exploring the use of sensor networks, on-site computing capabilities, and communications over distances in order to effectively predict and monitor floods and their impacts. As a teaching as well as a research institution, we must ask how we can most effectively instruct students in a highly multi- and interdisciplinary area. As well, we need to be a part of community education to help mobilize community response in extreme events and to cultivate citizen scientists.

I take great pride in the leadership that took place at our institution during the flood, during our immediate recovery, and currently during our campus renewal. That pride comes largely from being able to put together an incredible team that has shown masterful talent and coordination. I do make decisions, and I do direct people on how to proceed. But I could not possibly do it, or could not possibly have done it, without the spirit of partnership and cooperation that our university community and beyond have displayed, resulting in the best advice I could—and can—get.

We are still far from being finished, although the news media and attention are no longer focused on this disaster. The teamwork must continue. As a leader, I know that the key is bringing people together for the best possible outcome. None of this can be done alone. In the next few years, as a result, the University of Iowa will actually become stronger as a university community and as a physical campus. In fact, we already are. The flood of 2008 was perhaps our darkest hour, but it has also been, in many ways, our finest hour. That has happened because I had the wisdom, and some good fortune, to find the best people, coordinate and decide when needed, but mostly to get out of the way and let talented people do their jobs.

6

PREPARATION, RESPONSE, AND RECOVERY

The Everydayness of Crisis Leadership

Mark D. Nelson

The marking of time is often dictated by major events. Those who were alive at the time President Kennedy was shot will forever remember the exact moment when they heard the news of his assassination. The same holds true for events such as the *Challenger* disaster and the terrorist attacks of September 11, 2001. For the faculty, staff, and students at the University of Alabama (UA), April 27, 2011, bears a similar significance. After days of speculation and alarming forecasts, the city's worst fears were realized, as a violent EF-4 tornado ripped through Tuscaloosa late Wednesday afternoon. The tornado cut a path of destruction 1.5 miles wide in the city, ultimately injuring hundreds and claiming the lives of 52 residents.

Today, the effects of the storm are still evident. Far beyond the bent trees, vacant homes, and hollowed-out businesses, we are a community forever changed. Reports of severe weather are met with an informed anxiety; students relive and retell their versions of the story during the city's monthly emergency alarm tests, and all the while university administrators are still processing and improving the plan that carried them through the harrowing days after.

This chapter will detail the impact of the storm on April 27, 2011, the strategies and guiding principles used by the university's Emergency

Preparedness and Response Planning Group (EPRPG), and the lessons learned through the process.

Background and Impact of the Storm

Tuscaloosa had suspended operations about a week earlier when news of severe weather and area tornadoes threatened western Alabama. Students, huddled in university basements, had been directed by campus public address (PA) systems to remain on campus until the line of storms had passed. Nearly a week later, reports resurfaced about conditions that could ultimately support a "super-storm" system with the ability to wreak havoc on the Southeast. And it did.

The National Oceanic and Atmospheric Administration listed the tornado outbreak on this day as the fourth deadliest natural disaster in the history of the United States, with a total of 205 tornadoes touching down that day. According to the National Weather Service, the four days including April 25–28, 2011, recorded the largest outbreak of tornadoes in America's history. Four of the tornadoes were rated EF-5 (the highest ranking possible) and 348 people were killed throughout six states in the southern, midwestern, and northeastern United States. In Alabama alone, there were 238 tornado-related deaths.

At 5:10 p.m. on April 27, 2011, the exceptionally large and destructive tornado struck Tuscaloosa with 6,700 students in its path.[1] In less than 6 minutes, 12 percent of the city was destroyed, 1,261 students and 300 employees were left homeless, 1,200 individuals were injured (200 critically), and 800 were missing. In Tuscaloosa, 7,000 residents became unemployed owing to the excessive commercial damage, which included 114 businesses destroyed and 240 businesses severely damaged. Additionally, the city's emergency response infrastructure, including communication towers, the fire station, the police precinct, the emergency management agency, and environmental services, was severely damaged—all of the emergency first responder agencies were destroyed. In the end, 52 people in Tuscaloosa died, including 6 university students and 1 employee.

Alabama was in a federal state of emergency, and the University of Alabama was among the cities and towns at the center of attention. Although the campus itself did not suffer structural damage (only loss of power and trees), many of the residential areas where faculty, staff, and students lived were destroyed, and a large number of Tuscaloosa's support infrastructures and schools were severely damaged or destroyed. The mass destruction of the surrounding area and the devastating impact on faculty, staff, and students called for an immediate response on campus and the beginning of a major coordinated effort on the part of the university's leadership and the city of Tuscaloosa.

Emergency Preparedness and Response Planning Group

On April 25, two days before the actual tornado, the university's Emergency Preparedness and Response Planning Group (EPRPG), composed of the provost, the vice president for financial affairs, the vice president for student affairs, the assistant vice president for university relations, the assistant vice president for public safety, the chief of the university police department, and the director of emergency preparedness, began monitoring reports from the National Weather Service and preparing to implement the emergency response plans for severe weather. The following is a timeline of what unfolded on campus:

On April 27, by 10:35 a.m., the campus was issued a warning of possible severe weather, and by 11:30 a.m., the university's Emergency Operations Center was activated and staffed. A full two hours before the tornado hit the Tuscaloosa area, all university classes and operations were suspended. Students, faculty, and staff were notified through a variety of media, including text and phone call alerts, PA systems throughout all indoor and outdoor campus areas, e-mail alerts, the university homepage, Facebook, Twitter, digital signage across campus, marquees on campus buses, the campus cable network, and notifications to the Tuscaloosa/Birmingham broadcast media. Messages regarding the tornado warnings and university operations were updated and repeated approximately every 30 minutes until the passing of the storms. During the time leading up to the storm, parents were receiving much of the same information as their children via updates through the Parents Association's media accounts. Likewise, communication between and among parents, students, and university employees had increased and intensified. That is, until the storm hit. Immediately, after the tornado, most of the traditional modes of communication were rendered ineffective.

Critical to the success of the EPRPG during this time was the preparation of the group well before the storm was ever a factor. Routine, monthly meetings and emergency tabletop exercises were valuable tools in developing critical competencies before they were needed. The EPRPG and various campus partners were certified through the National Incident Management System, which helped to provide a structured framework, a common language, and an understanding of the various roles and duties among all involved. The advance preparation and the development of relationships with key players before the incident were instrumental in the success and ability of the EPRPG to provide an immediate and coordinated response to the events of April 27, 2011.

In addition to the advance preparations and relationship building, the EPRPG was guided by five core principles in their communication response:

1. Activate timely and early alert messages
2. Provide frequent updates
3. Incorporate a variety of tools and media
4. Leverage the university's homepage
5. Educate and involve stakeholders such as parents, leadership councils, and alumni

These five principles guided the EPRPG not only before and during the crisis but also after the crisis. The minutes and hours after the tornado were critical for the safety and well-being of our campus community. The campus PA system was used for an hour after the storm until the emergency backup was exhausted because of the loss of electricity on campus. The campus electrical outage lasted for two days. In the meantime, social media, e-messaging, and news outlets were critical to notifying the campus community and stakeholders regarding the variety of issues of immediate importance. The student health center was used as a shelter for students and employees whose off-campus housing was damaged or destroyed. At 8:03 p.m., messages were sent regarding the opening of an emergency call center on campus to provide information to students and parents, and at 8:05 p.m., the call center received its first call. Classes were canceled for the remainder of the semester, and students were given the option of accepting their existing grades as of April 27 or taking a final exam at a later date. Residence halls remained open, but students were encouraged to return home if they could do so safely. To help facilitate their return, students were provided with shuttle service to the Birmingham airport. One dining hall remained open with limited food and beverage selections, and normal university operations were suspended with only essential personnel reporting to work. Frequently asked questions (FAQs) were added to the university's homepage and updated daily.

Normal university operations remained suspended until May 2, 2011, just five days after the tornado. By this time, the call center had received more than 1,800 calls, and all volunteers and volunteer efforts were being directed to and coordinated with the city of Tuscaloosa. Students and employees who were sheltering in the recreation center were relocated to other housing options, and the UA Acts of Kindness Fund was receiving donations for emergency assistance to students and employees. Additionally, members of the university community were encouraged to donate blood and volunteer with relief efforts, and the university announced that all interim, summer, and fall classes would resume as scheduled. Sadly, also by this time, the university had confirmed the six student fatalities, and on May 3, a memorial page dedicated to the student victims was added to the university's website. By mid-May, the university's police department ended its role as incident command, and throughout the month, University Relations posted daily updates via e-mail, websites, and social media on the status of the university and its recovery efforts.

Lessons Learned

Throughout any crisis, it is important to take the time to identify the successes and failures that ultimately become lessons for the future. The most obvious and overwhelmingly true aspect of each of these observations is that we must keep our energy and attention in a crisis on the crisis. If situations like this are viewed as a journey—literally a group of people moving from point A to point B—then it is too late to focus on building the roads. The relationships, the planning, the reporting structure—all of it should be determined before the event. When you are in the middle of this kind of experience, you must rely on trusted connections and procedures to calibrate your progress.

Through the process of reflection, six major lessons emerged that will continue to guide the University of Alabama in its emergency preparedness and response initiatives. The lessons include the following:

1. Use whatever communication tool you have to point to sustainable, reliable information. In times of crisis, information is both the destination and the roadblock. When access to information is compromised, people have a tendency to gravitate to anything being widely and regularly circulated, with little regard to authenticity or source. One of the University of Alabama's greatest accomplishments was the establishment of an online repository for facts related to the crisis—our web page. Our communication staff worked to validate and update the information provided there so that we were able to maintain a credible voice in the discussion of policy, facts, and future planning. In today's increasingly flat digital landscape, we have more individual publishing power than we've ever had. Outdated communication plans might not allow for one of the most successful practices that sustained us throughout the tornado crisis: We used any kind of social media—Twitter,

Facebook—to point users to the website for validation of facts. Building a following that looks to these outlets as trusted and credible sources of information is critical to the success of relying on these media during the times of crisis.

2. Establish a digital crisis plan with off-campus partners. Much of how we communicate with our various campus constituencies is influenced by partnerships with off-campus providers of contact software and e-mail marketers. During a crisis, those in charge of disseminating information may need to relocate to off-campus locations and are likely to need to arrange for temporary computer access. It is important to make these arrangements in advance and to notify third-party providers, such as those that offer e-mail services (e.g., MailChimp, Constant Contact) regarding alternate crisis location(s). Safeguards put in place to protect communication can ultimately inhibit the ability to reach all audiences when they are most in need of information. Time spent convincing these e-mail providers that you are not a hacker is an unnecessary stressor during times of crisis.
3. Embrace a new kind of volunteering. In addition to a call center, we learned that digital volunteers are critical to responding to e-mailed questions from family members who have been disconnected from their students. These digital volunteers are also able to work from a variety of locations to handle the onslaught of e-mail and posts to our social media accounts. University administrators can also become aware and alleviate miscommunication when digital volunteers are monitoring message boards, Twitter accounts, and Facebook posts. The most effective use of multiple digital volunteers is to agree on a strategy (in our case, we referenced confirmed and authenticated information from our website and reinforced that as our official communication channel).
4. Take time to process the information as humans, not just professionals. In the midst of responding to a crisis, those in charge may be so busy ensuring that the details of their task are carried out that they forget the human factor. The truth of the matter is that in most crisis situations, emotions are high (even raw), and people are hurting. These are the moments when taking a time-out to provide a sympathetic ear or a shoulder to cry on is important. Likewise, during such tragedies it is important to mourn together as one community and to recognize the many forms that people may need to express their grief. Providing and supporting blogs, Twitter feeds, and online bios provided our community with a variety of media through which to participate and express

their support for our loss. Additionally, once the majority of our students returned to campus for the following fall semester, we organized a memorial service as a means of remembering those whom we lost and helping the students and campus family to provide an immediate response to the tragic event. One year later, we honored the victims of the storm with a campus-wide day of service.

5. Celebrate students' involvement and innovation. As educators, we know the value of reinforcing the behaviors we want to see replicated on our campuses. They become part of our identity—how we describe the "heart" of our institutions. These stories become the reality of a student body by becoming the legend of the campus. Although most of our students were urged to return to their homes after the storm, many decided to stay and volunteer to help with the relief efforts. One of the major student initiatives during this tragedy was UA Greek Relief, a student-led relief effort responsible for preparing more than 52,000 hot meals; for distributing hundreds of thousands of pounds of canned goods, clothes, and hygiene products; and for raising $180,000 in donations. At one point, the UA Greek Relief volunteers were responsible for preparing more than one-third of the total hot meals distributed throughout the city of Tuscaloosa. From April 29 to May 6, UA Greek Relief registered more than 600 volunteers, including students (both Greek and non-Greek), alumni, community members, and volunteers from across the country. Following the weeklong effort to prepare hot meals and distribute relief items, the organization shifted its primary focus to disaster relief fund-raising. As a result, UA Greek Relief is still in operation today. By embracing student involvement, we were able to help more people and build a sense of community on our campus that would not have otherwise been possible.
6. Take time to ask for help and prioritize work for volunteers. During a crisis, the group tasked with identifying all the major areas of crisis work often begins implementation of those projects in addition to directing the efforts of the larger institutional response. The best piece of advice for leaders is "Do only what only you can do." This is especially true in a crisis situation. Ask for help. Get the best person to accomplish the specific task you wish to accomplish. Communicate clearly with volunteers and help them prioritize the task list in front of them. And train them to do the same. In crisis situations, a few get burned out and the majority feels helpless. Engage more individuals with specific tasks and ignore the reflex of "just doing it yourself" because of expediency. Also, it may be helpful to establish a volunteer corps leadership team. Such a team may be able

to alleviate the need for essential personnel to meet with, organize, and educate each new group arriving to provide assistance, saving valuable time for more critical needs.

Although April 27, 2011, will always mark devastation in our community, it also represents the resilience and the dedication of university students and employees. In response to the tragedy, the choice to collaborate rather than to separate, to inform rather than to remain silent, and to inspire rather than to distance a grieving community shapes who we are as a university. We cannot undo the tragedy the tornadoes wrought on our community. We can only vow to become better stewards of this opportunity we have as leaders of our university to guide our students, our colleagues, and ourselves through the healing process. The nature of a crisis is to test the core of an entity, an institution. It is our fundamental belief that everyday excellence forged our relationships, informed our decisions, and sustained our processes. And that hope fuels us to become better versions of ourselves—our institution—for the generations that follow.

Note

1. All times reported in this chapter were obtained from an archived log of events.

7

RESPONSIVENESS IN TIMES OF CRISIS

Campus, Mission, and Community

Joseph Urgo

All of us prepare for campus crises; we have our emergency response team, our protocols for bomb threats and shooters, severe weather, pandemic outbreaks, and other known risks to residential campuses. However, although it's not possible to prepare for every imaginable crisis that may hit the campus, it's less likely that we are remotely prepared for a crisis that never occurred to anyone. For example, how many of us maintain on our campus, in reserve, a spare classroom building, an extra dining hall, or an empty residence hall or two? What would happen if we needed one of these facilities with no advance notice?

St. Mary's College of Maryland is situated on a bend in the St. Mary's River, a tributary to the Potomac River, a few miles away from where the Potomac meets the Chesapeake Bay in St. Mary's County, Maryland. We are barely above sea level, and there is a lot of water around us in the river and in the ponds and marshes on campus. The county, like the state, is named for the original colony, established in 1634 and distinctive among American colonies for its experiment with religious toleration. The colony was named for Queen Henrietta Maria (1609–1669), the wife of Charles I, and Henrietta Maria was named for the Catholic saint. In 1840, the state of Maryland established St. Mary's Seminary for women, a public boarding school, as a "monument school" to the original colony, a place where young women, future mothers of Marylanders, would learn and then teach their sons and daughters the colonial legacy values of freedom and tolerance. The high school, named after the county, expanded to a junior college in the mid-twentieth century and became a coed four-year college in the 1970s.

Today we are a public liberal arts college, and since 1992, we have been the state's designated honors college. A predecessor of mine referred to us as "the public Swarthmore." Waggish students responded with a counter-tagline and referred to the campus as "Swarthmore in the swamp." Sailing, kayaking, swimming—these are all integral to our competitive and recreational sports programs. Students, faculty, and staff can check out a boat with a college ID card, much as one would check out a book from the library. Our campus has 53 buildings and about 1,900 undergraduate students, 1,600 of whom are in residence. We are neighbors to Historic St. Mary's City, the site of Maryland's state capital until the end of the seventeenth century, when the capital moved to Annapolis. We are one vast archaeological site, because when the capital moved, the colony was abandoned. We know a lot about the historic site, but what's to be learned in the future is largely subterranean. Existence here is close to the earth and closely associated with the water.

Hurricane Irene arrived on August 28, 2011, on the same weekend students were returning to campus for the fall semester. We received 10 inches of rain along with winds in excess of 60 miles per hour, extended over 2 days. Students were confined to their residences for the most severe portion of the storm. We convened our emergency response team, followed the established protocols we'd rehearsed in the past, and managed the crisis without significant trouble. Tropical Depression Lee followed a week later, with another 10 inches of rain, and we managed that with little incident as well.

Twenty inches of rain in two weeks left things pretty damp on campus that September. During Irene, power was out for 42 hours, and it became extremely hot and humid in the residence halls. Students, of course, opened all their windows, which brought the high humidity indoors. When power was restored, jubilant students turned their air conditioning units down to the lowest settings, and room temperatures dipped below the dew point. Saturated building materials, plus high levels of humidity and the introduction of very cold air, led to unprecedented amounts of condensation on HVAC pipes and in air conditioning units, which led to the growth of mold in both visible and non-visible areas.

In late September and into October, students in our air-conditioned Prince George and Caroline Hall residences began to complain of respiratory problems typically associated with allergies. We took mold readings in the buildings, which returned at high levels. In response, we undertook an aggressive cleanup of the two residence halls over the fall semester break. After the cleanup, we retested and were surprised and dismayed to see the high levels remain. At this point, we were able to confirm the worst-case scenario: that mold had grown on the HVAC pipes behind ceiling tiles and inside the mechanisms of individual room cooling units. We consulted with a medical expert on mold who advised us that although there were no specific thresholds for a "mold crisis," the levels were clearly at a point where student health was endangered. He recommended evacuation of the 350 students who lived in the two affected residence halls. We no longer had a problem; now we had a crisis, one that extended from a facilities failure to a potential respiratory epidemic.

We were also in for a prolonged crisis as we contemplated the logistical implications of an extended student relocation. Worse yet, most of the affected residents were first-year students, in the midst of their transition to college life. Homesickness is not welcoming of displacement and uncertainty. Emergency meetings were convened to think through our predicament at various levels of the campus administrative structure. Where would students live? Was there room on campus for some of them? How could students go to an off-campus site and still be in residence? How would students get on and off campus? What will students do with all their personal belongings? What strings are attached to hotel accommodations? What needs to be done to restore residence halls? How fast can residence halls be restored? How do we pay for all of this? And most destructively to the will to solve problems, who was to blame for this situation?

Mold is nothing new on our watery campus, and our mold expert was quick to point out that high levels of mold readings could be acquired outside in the open air. Those same levels indoors are unhealthy. Each summer, we clean up isolated mold outbreaks in buildings vulnerable to high heat and humidity. So who missed the mold that grew in these two residence halls? I can distinctly recall a meeting during which we decided on a "moratorium on blame." Tensions were high within student affairs, within physical plant and housekeeping, and among these divisions, all regarding "how this happened." We needed to act quickly and with clear heads, and the decision to hold responsibility for the situation in abeyance was critical to restoring the confidence and security necessary to good thinking. Also, it was clear that the existing emergency response team was not what we needed. Instead, we assembled a group specific to the unprecedented combination of factors, from mold remediation to travel and logistical support, and as the situation unfolded, we added personnel with needed expertise—such as our museum neighbors. We needed everyone to see one another as resources for solutions, not as unwitting agents of responsibility for the crisis.

Our immediate task was to relocate 350 students from the Caroline and Prince George residence halls. We placed 100 students in on-campus housing, turning doubles into triples, occupying lounge areas, and allowing students to find creative solutions with willing hosts on campus. We moved 250 students to three local hotels, renting 125 rooms. That gave us breathing room, but we were not breathing easily. The hotels were anywhere from 10 to 20 miles away from campus, and placing half the first-year class and their resident assistants (RAs) into commercial hotel rooms represented a potentially fatal assault on our residential mission. Students treated the hotels like dormitories, which was sweet in some ways (the management put out snacks and turned lounges into study halls) but also dangerous, as students socialized in hallways often leaving their doors unlocked, trying to re-create dorm life in the hotels. But the general anonymity of a commercial hotel clashed with the open, curious, and exploratory lifestyle of college students in residence. We placed off-duty police protection at each location from 7:00 p.m. until 7:00 a.m.; we ran a continuous shuttle loop for 18 hours a day. The commute to and from campus, with three stops, in high traffic times could take as much as an hour.

Life in the hotels, after the novelty wore off, was just hard. Students had to haul their laundry to campus and back and had to return to campus each day to use their meal plan; they lost the spontaneous, unpredictable social and educational interaction that is integral to residential college life. Students could not fit all their belongings into the hotel room, so we provided storage on campus, and inevitably what was needed after moving was in a box somewhere in the storage unit. As the days went on, we sensed a growing urgency to get students back on campus. As president, I made it clear to my leadership team that students in hotels was an unacceptable situation—it was a life preserver, not a long-term solution. We asked everyone to work on the challenge and to bring ideas forward. A number of options were considered, and cost and logistics estimates were gathered, including renting temporary buildings, bringing in Federal Emergency Management Agency (FEMA) units, installing partitions in the gym, and setting up air structures (otherwise known as tents). It was in this frantic atmosphere of pitching solutions that our sailing coach, Adam Werblow, heard from an alumnus about a wild idea and took it to Charles "Chip" Jackson, our associate vice president for planning and facilities, who brought it to me.

Chip Jackson (now vice president for business and finance) sat across my desk with our CFO, Tom Botzman, and said he had something to ask me. Within a few days, the *Sea Voyager*, a 286-foot oceangoing cruise vessel, would pass by the mouth of the Chesapeake Bay on its way south from Nova Scotia to North Carolina. The ship was for sale, and while it was for sale, it was also available to rent. It had just completed a rental agreement that allowed workers to live on board while employed on a construction project. The ship has 110 cabins, 220 beds, and 36 crew cabins with another 72 beds, not all of which would be used by a scaled-down crew—we'd not need waiters and servers because students would get their food on campus. A shared, if audacious, vision began to unfold. Chip had done his homework and answered my two questions: Were there enough beds for all the students? That answer was yes, probably, if we counted freed-up crew cabins. How much was this going to cost? Allowing for unforeseen costs to prepare the dock and for other incidentals (and there were plenty of these), it looked to be—and here's where we smiled—it looked to be a wash. That is to say, relative to the cost of hotels, security, and transportation, the cruise ship solution appeared to be (and eventually was, in fact) cost neutral, and for that reason, we agreed to proceed.

So much of life at St. Mary's College of Maryland involves the river, the ponds, and the marshes on campus—and the sunsets, the beauty, and the force of water. My office on campus overlooks the river, and my office at home looks back at the campus, across Horseshoe Bend. Hundreds of boats compete in the Governor's Cup sailing race each August, which finishes on campus. European settlers established the first colony in Maryland on the site of the campus, arriving on the *Ark* and *Dove* transport ships. A re-creation of the *Dove* may be toured on the museum dock or sailed on in the river's bend. In the nineteenth century, young women who attended St. Mary's Seminary arrived by steamship, vessels that looked a lot like this *Sea Voyager*. Knowing nothing about maritime law, having no experience renting oceangoing cruise ships, hearing Chip Jackson's cautious assurance that the ship could probably dock on either our or the museum's dock, I relied finally on the one resource from which a president must draw on occasion when the path just is not that clear or obvious. All risks aside, my instinct was incontrovertible: In my gut I knew our ship had come in.

As I look back on the events that followed our decision to lease a cruise liner, I can say that only a gut response would have produced an affirmative response. There were numerous complications, and more than once we seemed done in, but the response team and the campus as a whole found the solution to the crisis so cool, so emblematically St. Mary's, that it was not possible to lose the will and the enthusiasm to make it work. As it was, we were not fully confident that the water at either dock was deep enough (as it turned out, the museum dock had a foot to spare in low tide), or that the dock itself would be large enough to accommodate the *Sea Voyager* until the day it arrived. And no matter what we thought about it, our judgment was solely ours and was not authoritative—it would be up to the Coast Guard to sign off on the ship's docking and on our capacity to keep it docked safely. If we could not, we'd need to anchor it in the river and arrange a ferry or barge service. And then there was the matter of Homeland Security. The *Sea Voyager* was registered in the Bahamas, which makes it a foreign vessel, and this opened our logistical arrangements to the scrutiny of Homeland Security. For example, even though the boat would never leave the dock, and even though the only people allowed on board were students and staff with St. Mary's identification, every tenth person to board would be subject to a security search.

Among the initially unforeseen expenses we incurred were physical improvements to the dock facilities, running Internet cable to the ship to provide wireless access, and arranging for waste removal so that nothing was deposited in the river (students had amusing names for this last service, which I'll leave to the reader's imagination). And although the museum dock is only a 10-minute walk from the center of campus, the walk from the edge of campus to the river is not lighted. We installed electric lights to accommodate our students' nocturnal habits and maintained a Public Safety presence around the clock.

The ship arrived in late October, and we decided that no matter when the residence halls were ready for reoccupation, the students would stay on board the *Sea Voyager* for the remainder of the semester. There would be no more displacement until January, when students would return to their original rooms. The decision made sense financially because by slowing down the pace of mold remediation we saved on overtime costs, and it also allowed us to negotiate a firm end date to the cruise ship contract. In round figures, the ship (and all expenses incurred to dock it) cost $1.5 million; the mold remediation cost another $1.5 million, for a total of $3 million—which was about 60 percent of our fund balance for emergency use.

Students' reaction to their new home on the cruise liner was mixed. Some were simply weary of relocation: They'd moved out of their rooms once for cleaning, a second time to move to a hotel, and a third time to move into a cruise cabin. The cabins varied in size, as one would expect, from luxury class to crew cabins, the latter of which were pretty snug. None of the rooms was as large as rooms in residence halls or hotels, and they were not designed for extended stays. Indeed, most of waking life on board is designed to take place in the well-attended Rosecliff Restaurant, with a capacity of 300; the Fog Cutters Pub, with a piano and a capacity of 150; the Harbor Lights Lounge, also with a piano and capacity of 300; and, out on deck, the Lighthouse Keepers Bar, with a capacity of 120. We turned the restaurant into a "quiet room" for study, and equipped it with computer stations and printers. The pub and lounge were used as social spaces, and our campus's Daily Grind coffee bar established a local branch on board in the Fog Cutters Pub. Students made great use of these public spaces and found the Harbor Lights Lounge and the Rosecliff Restaurant to be conducive to study, with their comfy chairs, marble floors, and fancy chandeliers—not to mention the expansive river view on a western exposure. In the end, the first-year student fall-semester grade point average on board the *Sea Voyager* was slightly above the non-displaced first-year student average.

Because the number of beds available on board matched almost to the pillow the number of beds we needed, the ship was at capacity. This meant that visitors to the ship had to be limited to no more than 20 at a time—and this meant that life on board took on the nature of an extended family or clan. Students knew everyone on the ship and could interact socially and work on their school assignments in an atmosphere of safety and familiarity. Public areas were comfortable, open, inviting, and conducive to concentration without isolation, settings that we know students today value. The quality of the study areas in the abandoned residence halls would come under scrutiny as a result, and we are looking at the quality of the public areas we maintain in our living areas.

Nonetheless, we did field a steady stream of complaints from students and parents, whose capacity for patience and flexibility varied widely. For some students, just going on board a ship was terrifying, let alone living on one, and these students easily traded accommodations with students on shore who were attracted to the novelty. Calls for "compensation" arose regularly among consumer-minded students who claimed to have purchased a residence hall room, not a cruise cabin, and wanted partial refund of their room fees. We assigned rooms by lottery, and some of those who fared less well than others complained of the unfairness of chance. And the Coast Guard mandated regular emergency drills, which were, to say the least, annoying to students as they involved loud alert noises and necessitated physical responses. While we were arranging the arrival of the ship on campus, we did not communicate a timeline for arrival and boarding because we could not predict with certainty whether and when the docking would be successful. Our uncertainty fueled anxieties in ways even now I am not sure we could have alleviated. As it turned out, the day we were to board we experienced a one-day delay because the ship was found to be listing to one side—a fixable problem, but one that would make boarding 250 students unsafe until addressed.

We had scheduled a press conference for the day of the boarding, and the result was stories about the delay, followed by stories of the boarding the next day. While the campus prepared for and then installed 250 students on board the *Sea Voyager*, the story of the "floating residence hall" captured media attention nationwide. As with any crisis, this one was a public relations challenge as well as a crisis in residence life. The headline in the *New York Times* on November 14, 2011, captured the way media coverage unfolded: "Staterooms, Not Dorms, All Thanks to Mold" (Southall, 2011). For all the same reasons why chartering the *Sea Voyager* struck us as so right for the college, the media found the story irresistible. As a result, the problem of "mold" was not the story—the story was in the response to the problem by the college.

In managing media coverage, we stressed the normalcy, to us, of the response we mounted to the displacement of students. The 286-foot *Sea Voyager* shared its dock with the *Maryland Dove*, a replica of the 76-foot trading ship that accompanied settlers to St. Mary's City from Europe in the seventeenth century. Not far from the site was the dock where steamships from Baltimore and Annapolis brought students to the female seminary in the nineteenth and early twentieth centuries. The river is the source of so much of what enlivens campus life and fuels our shared imaginations. It inspires our sailors and our poets—of course we would turn to the river when we had a problem. The same phenomenon of an excess of water that got us into our predicament would deliver to us our solution. We called the *Sea Voyager* our "floating residence hall," and campus life for the 250 displaced students returned to something close to normal for the final six weeks of the fall semester.

In times of unforeseen crisis, no one will find fault with victims. The rains and the wind and the humidity came; the HVAC systems failed; the students were moved for their own safety and well-being. Judgment commences with reactions to the responses we undertake. Throughout the extended crisis, we grounded our decisions in the college mission. The hotel solution was the life preserver, thrown out to the students to provide shelter—but living in a hotel miles away from campus was unacceptable as a solution because it violated our residential campus mission. We kept saying that. When the ship was contracted, we stressed its inevitability, again because it rescued and fulfilled our mission organically. What happened as a result was that our solution to the problem was a much more compelling story than the problem itself. Instead of stressing victimization, instead of looking inward to find sources of blame, we concentrated on what we had to do in response in order to uphold our sense of community.

We never defined the problem as belonging to the president, or the senior staff, or residence life—we defined the problem as a campus crisis, a crisis of mission and purpose. At every step, we called for campus cooperation. Dozens of staff and faculty assisted students when it was time to move out of their rooms or on board the ship. We held a series of open meetings to educate the campus about mold and its remediation, and we invited parents to attend. We hired experts and consultants as needed, for advice and guidance. And we used the opportunity to satisfy public curiosity by leading the media to see the solution as emerging from who we are as a community and allowing that definition to inform the storyline.

At the same time, yes, of course, there was a lot of squabbling. Even a shared mission and purpose is subject to the vagaries of human sensibility and response. In the office of the president, I understood my function to be one of continuous elevation to the level of mission.

What this meant was to encourage all involved to see themselves as contributing to something much larger than their individual role, something larger than any one of us, and something that needed all of our contributions singularly. To a student who complained to me about getting assigned to one of the tiniest crew cabins, I reminded him of how much richer his story would be when, twenty years hence, he could tell how he managed to live in a single room because it was impossible to fit another human being into it. We encouraged an endless series of seagoing metaphors in our daily speech; on our website and on Facebook, we placed photos of nineteenth-century steamships docking on campus and delivering students. We celebrated creativity, risk taking, and student resilience. My holiday card featured a photo of the ship and wished friends of the college "a buoyant new year." As a result, for those who put in hours and hours of additional work, who stretched their capacity and their endurance, there was a shared sense of community response that has left us all, long after the ship departed, with an enhanced sense of what this public liberal arts college can do when faced with a threat to our shared sense of mission and purpose.

Reference

Southall, A. (2011, November 15). Staterooms, not dorms, all thanks to mold. *New York Times*, A14.

8

A SHELTER IN THE TIME OF STORM

Bonita J. Brown

In the past few years, the United States has seen what seems to be an increase in the number of natural disasters. Floods, hurricanes, tornadoes, mudslides, and fires have become all too familiar headlines in the news. Most discussions about emergencies on a university campus focus on what to do when the emergency (hurricane, tornado, fire) directly impacts the campus. Little attention is paid to those universities that work behind the scenes to support other universities, states, or regions in the time of emergency. Many universities provide volunteers and supplies and often serve as shelters for people displaced by natural disasters. This chapter will explore the inner workings of hosting a shelter on a university campus, focusing on external and internal considerations.

Scenario

In 2008, the Texas Gulf Coast was hit by two significant hurricanes within a week of each other. Hurricane Gustav, a Category 2 storm, made landfall on September 1, 2008, and Hurricane Ike, another Category 2 storm, followed on September 13, 2008. Much attention was paid to Houston, New Orleans, and other areas directly impacted by the storms. The cities were evacuated, causing many thousands to flee their cities and move north. After learning valuable lessons from the incidents that transpired after Hurricane Katrina, the Federal Emergency Management Agency (FEMA), state and local governments, and other humanitarian organizations were better prepared to assist those forced to leave their homes.

The University of North Texas (UNT) is a state institution located 30 miles north of Dallas. The campus is home to more than 35,000 students and includes more than 168 buildings and 14 residence halls, covering approximately 848 acres. The campus has a football stadium, coliseum, and other facilities and is centrally located in Denton County. Owing to the size and complexity of safety precautions to keep the campus safe, the university employed an emergency coordinator. The role of this staff member was to plan, review, and execute the university's emergency planning. This process included safety precautions for incidents that may happen on campus, such as fire, storms, chemical leaks, active shooter, and many other possible hazards. At UNT, the emergency coordinator directly reported to the director of health and risk management, reporting to the vice president for business affairs, with a dotted line to the chief of staff of the university. This dual reporting line was critical in being able to maneuver university resources in unprecedented ways.

As the weather forecasts for Hurricane Gustav/Ike advanced, the emergency coordinator participated in daily conference calls with the Texas Governors Division of Emergency Management (GDEM). These calls updated emergency coordinators across the state about the status of the storm, resources that were being made available, or resources that were needed. On one of the calls, GDEM informed us that thousands of people from New Orleans and Houston would need to be sheltered in the Dallas area and solicited entities to host shelters.

The emergency coordinator brought the proposition back to the campus to determine if UNT would like to participate as a shelter. These discussions were held at the cabinet level of the university because the coordination of resources necessary to run a shelter would cross all divisions. The cabinet unanimously agreed that hosting a shelter was "the right thing to do" and exemplified the university's mission of producing engaged citizens of the world.

Once the decision was made to host the shelter, it was necessary to develop a plan of action. It was determined that the UNT Coliseum would be used as the sheltering site. It had the largest open space, multiple bathroom facilities, and entrances and exits that could be secured, and it was on the outer fringes of campus. Running a shelter of this size would require the involvement of many external organizations, such as FEMA, the Red Cross, the Denton County government, GDEM, and the university. During this sheltering event, the University of North Texas successfully hosted 3 separate shelters over the course of 19 days, sheltering 358 evacuees, including 80 students from Lamar University.

What should universities know or consider when agreeing to serve or serving as a shelter? What types of challenges or situations should a university expect to face? The following outlines considerations on two levels: the external and the internal.

External Considerations

What is meant by *external considerations*? In this chapter, external considerations are items and actions of those outside of the university, beyond the university's control. These include federal and state agencies, the community, media, other universities, and legislators. It is important to be aware of these considerations because they are a major factor in running a successful shelter.

Establishing Relationships With External Agencies

Universities, especially in "college towns," are often engaged with external agencies for a variety of reasons. It is imperative that the president have a good reputation and relationships in the community and with legislators in advance of emergencies. What this does for the university in times of emergencies is facilitate access to resources and increase the trustworthiness of the entire university. The president having good relationships with the mayor, county officials, and state representatives could be the difference between the university getting what it needs or making enemies. Also, the relationships that the emergency coordinator, the campus police, and the media have with their counterparts will be critical in the management of a very fluid situation. Universities or presidents of universities that have not fostered good relationships may find themselves lacking the external support in the greatest time of need. The president at UNT was very well respected, which directly resulted in the overwhelming offer of support that was received from agencies and individuals in Denton and across the entire state.

Setting Parameters for the Campus

The university must have a strong leader of the sheltering effort and must set parameters for the campus. The institution's goal of hosting a shelter is to provide relief while minimizing the day-to-day impact on the campus. Multiple agencies will be involved in this effort, and all of them will be asking the university for something. The institution must maintain control and lay out the plan of action. Do not be afraid to say "no" and to set boundaries. This will be very difficult. Although everyone wants to do what is best for the shelter, the university also has constituents that it must keep in mind—the students, faculty, and staff. The staff will have to be very diplomatic in implementing the plan and determining boundaries.

A perfect example of setting boundaries involved background checks. GDEM and FEMA determined which busloads of individuals would be coming to UNT. As the bus was en route, we tried to determine what screenings should be done for the evacuees. This was important for us because we didn't believe that we would be serving the campus well if we did not have information about the individuals who would, for all intents and purposes, be living among our students. We demanded that background checks be conducted on all evacuees. The state and federal agencies indicated that they would not be providing that service and that if we wanted it done, then we would have to bear the costs. We were adamant that the individuals would not stay on our campus until they had background checks. This was a tense discussion, but we had to stand firm in our position in order to protect our students. We partnered with the local police department, and background checks were conducted. There were at least two individuals in the group who were identified as sexual offenders. We found a local agency that agreed to pay for hotel rooms for these two individuals away from the campus. If we had not stood our ground, and a sexual assault had taken place on our campus, the university could have been embroiled in legal matters and questions as to why the safety of our students was not a major consideration.

Another example involved the setup of the shelter. The Red Cross provided the cots, blankets, and food for the shelter, with the understanding that they would also provide volunteers. The university had also agreed to provide volunteers. As the volunteer schedules were being made, it became apparent that the Red Cross wanted to fill the "prime time" hour slots during the day with their volunteers and wanted university volunteers to cover the overnight shifts. This proposition was not acceptable to us for many reasons. We did not want our students or staff members to work overnight for extended periods of time. Also, we wanted our faculty and staff to be able to work their community service hours during the normal workday, and we wanted them to get the recognition for their service. This was a delicate situation in that we needed the Red Cross as a partner, but we did not want to feel as if the university was being used and being given the least desirable work. We successfully addressed this with the Red Cross and created a volunteer schedule that was balanced and acceptable to everyone. Again, agencies and volunteer organizations will ask for everything that they need to fulfill their role. The institution must set the boundaries and protect the interest of the university, while maintaining external relationships.

Expecting the Unexpected

As FEMA and GDEM were routing buses to various locations in the Dallas area, we received a call that a bus was headed toward us with approximately

70 people. When the bus arrived, we immediately assessed the situation and determined that we did not have the capacity to serve these individuals who had severe medical needs. Although we were prepared to serve, we were not in a position to provide urgent medical attention. The emergency coordinator called FEMA and explained the situation, and the bus was rerouted. The buses that arrived next contained 131 people, including children and babies. We were prepared for adults but had not planned on receiving babies and children. As evacuees, they had very few of their belongings. We found ourselves in urgent need of baby items—diapers, milk, formula, cribs, and baby clothes. Every hour identified a need that we had to figure out how to address. Some people brought medication that we later determined required refrigeration. Some did not have any of their medicines. Others did not bring enough clothing. Many did not have basic toiletries. One of the biggest challenges we faced was the fact that many people did not have their cell phones or did not have chargers for their cell phones, and therefore they could not find family members from whom they were separated. We immediately mobilized our information technology (IT) and telecom staff to set up a phone bank and computer labs to give them communication with the outside world. By day two, the children were bored, so we set up a TV and game room and found things for them to play to occupy their time. Many of our early childhood education majors volunteered their time to stay with the children so the parents could rest, take care of business, or look for their loved ones. We had to learn the dietary needs of the individuals and ensure that they received food that they could eat. In essence, we had to be nimble and ready to address anything that came up. This could not have been done without a high level of coordination with the campus and the community.

Another example of being prepared to address whatever issues may arise involved a university located in Houston. Approximately 80 student athletes from Lamar University were traveling for a competition and could not return to the university because their campus had been damaged by the storm. They were stranded. The athletic director from Lamar contacted the athletic director at UNT and asked if we could provide assistance. As a matter of course, most universities have partnership or interagency/mutual cooperation agreements with another university that is a safe distance from their campus. These agreements are often sought out by the universities located in risk areas as a part of their emergency planning processes to ensure that they have a place for their students to go in the event of an emergency. Although we did not have such an agreement with Lamar University, we did have agreements with other universities and used those agreements as the model for hosting the students from Lamar. Because the UNT Coliseum was already in use for a shelter, we used other athletic facilities on campus to host the students at the same time we were hosting the large shelter in the coliseum. Although this may be an extreme case, it illustrates the point that you have to be ready to address whatever may arise.

Developing a Plan for Involving the Community

During times of major disasters, everyone wants to lend a helping hand. Once the word gets out in the community that the university is hosting a shelter, they will want to help. You can't stop them. And you need them. What you can do is be prepared with a plan for what you need from the community. Once it became clear that the shelter was going to be a reality, we created a drop-off location for donations. We kept a running list of volunteers and organizations that wanted to help and were able to target our requests. People had already begun calling, wanting to drop off items, so we asked for community volunteers to help sort and organize the supplies. Once the drop-off location was organized, we immediately sent out a call specifically for toiletry items. A specific call was necessary because people saw the donation call as an opportunity to get rid of items that they no longer wanted, and this was not what we were seeking. We only accepted items that were on the "call for supplies" list. Once the evacuees arrived and we were better able to determine their needs, we were able to put out more specific calls for items. This process created a few tense moments, with people being frustrated when their donations were turned away, but the university had to be smart and not accept items that would have a high disposal cost. The community was most helpful with the baby supplies. We were overwhelmed with the donations of baby chairs, baby food, toys, and diapers. We also needed the community to transport the evacuees to stores, to the doctor or hospital, and to visit ministers or counselors. Hosting a shelter is not possible without the service and donations of the community, but the coordination of those services is of vital importance.

Holding External Agencies to Their Promises

During an emergency, the situation is so fluid that a turn of events can change the entire situation at a moment's notice. Federal agencies often promise support in exchange for an agreement to provide some type of service. It is very easy to find yourself agreeing to take on more responsibilities than initially discussed because a state agency assured you that you would get reimbursed for the additional expenses. Do not get left holding the bag. Document your conversations, send e-mails to document conversations, get a contract of written agreement if possible, and keep receipts. Our total cost for two of the three shelters was approximately $50,000. FEMA guaranteed us that we would be reimbursed at 100 percent of our expenses. The emergency coordinator was dogmatic in pursuing this reimbursement. He was given the run-around for many months and sent to different departments and had to submit the same paperwork three or four times. Finally, eight months later, we received 100 percent reimbursement for our expenses. The staff must be dedicated to the reimbursement process and to holding agencies to their promises.

Managing Visits From Government Officials

In times of emergency, government agencies and officials are called upon to service the public need. As a result, many political figures and heads of agencies will want to visit the emergency site or sheltering site to see the work in action and to take photographs to document the happenings in their area. Although this is to be expected, it has its pros and cons. Photo ops are great in that they highlight the good that your campus is doing. Be sure that the school logo or image is visible throughout the shelter and encourage public officials to state the name of the institution in their interviews. This will bring publicity to the university in ways that you cannot imagine. It also shows the university as a good citizen. There are also challenges that come with photo ops at a shelter. Remember: the shelter becomes the home of the evacuees. The evacuees are exhausted, worried, and often emotional—but still trying to carry on with their lives. Government officials are often working on their own timetable and feel that they can come and take the photo ops whenever it fits their schedules, with no thoughts about others' circumstances. There will be times when you may have to turn away a government official to protect the privacy and respect of the evacuees. This is a tricky proposition because you do not want to make an enemy out of someone that the university will need for future ventures. It is recommended that you involve your government relations person early in the process. Be proactive. Keep this person informed of the sheltering efforts and, if possible, have them call and invite the officials to come at designated times. You may also want to schedule conversations with specific evacuees and allow the government official to tour the facility at an appropriate time. If a government official just shows up, you must be nimble and figure out how to create a successful visit for the official. This may require creativity on your part. Have a well-trained volunteer or media relations staff member, a memorable evacuee, or someone from one of the partner agencies ready to speak at all times. These officials often ask what they can do to be of more assistance—be ready with a list of one or two items that you really need. Then use whatever it is they provide and follow up and let them know how it was used. This brings goodwill to all involved.

Managing the Media

The media presents an ever-present challenge that has both external and internal implications. Although a university hosting a shelter is a great humanitarian story, the media also loves stories about the internal struggles behind the scenes or stories about the university turning down the request of the local beloved agency. Involve your media relations department from the beginning. They should create talking points for the president, the emergency coordinator, board members, and any others who may be asked to speak on behalf of the university. You should make sure that the media coverage is positive and even write stories and press releases to send to the media outlets. If negative stories happen to make it to the media, be prepared to cast the story in a better light and highlight the giving nature of the university. It is recommended that you have a media relations person present during the daytime while the shelter is in operation. The media must be managed very carefully because it is possible for the university to be shown in a less than favorable manner despite the fact that it is providing a public service. Take deliberate steps to protect your university.

Internal Considerations

As significant as the external considerations are to this entire process, the internal considerations are just as important. Internal considerations involve the policies, rules, culture, and procedures that occur inside of the university. Dealing with internal considerations is tricky at best because you may have to bend a few of your rules while holding firm to others. This is particularly challenging for public universities that are governed by state rules and regulations.

Using University Resources

Hosting a shelter on a university campus evokes a lot of emotions. Many people will want to go overboard and do anything that is necessary to help, whereas others will want to protect their departments and their resources. This creates a very interesting dynamic on the campus. The first step in this process is to get the approval and buy-in from the president and the president's cabinet. Once they are in agreement that the campus will host a shelter, a central committee must be created to coordinate all efforts. Membership on this committee should include decision makers from each unit of the campus. This is important in that decisions will need to be made in real time, and there is no time to wait for approvals to be received through the various channels that may exist in a department. Information will also need to be disseminated deeply within the university so that everyone is aware of what has been decided and will understand, when they receive requests for assistance, that it is a university-wide approved event. The emergency coordinator should take the lead on the resources effort. The campus should also be in constant contact with FEMA or the state agency to understand the reimbursement options. Although it is hoped that 100 percent of funds spent will be reimbursed, each department should set a baseline of how much funding they can dedicate, with the underlying knowledge that all monies spent may not be reimbursed. This is particularly difficult for a state agency, in that state agencies cannot give away state resources. The president may have to cover expenses out of the university discretionary funds or raise funds for the sheltering effort. The campus must be very creative in how they provide support.

Another challenging decision surrounding use of university resources relates to deciding where to host a shelter. This is a very delicate balancing act on a university campus in that you need enough space to host a proper shelter, but at the same time, you cannot take resources away from your faculty, staff, and, most important, students. At UNT, we looked into the use of multiple facilities, such as the recreational sports gyms, the Coliseum, and the Research Park. Some of the considerations included egress and ingress options, how to get food to the evacuees, shower facilities, proximity to students and classes, and the overall amount of space available. The Coliseum was chosen as the location because it provided the best options for the considerations previously listed. Had it been basketball season, or if other large events had been scheduled for the Coliseum during the dates of the hurricane, use of the Coliseum may not have been possible. There also had to be a lot of discussion with the head coaches of the basketball teams because they raised concerns about the use of the Coliseum in this manner. Understanding that this was something that the university was in favor of, and being reassured that we would consult with them on day-to-day decisions about the use of the facility, they fully supported the effort. Use of university resources is one of the most significant internal considerations in the decision to host a shelter.

Managing Student and Faculty Involvement

Many of the same considerations about community involvement hold true for the campus community. Faculty, staff, and students will all want to be a part of the sheltering activities. Student groups are a great resource for key parts of the sheltering process. At UNT, many of the student athletes and Greek organizations assisted in the setup and breakdown of cots, they helped manage the distribution of supplies, they worked with the children of the evacuees, they took photographs, and they volunteered in many other capacities. The UNT Center for Leadership and Service served as a connectivity resource, linking the students, faculty, and staff with the community agencies and individuals in need of volunteers. This office was very active during the sheltering process and assisted by coordinating the efforts of our students. For students who needed community service hours, the center allowed their work at the shelter to count toward their community service requirements. More than 300 student volunteers participated in this shelter. Faculty and staff will also want to volunteer their time, skills, and resources, and the university should be organized in a way to accept their services. One of the highlights of faculty involvement in the shelter involved the Department of Speech and Hearing Sciences at UNT. Many of the elderly evacuees had hearing aids. In the rush to evacuate, they did not bring extra hearing aids or batteries for the hearing aids. When the faculty in the Department of Speech and Hearing Sciences heard about this, they took immediate action. They contacted the emergency coordinator and asked if they could set up a hearing clinic. They brought a portable sound booth and tested hearing aids, provided free batteries, and assisted everyone who was having a problem with their hearing aids. The evacuees were most grateful. This was a circumstance that I do not think we would have even thought to plan for, but the faculty saw the need and freely offered their expertise. There were numerous examples of volunteerism during the 19 days the shelter was open. Much of the work that needs to be done to provide a shelter cannot be done without the service and resources of the faculty, staff, and students.

Reviewing and Establishing University Policies

Sheltering is often a response to an emergency situation that is occurring in a different location. Because of this, a "state of emergency" is often not in existence for the sheltering area. In a state of emergency, state laws and normal procedures may be suspended in an effort to contain and address the situation. Outside of a state of emergency, normal state policies and rules apply. This directly impacts the policies, laws, and rules for state employees. It will be important to review the university's community service policy, volunteer policy, overtime policies, workers' comp policies, and vacation or leave policies. These policies regulate when faculty and staff can volunteer, whether or not they get paid for their time, and what happens if they are injured during the course of their service. If the university does not have clear policies in these areas, such policies should be established because it is challenging to create or revise a policy in the middle of a sheltering event. Many policies may need to be reviewed, revised, or created, and the university should document the ideals of the university on volunteering through well-written policies.

The human resources staff should be well versed in the university policies so that they can provide uniform advice to supervisors across campus. Policies can be interpreted in different ways, so it will be important to have a single interpretation of the policies. This will help in preventing situations in which staff members are treated differently across departments. Being knowledgeable about internal policies and procedures about volunteer and employment matters will go far in decreasing internal frustrations about volunteer efforts.

Considering Liabilities

A sheltering event will bring the general counsel many sleepless nights. There are many areas of possible liability that could arise through this process. While the events coordinator and other staff are thinking about the immediate day-to-day happenings, the general counsel will be imagining numerous scenarios that could result in liability for the university. Legal representation is critical on the Emergency Coordinating Committee. The university should enter into a sheltering agreement with the Red Cross or other leading agency. This agreement should include language addressing insurance requirements for both parties, joint liabilities, payment terms, if any, and it should clearly define who is responsible for what. Sheltering in and of itself is a risk, and if the university has decided to accept this risk, the attorney's role is to help the campus mitigate the risk and avoid creating larger problems. Legal matters such as slip and falls of volunteers, employees, or the evacuees are a possibility, as are workers' comp claims for employees of the university. Would working at the shelter fall under their job responsibilities, making them eligible for workers' comp, or is this outside the scope of their employment? What if someone gets physically assaulted in the shelter or gets sick from the food that is provided, or what if a child goes missing? What if someone is assaulted or their items are stolen? Does the work of the emergency coordinator and other university employees constitute the "giving away" of university resources? Unfortunately, these are questions that may not be able to be addressed until the middle of the process, but the questions should be asked and should be considered during the planning and implementation of the shelter.

Breaking Through the Red Tape

Any large event on a university campus calls for extraordinary coordination of university resources. Operations that normally take weeks to achieve will need to be done immediately. The emergency committee should contain representatives who have the power or authority to make the critical decisions that impact their areas. As an example, for the shelter at UNT, we requested that IT set up phone banks and computer labs in one day. A high-ranking IT staff member served on the committee and was invaluable to the process.

He had the department immediately assess their resources, and they were able to set the phone banks and computer labs up within hours after the evacuees arrived. In setting up a shelter, there are many legal agreements that will require immediate review and signature. General counsel will need to be available and that office must be willing to move these documents to the top of the review list. The president or designee also has to be available to answer questions and discuss the risks with the attorney. Outside of the emergency coordinator, the chief of staff or the president's designee should be able to use their connections, influence, and relationships on campus and in the community to secure any needed resources. This includes directing the flow of information, garnering support, and diplomatically moving resources on the campus.

Keeping Records

Record keeping is essential throughout the entire sheltering process. For state agencies, it will be important to keep track of costs and hours worked by employees in the event that a public records request is received. Sheltering requests are often made by FEMA or a state agency, and along with the request often come reimbursements. It is important to ask about the reimbursement rate prior to agreeing to the shelter and to get the agreement in writing. Once the campus has determined what the reimbursement rate is, the documentation must be provided in exactly the manner requested by the federal or state agency. Whether it is intentional or not, government agencies tend to deny reimbursement requests for the slightest of reasons. It is important to understand up front how they want the documentation to be presented and give it to them in exactly that manner. Documentation could include time sheets, cost estimates, actual costs, rental fees, security costs, equipment costs, and so on. The emergency coordinator should be most familiar with the reimbursement requirements and should work with all campus participants to assist them in tracking their costs, time, and resources. Probably one of the most important records that can be created is an after-action report. This report should document the entire sheltering process, including but not limited to challenges, committee lists, creative solutions, lists of participants, total costs, volunteers, and so on. This will be the best record of the university's participation in the event the university decides to provide a shelter in the future.

Conclusion

Hosting a shelter on a university campus is one of the most rewarding and altruistic services a university can provide. The University of North Texas hosted 3 separate shelters over the course of 19 days, sheltering 358 evacuees, including 80 students from Lamar University. The entire shelter operation involved 141 role players, 14 internal departments, 20 external organizations, 20 American Red Cross volunteers, and more than 300 student volunteers. A university must balance the risks versus the costs and apply that same analysis to the many internal and external considerations. Although hosting a shelter may be a daunting effort, when done successfully, it exemplifies the heart of a university.

PART THREE

BUILDING A TEAM

Shared Responsibilities

Leveraging resources during a campus crisis will help turn a chaotic situation into a more manageable event. Essential resources that are found internally include the knowledge and expertise of the staff, tightly crafted crisis and communication plans, and the availability of emergency funds to help support the immediate actions that are often necessary during the acute phase of a crisis. External resources are equally important and can include crisis management firms, crisis communication consultants, and national higher education associations and organizations, as well as external legal counsel in addition to the general counsel from the college or university. Campus leaders need strong internal resources as well as strong external resources for the successful resolution of campus crises.

As the main decision-making entity during times of emergency, campus crisis teams are on the front lines during the crisis. They are essential resources because they allow institutions to respond immediately and effectively to the crisis and encompass diverse perspectives and expertise from the campus community. Because the crisis can hit while the president and other members of the senior leadership team are away from campus, it is critical to have backups for each member of the crisis team. This allows for coverage of all critical roles and more flexibility within the team.

Campus leaders should also consider having multiple crisis teams depending on the type of crisis. The staff members who serve on the crisis team during a natural disaster may not necessarily be the most appropriate candidates to handle an active shooter situation on campus. As conveyed by Dianne F. Harrison, role differentiation, cross-divisional collaboration, as well as a clear understanding of the chain of command can be the difference between success and failure in the handling of a campus crisis.

Often overlooked, trustees or board members of colleges and universities can play an important role when the campus is in crisis. First and foremost, presidents need to inform the board of the situation and remain in contact with the chair. As stated by Patrick T. O'Rourke, governing boards have a fiduciary obligation to ensure that proper reporting procedures and structures are set in place to ensure timely and effective disclosure to the board of major risks to the institution. Chapter 10 uses the Pennsylvania State University athletics incident as a case study of communications with a governing board and provides practical recommendations for governing boards of colleges and universities targeted at setting effective structures that will allow the institution and its board to respond appropriately in a time of crisis.

When a crisis hits, campus leaders may feel the need to manage the situation with only the resources that are available to them on campus. However, many crises are extremely complex, and it can be unrealistic to expect internal staff to have the expertise needed for all types of crises. It is important for the campus to reach out beyond the institution for specialized expertise. When doing this, seeking out consultants who have experience working with higher education institutions can complement the existing knowledge base on the campus. If presidents choose to go this route, they need to be proactive during the planning stages of crisis management and establish relationships with individuals or organizations that can be of assistance when the campus is dealing with a crisis.

Janice M. Abraham, president and CEO of United Educators, provides a road map for equipping campus crisis teams with the tools to manage, recover from, and, ultimately, thrive after a crisis. Abraham stresses several critical building blocks—teamwork, shared values, preparation, and the establishment of a culture of candor and trust among members of the senior team and the governing board—as being essential for the effective handling of campus crises.

Presidents can also reach out to a network of their peers, either from like-minded institutions or from local colleges and universities. Because being a college president can be an isolating and challenging job, it is important for presidents to be able to call upon their peers and ask for advice and support during a crisis.

One area that is often overlooked is maintaining strong relationships with leaders in the local community and beyond. These individuals may represent the local media, police, religious leaders, as well as local, state, and federal governmental officials. It is important to have strong relationships with individuals who are highly regarded in the community because they can speak out in favor of the campus and can offer critical advice that may help in the proper handling of a crisis situation.

From the moment she learned of the near-drowning of an international student on her campus, Connie J. Gores and the members of her institution's crisis management team had to rely on the strong ties they had built with key members of the broader community to manage the situation with the utmost cultural sensitivity, care, and compassion. This involved working closely with the student's family and home university in China, with staff from the U.S. Embassy in China and the U.S. Department of State, as well as with a local Muslim cleric who provided advice on the proper religious protocols to be followed.

Leaders also need to be mindful of the stress brought about by incidents on the campus, both for themselves and the leadership team. If a leader can't get to campus because of bad weather, what provisions have been made for contact? If the information technology network is affected by a power outage, what is the backup plan? If the campus is in lockdown, where is the alternative meeting place for the crisis team? If all of these questions are answered ahead of time, there is less stress on the team. Every team should engage the services of the Employee Assistance Program when needed—for the administrators as well as the faculty, staff, and students. Campus leaders must be mindful of the fact that they must take care of themselves in order to be able to take care of others.

9

LEVELS OF CRISES AND LEADERSHIP RESPONSES

Role Differentiation and Collaboration

Dianne F. Harrison

The January 17, 1994, Northridge earthquake remains a seminal event in the history of California State University, Northridge (CSUN). With the epicenter of the quake located within two miles of the campus, the natural disaster caused $400 million in damage, the most serious for a university campus up to that time. Nearly all 107 buildings on campus were impacted—a parking structure collapsed and buildings were severely damaged. Several of those buildings eventually had to be razed when they were deemed irreparable, and others remained closed for an extended period.

CSUN was fortunate that the event occurred at 4:31 a.m. on a Monday holiday (Martin Luther King Jr. Day), while the university was still in winter break. One shudders to think about the different outcome that might have occurred had the earthquake struck during the middle of the day while classes were in session. Seventy-two people died as a result of the 6.7 magnitude earthquake, none on campus. Of the victims, two were CSUN students, killed while they slept in their beds in a privately owned apartment complex across the street from the university.

Under the determination and courageous leadership of the university's then president, Blenda J. Wilson, the university reopened for the spring semester on Valentine's Day, February 14, just two weeks later than scheduled. This was achieved through the creativity and adept logistical planning of President Wilson and the university's talented and committed faculty and staff. The effort included bringing more than 350 temporary structures on campus, which required the university to manually reschedule nearly all classes in the trailer parks that now populated the campus, and communicating updates in an era before there was the kind of critical mass of Internet connectivity, e-mail, and social media we now take for granted. CSUN's experience and accomplishments in overcoming such a major catastrophe have been deservedly honored and recognized—including with visits shortly after the disaster by Vice President Al Gore and, at a ceremony on the first-year anniversary of the earthquake, by President Bill Clinton.

As one can imagine, this experience has infused into CSUN a culture of emergency and crisis preparedness. Begun by President Wilson and further developed under her successor, Jolene Koester, under whose leadership the university in 2007 officially completed its recovery from the earthquake, CSUN has developed a mature and comprehensive preparedness plan. When I was appointed president of California State University, Northridge, in 2012, it was my second presidency, and knowing the high expectations and increased obligations required of university presidents to act quickly and decisively in a crisis, one of the first people I met with on campus was our chief of police. I was pleased to learn about the university's level of emergency preparedness and the extent of training, commitment of resources, and ongoing review and updating that went into keeping plans relevant and effective. I also quickly understood that, in large part owing to the earthquake and eventual rebuilding of the university, campus employees developed and handed down a culture of resiliency and a "can-do" and collaborative outlook across the university.

As I write this, I am slightly less than a year into the CSUN presidency. Yet already the campus has faced the report of a potentially armed individual that resulted in the temporary evacuation of the university library, one bomb threat, one death threat (to me), a student hunger strike, a student suicide with witnesses, and an emergency crash landing of a small airplane on a recreational field, among others. In the latter event, when I arrived at the scene of the plane crash, knowing in advance there were no fatalities (pilot and passenger sustained minor injuries and no students or employees were involved), I commented to my chief of police that we were extremely fortunate that this accident happened on the Sunday afternoon of Thanksgiving weekend before most students had returned from the holiday. She agreed and also informed me that she had selected this seemingly remote incident (plane crash on campus) as the subject of a training exercise for the university's annual Emergency Operations Center (EOC) drill three years prior. I was extremely reassured and further convinced of the necessity to practice various scenarios. I also quickly developed confidence in the chief's extraordinary expertise.

Even with these careful preparations and team expertise, I have learned to apply an important principle: Not every crisis or emergency requires the same action. Every situation is different and necessitates different kinds of expertise and responses. Thus, having plans in place that are flexible, understanding everyone's role differentiation and the chain of command in such situations, practicing responses repeatedly, and having a strong culture of cross-divisional collaboration and trust are essential to effective emergency and crisis planning.

Crisis Levels and Leadership Structure

CSUN is one of the largest and most diverse universities in the nation. Part of the 23-campus California State University system, we are an urban-serving university that serves 36,000 students and nearly 4,000 employees, situated in the San Fernando Valley in the City of Los Angeles. Given our size, like many large universities, our daily operations and services are comparable in size and scope to a small city.

The range of crises and emergencies that universities may experience vary greatly. There are the obvious catastrophes we hope never to face, like a major earthquake, wildfire, or shooting. There are moderate issues that may affect the health or safety of part or all of the campus, like local fires, heavy storms, and bomb threats; minor emergencies that can be dealt with by first responders and are immediately "contained"; and crises and issues that may not impact health, safety, or resources but must be nevertheless managed carefully because they may affect an institution's reputation and credibility. Being responsive to both fast-moving and "slow-simmering" crises as diverse as budget reductions, racial incidents, athletics infractions, employee misconduct, labor and personnel issues, student protests, and the like can be as important and happen more frequently than the larger catastrophic events for which we tend to prepare and practice. In fact, these typically "lesser" emergencies and issues provide valuable preparation and training for more serious crises and can help develop a high level of trust and cooperation that will pay off if and when a significant catastrophe does strike.

As examples of what we have put in place at CSUN, the following sections provide overviews of the university's formal Emergency Operations Plan (EOP) and, for less dire circumstances, our Campus Closure Integrated Communications Protocol and issues management process.

Emergency Operations Center

The centerpiece of CSUN's comprehensive emergency management program is our risk-based Emergency Operations Plan. The plan is written in compliance with California's Standardized Emergency Management System (SEMS) and the National Incident Management System. It was developed with a multi-hazard perspective to make it applicable to the widest range of emergencies and disasters, both natural and human caused. However, incident commanders at the scene of an emergency and the Emergency Operations Center director retain the flexibility to modify procedures or organizational structure as necessary to accomplish the emergency/disaster response and recovery missions in the context of a particular hazard scenario.

SEMS was developed to create a consistency of training and roles and to improve the coordination of state and local emergency response efforts in California. At CSUN, the responsibility for campus-wide emergency management has been formally designated by the university president to the department of police services, under the leadership of its director, the chief of police. Understandably, the university's experience with the Northridge earthquake has instilled in us the priority to have a comprehensive emergency plan in place, and perhaps more important, to take seriously the need to be prepared, practiced, and collaborative on the part of every university division.

The California SEMS incorporates the Incident Command System (ICS) and describes how it should be used in the field (the scene of emergency), including the interface between the field incident command post and the Emergency Operations Center. Thus, the CSUN Emergency Operations Center operates on the ICS structure and uses the standard five major sections of ICS: management, operations, planning, logistics, and finance. The university's chief of police serves as the director of the EOC and has overall responsibility for the management of the EOC. The director of the EOC directly oversees the management section, and other university staff lead the remaining four sections. When the EOC is activated at the university, the president and president's cabinet serve in a separate section from the EOC known as the Policy/Advisory Group, with whom the EOC director (or the director's liaison) frequently briefs and consults during the course of the emergency. In the event of a major emergency, this structure defines the supervisory authority and reporting relationships and provides a unity of command.

When an event arises that may require the eventual activation of the EOC, the Crisis Action Team is first called together. At CSUN, the Crisis Action Team is made up of the president and the president's cabinet, which consists of the university's main executive leadership team (the university's five vice presidents, the president's chief of staff, and the executive director of the University Corporation, our auxiliary organization that oversees housing and food service), as well as the chief of police and the associate vice president for marketing and communications. The Crisis Action Team determines whether the university has the necessary resources to deal with the situation or whether a partial or full EOC activation is warranted. It should be noted that although there is this command structure, depending on the event, the timing and availability of the president and cabinet members, the full EOC may be activated by any member of the Crisis Action Team.

In addition to outlining the organizational structure of the EOC, the EOP also identifies three levels of emergency: a minor emergency (Level 1), a moderate emergency (Level 2), and a major emergency (Level 3):

Minor Emergency	A situation that can generally be handled at the scene of an incident, usually with the assistance and support of a local emergency response organization, that is, law enforcement, fire and rescue, or paramedics (e.g., student injured by vehicular traffic on or near campus).
Moderate Emergency	A significant emergency or multiple events commanded by incident commander(s) that require more extended conferral with the Crisis Action Team. The EOC team may be partially activated, with the level of staffing based on the situation (e.g., "isolated bomb threat," extended power outages campus wide).
Major Emergency	An area-wide emergency with severe potential impacts on the health and safety of students, faculty, staff, the public, facilities, and/or the environment, commanded by law enforcement, fire department, and emergency medical services, in coordination with the university and local, city, or county EOCs (e.g., earthquake or active shooter).

Other key factors that will normally trigger the activation of the EOC include emergency response resources needed beyond the university's capability, an emergency of long duration that may require major policy decisions, and the declaration of a state of emergency.

Logically, the nature of the emergency and its impact on the university will often determine the scale and staffing of the EOC activation—only those people whose services and expertise are needed, as determined by the EOC director and the Policy/Advisory Group, are activated. At CSUN, the communications and public information team is part of the management section, which not only includes the traditional public information officer/media spokesperson role, but also members of the web management team and staff with social media skills so that updates may be posted to the campus website and social media monitored for comments, trends, and the morale or general tenor of the campus community constituents, including students, faculty, staff, and parents. Team members are cross-trained as much as possible.

At CSUN, we have designated a room within our police services facility—as well as backup locations, including University House, where I reside—to serve as our EOC, with the rooms and location of each section already mapped out. Once a year, we test the EOC in a real-time, realistic drill: The chief of police prepares and designs a sophisticated scenario that uses enacted TV coverage and footage broadcast into the emergency facility, reporters from our student newspaper, people commenting on social media, and so on, in order to create a realistic environment for the drill.

The process includes keeping a chronology and documenting decisions and actions. The expectations of the public (as well as federal and state requirements) oblige the university to demonstrate it acted quickly in responding to situations and informing its constituents of threats to health and safety. As an institution that received support from the Federal Emergency Management Agency to recover from the Northridge earthquake, we also know that keeping meticulous records of emergencies, especially those involving destruction and the use of resources, is essential.

Campus Closure Integrated Communications Protocol

As the university developed its emergency plan, the administration encountered situations in which the activation of the EOC was not warranted but action still needed to be taken, particularly in communicating the cancellation of classes and/or the closure of all or parts of the campus. On any campus with residential students (who still need food and shelter), the institution can never fully close, except in the event of full-scale evacuation. Yet there are instances when either some or all classes, offices, and university functions must be declared "closed." Because of confusion about what a "campus closure" meant, the Campus Closure Integrated Communications Protocol was developed to describe the command structure, create a notification tree for the university's major constituents (students, faculty, and staff) and a broader communications plan, and define the levels of closure. This protocol is driven by the Crisis Action Team and superseded in the event of the activation of the EOC.

The levels of closure defined in the protocol are outlined in Table 9.1. In virtually every situation involving a level of closure, the president makes the decision with close advice from the EOC director.

TABLE 9.1

Levels of Closure, Campus Closure Integrated Communications Protocol (CSUN)

Degree of Closure*	Level of Activity / EOC Activated*
Open	All classes and offices function normally.
Partial Closure	In certain low-risk situations (e.g., power outage), the Crisis Action Team may keep the university open but will cancel classes. This action is determined on a case-by-case basis. Because circumstances vary widely, decisions regarding other faculty and staff activities will be made by the Crisis Action Team on a case-by-case basis. Classes that are in session at the time of the decision will be canceled immediately, and all students will be dismissed to leave campus without penalty.
Closed	When the campus is closed, the EOC is normally activated. In this situation, • All students, faculty, and staff (except essential emergency personnel) leave campus. (The Crisis Action Team will make a separate determination regarding other campus activities, e.g., athletic events, performances, rehearsals, contracts with external organizations, etc.) • Essential emergency personnel include but may not be limited to: o University Management Team (president's cabinet, associate vice presidents, deans, directors) o University police o Parking and transportation staff o Environmental, Health, and Safety o Physical plant management and facilities o Information Technology emergency response team o Personnel essential for specified functions (e.g., food service, residence hall managers) o Other personnel determined to be needed by the particular emergency (e.g., counselors, interpreters)
Evacuated	When the campus is evacuated, the Emergency Operations Center is activated and all campus personnel are subject to the directives of Emergency Operations Center director. All campus occupants, except administration specifically assigned as liaisons to the Emergency Operations Center and essential emergency personnel, leave campus immediately. Buildings are secured with no reentry permitted until the controlling emergency agency provides clearance.

(*Continues*)

TABLE 9.1 (*Cont.*)

Shelter in Place	This advisory instructs individuals to seek immediate shelter inside a campus facility or residence hall. This course of action may be required during an emergency situation, such as an act of violence, weather emergency, chemical spill, and so on, as directed by emergency personnel. Sheltering in place will keep individuals inside an area that provides more protection. Any notification to shelter in place will be incident-specific and may apply to the entire campus or just certain facilities. Because of this, the mode of issuing a shelter in place notification will be determined by the emergency team in place (i.e., Crisis Action Team or EOC), using any or all of the communication protocols described in the document.

* *Decided by the Crisis Action Team*

Issues Management Process

CSUN's internal issues management process was developed to address a need for specific kinds of situations not covered by the other protocols. Used on a more informal and ad hoc basis, and usually involving a smaller number of key players, the protocol was developed to coordinate an effective and timely way to manage issues and develop public responses for situations that may not necessarily fall into the other contingencies discussed previously but still may threaten health or safety or require the coordination and commitment of resources. This process applies primarily to the kinds of issues that are anticipated to garner media or public attention among internal or external audiences, or that have already attracted such attention. Though issues management at CSUN has been applied primarily to negative issues or threats, this process has also been used to leverage opportunities to communicate positive developments, such as the appointment and introduction of a new vice president or athletic director.

Under the issues management process, all members of the university's senior leadership are expected to routinely monitor internal and external issues of actual or potential media or public interest (including those of interest to internal constituents). Vice presidents, for example, may identify issues emanating from their areas that may warrant a university-level response because of the issue's potential to generate negative or positive impact on the university as a whole. Any of these individuals have the authority and discretion to call together an issues management group if deemed necessary.

The issues management group is an ad hoc structure, composed of senior university administrators and other staff with particular expertise and responsibilities relevant to the issue at hand. It is an extremely effective way of getting out in front of situations that, left unattended, could potentially "simmer" or "boil."

The group provides a cross-divisional forum for information gathering and sharing, strategy discussions, decision making, and task assignments. The group coordinates the communication of information and university actions to internal and external audiences, as appropriate. Though primary responsibility for communications resides within university advancement, with the guidance and leadership of the vice president for university advancement and/or the associate vice president for marketing and communications, all members of the group contribute to the effort to develop and articulate the university's position and the most effective ways to communicate it.

The issues management group consists of a small core team and others who will be engaged depending on the specific issue. The group's ongoing core members are shown in Table 9.2. In the event of unavailability, each member has a designated alternate. Any member of the president's cabinet or the associate vice president for marketing and communications may call together an issues management group.

Before my arrival, this group would make recommendations to the president concerning a particular course of action. My own preferences were that I should be directly involved in the discussion, problem solving, and strategizing in two types of circumstances: (a) if the issue directly involved me

TABLE 9.2
Issues Management Group Core Members (CSUN)

• The vice president for university advancement and/or the associate vice president for marketing and communications
• The president's chief of staff
• The vice president or other executive officer responsible for the campus unit from which the issue has emanated or that is most affected by the issue: o Depending on the issue, additional members may include ▪ University counsel for legal consultation ▪ The director of police services for law enforcement matters
• The associate vice president for human resources and/or the senior human resources manager for personnel and employee relations issues
• The associate vice president for faculty affairs for issues involving faculty members
• The dean of students for student discipline issues

(e.g., statewide press criticism of several newly appointed CSU presidents' executive compensation) and (b) if the issue were likely to tarnish the reputation of the institution publicly (e.g., employee accused the university and several administrators of discriminatory employment practices that appeared on front page of local newspaper).

Other than these types of situations, that is to say, those we are likely to read about in the print or electronic media, the issues management group will meet on their own and make recommendations to me for actions. Obviously, by convening senior leadership, principals at the operating unit level, subject matter experts, and the university's public relations staff, the issues management group gives the university timely and accurate assessments of the situation, develops strategy recommendations, and executes and communicates the university's coordinated response. My approach is to get ahead of situations by anticipating the worst-case scenarios and planning from there. If a situation lessens, we are covered. In determining the communications strategy, a university spokesperson is designated (often the vice president whose division is directly involved and becomes the "content expert" and/or the public information officer). Under the leadership of the associate vice president for marketing and communications, Public Relations develops written message points for timely distribution to the president and all members of the issues management group.

The group meets at the request of any member as the situation changes and until the issue is resolved. Message points are also updated as the situation evolves.

Special Circumstances

Although careful and repetitive/redundant planning is essential, it is also important to prepare for the unexpected. Most planning drills take place when key players are scheduled to be in town. A more likely scenario, however, is that one or more of the key players, such as the president, the chief of police, or a vice president, will be away. (It became a gentle ribbing between the chief of police and me that something always happens when she is out of town.)

Modern communications technology, like cell phones, texting, video chat, and satellite phones, of course, has made crisis management from a distance more manageable. Yet there will still be times when key players are unavailable and incommunicado and when being on-site and having "boots on the ground" are essential to handling a situation in a timely manner. My strongest suggestion is to not only identify "backups" in all key positions but to rehearse with backups as well. The middle of a crisis is not the time to learn that a backup to a vice president does not follow protocol or understand shared responsibility and collaboration.

In addition to the previously described protocols that clearly define the chain of command and management structure in a variety of crisis situations, the president also regularly issues to senior administrators a "line of authority" memo, outlining the university's succession plan in the event the president or other chief administrators are "incapacitated, incommunicado, or unavailable to respond to a crisis or potential emergency that requires immediate action." Although in many cases this chain of command seems common sense and is indeed based on the roles and responsibilities of the president's cabinet, the experience and seniority of the members are also considered, and this provides the cabinet with a clear succession plan.

Like many universities, CSUN also has unique characteristics that require special preparation. For example, CSUN is distinguished by having one of the largest hearing impaired student populations among "mainstream" universities in the United States. As such, our plans also address the need for assisting and communicating with students and faculty with various disabilities. Our Campus Closure Integrated Communications Protocol, for instance, explicitly gives each unit "the responsibility for ensuring communication with individuals with disabilities, including students, staff, and faculty. In the case of campus closure or evacuation, the building marshals [and each building has a marshal and a backup] are responsible for locating individuals with physical disabilities in the facility and assisting them to the designated area for evacuation."

This past fall semester our emergency responders practiced an "active shooter" scenario that involved students, faculty, and staff at the building that houses our National Center on Deafness. Having campus police as well as local area law enforcement agencies participate was tremendously helpful and a learning opportunity for the law enforcement personnel who participated in the training. This spring semester we practiced a similar scenario with our EOC members, providing our leadership team a chance to think through the added resources and strategies needed for dealing with our deaf and hard-of-hearing students and their families. My advice is to anticipate and plan for issues related to the entire campus and all of the student and employee demographics. Do not underestimate the power and speed of social media to either undermine or enhance the campus efforts.

Ongoing Planning, Practice, and Pulling It All Together

Our plans are not static and are subject to ongoing review. As I mentioned earlier, all members of the EOC, from the Policy/Advisory Group, consisting of myself as president, the cabinet, section heads (associate vice presidents and deans), and their designated staff, participate in an annual real-time scenario drill. The plans are also reviewed annually, and staff are cross-trained as much as possible, with alternates who have the talent and skill sets to fulfill the responsibilities of the main designees if he or she is unavailable identified from across campus. Every semester, we also push out to students and employees the link to the university's emergency plan (www-admn.csun.edu/dps/emergency). At every freshman and new student orientation, I personally urge students (and their parents) to enroll their cell phone numbers in our emergency alert system.

Modern technology plays an important role in our process. Our website and Facebook and Twitter feeds are part of our planning, and we use online tools like Blackboard Connect and WebEOC for crisis incident management. We rehearse; are redundant; and vary our scenarios and backup plans, people, communication tools, and venues (e.g., satellite phones, landlines, security cameras, texts, and social media).

At the end of the day, however, what is perhaps the most important resource is the leadership support and the level of mutual trust and collaboration. Although the EOC is reserved for the direst of circumstances, our plans are put to the test whenever any kind of situation arises that requires a campus response and the activation of the Crisis Action Team, the Campus Closure Integrated Communication Protocol, or our Issues Management Process. "Lesser" emergencies need to be dealt with but also represent opportunities to identify weaknesses and gaps and provide valuable team-building opportunities. Recognizing the necessity of shared leadership, shared responsibilities, role differentiation, and, most important, collaboration and trust will serve the campus well. I am fortunate to have such a team at CSUN and have thankfully witnessed these principles in effective action.

IO

CRISIS COMMUNICATIONS WITH GOVERNING BOARDS

Lessons From the Penn State Experience

Patrick T. O'Rourke

In the aftermath of the proceedings that determined Gerald A. Sandusky, a former defensive coordinator for the Pennsylvania State University (Penn State) football team, had abused a position of trust and sexually abused young men, both in Penn State athletics facilities and elsewhere, Penn State's Board of Trustees commissioned a report to determine exactly where Penn State failed. Freeh Sporkin & Sullivan, LLP, an organization that former federal judge and FBI director Louis Freeh headed, determined that Penn State's highest leadership failed in its obligation to investigate suspicions of child abuse and abdicated its obligations to the community it served. Since the organization published the report on its findings (Freeh Sporkin & Sullivan, 2012; hereafter called the Freeh Report), the majority of the criticism and media attention has rested with Graham Spanier (Penn State's former president), Gary Schultz (Penn State's former senior vice president for finance and business), Tim Curley (Penn State's former athletic director), and Joseph Paterno (Penn State's former head football coach). Indeed, given that Spanier, Schultz, and Curley have been indicted for offenses that include perjury, obstruction of justice, and endangering the welfare of children, the focus upon their alleged failures is appropriate.

What has been less well publicized, however, is the fact that the Freeh Report does not stop with these officials and presents significant criticisms against Penn State's Board of Trustees. Among the Freeh Report's findings are the following:

- In 1998 and 2001, when members of the administration were investigating reports of Sandusky's misconduct, the Board of Trustees failed to exercise its oversight and reasonable inquiry responsibilities.
- The board did not have regular reporting procedures or committee structures in place to ensure disclosure to the board of major risks to Penn State.
- Because the board did not demand regular reporting of such risks, the president and senior Penn State officials in this period did not bring major risks facing the university to the board.
- Spanier and senior university officials did not make thorough and forthright reports to the board, which itself equally failed in its continuing obligation to require information or answers on any university matter with which it is concerned.
- After the Sandusky investigation became publicly known in late March 2011, the board did not independently assess this information or further inquire before the investigation erupted into a full-blown scandal.

In other words, although Penn State's Board of Trustees apparently did not have direct evidence of Sandusky's predatory conduct, it failed to create an environment where officials would take necessary actions in response to the concerns about him.

Although prosecutors have not alleged that the Board of Trustees' failures violated any criminal laws, the Freeh Report details how the Board of Trustees failed in its obligation to govern Penn State. And, make no mistake, the costs of those governance failures, both by Penn State officials and its Board of Trustees, are enormous. In financial terms, the Sandusky scandal has cost Penn State more than $20 million in attorney's fees and at least $60 million in penalties that have been or will be paid to resolve National Collegiate Athletic Association (NCAA) sanctions, and the Board of Trustees has authorized the expenditure of $60 million to resolve civil claims. Interestingly, however, in the first year after the investigations, alumni giving has not flagged, and it has actually increased in some sectors. Beyond the financial penalties, the Sandusky scandal will have noneconomic consequences, such as damage to the institution's reputation that will extend well into the future. Time will tell to what extent the Sandusky scandal will harm Penn State's enrollment, ability to attract students and faculty, and status as one of the most respected U.S. public institutions of higher education.

This chapter aims to use the Penn State scandal as a case study of communication with a governing board. In times of crisis, officials in institutions of higher education are often caught up in the day-to-day cycle of reacting to events as they unfold, which can make communications with a governing board challenging. Nonetheless, although it may not be the governing board's responsibility to address each aspect of a crisis as it unfolds, the governing board remains obliged to ensure that it is informed of these events and that it understands the administration's plan of response. Although this obligation would exist with any type of crisis, including natural disasters or violence directed at the campus community, it is most acute when an institution of higher education is responding to an ethical crisis involving its leadership. In those situations, the potential for conflict between the governing board and the administration is at its highest.

Key Facts Related to the Penn State Board of Trustees

To prepare his report, Judge Freeh and his team interviewed more than 400 witnesses and reviewed millions of documents. The report itself provides an exhaustive chronology of the events giving rise to the scandal, not to be replicated here. Instead, I will focus on a few key facts related to the Board of Trustees and its governance of Penn State.

The Penn State Board of Trustees is a body corporate that is responsible for governing the university. It is a large board, comprising 32 members, some of whom are politically appointed, others who are elected by Penn State alumni, and others that the Board of Trustees itself elects. Under the Board of Trustees' governing documents, it has delegated day-to-day management and control at Penn State to the president and his designees. As the Freeh Report notes, "This delegation of authority requires that the board rely on the judgment and decisions of those who operate under its authority" (pp. 98–99). Yet, this delegation does not serve as an abdication of the ultimate responsibility to govern. Consequently, the governing documents state that "the board shall receive and consider thorough and forthright reports on the affairs of the University by the President or those designated by the president. It has a continuing obligation to require information or answers on any university matter with which it is concerned." (Freeh Sporkin & Sullivan, 2012, p. 99). Because the Board of Trustees delegates significant responsibilities to the president, it is not surprising that hiring the president is one of the board's most significant, non-delegable duties.

The Freeh Report details the history of Sandusky's abuse, which occurred in 1998 and 2001, and the administration's concerns about it. The details known to the administration are less pertinent to this inquiry than is the fact that neither President Spanier nor any other executive briefed the Board of Trustees about their investigation into Sandusky's activities or their proposed courses of action. Consequently, the Freeh Report concluded that the Board of Trustees "failed to exercise its oversight functions" because it "did not have regular reporting procedures or committee structures in place to ensure disclosure to the board of major risks" (Freeh Sporkin & Sullivan, 2012, p. 101).

Similarly, in 2011, Spanier, Curley, and Schultz provided grand jury testimony in the criminal investigation against Sandusky. Judge Freeh again determined that "the board failed to perform its duty of inquiry, especially when it was on notice that the university was facing a major risk" involving the grand jury investigation (Freeh Sporkin & Sullivan, 2012, p. 101). Although noting that Spanier and Penn State's general counsel had briefed the Board of Trustees in May 2011, the briefing "downplayed" the significance of their testimony, and "the board members did not independently assess the information or demand detailed reporting from Spanier and Baldwin on this serious matter" (p. 101). When one board member asked Spanier for additional information, Spanier complained that "[the trustee] desires near total transparency. He will be uncomfortable and feel put off until he gets a report" (p. 101).

It was only in November 2011 that members of the Board of Trustees began to press Spanier about the potential charges against Sandusky. Even at that point, however, Penn State's reaction was muted, and some members reported that the board's meetings felt "scripted" or that they were "rubber-stamping" major decisions already made by Spanier and a smaller group of trustees. Indeed, even as Sandusky was being arrested on November 5, 2011, Spanier's position was that the Board of Trustees would hear "nothing more than what we said publicly" (Freeh Sporkin & Sullivan, 2012, p. 102). It was only in the ensuing days that the Board of Trustees began to assert any control over the situation by removing Spanier as president, removing Paterno as head football coach, and announcing that it would form an investigative task force to analyze Penn State's actions.

Fiduciary Obligations

To understand how Penn State's Board of Trustees failed in a time of crisis, one must first take a step backward and determine the nature of a governing board's obligations. Obviously, each governing board will face different challenges, but most commentators recognize that board members of public and nonprofit corporations owe fiduciary duties to the entities they serve. These include: (a) a duty of care; (b) a duty of loyalty; and (c) an emerging duty of obedience.

Duty of Care. The first of the fiduciary duties is a "duty of care," which requires members of governing boards to act in good faith and exercise the same degree of diligence and care that a reasonably prudent person would exercise when attending to his or her own affairs. Although the law protects board members who exercise their best judgment in light of the known circumstances, it will not protect those who fail to undertake their duties with the seriousness and attentiveness reasonably expected of them. Stated another way, although the law does not require board members to make perfect decisions, it requires thoughtful and informed decisions. Significantly, in most jurisdictions, a board member may rely upon information, reports, and statements prepared by others, as long as he or she has reason to believe that the person responsible for preparing and presenting the data is competent.

Judge Freeh concludes that a board breaches the duty of care when it "utterly fails to implement any reporting or information system or controls" or "consciously fails to monitor or oversee its operations thus disabling [the board members] from being informed of risks or problems requiring their attention" (Freeh Sporkin & Sullivan, 2012, p. 100). He reasonably incorporates the business judgment rule in his analysis and concludes that a board does not breach its duty whenever a mistake occurs, but instead breaches its duties when it "fails to provide reasonable oversight in a sustained or systematic fashion" (p. 100). It is important to note that Judge Freeh does not conclude that the governing board has an obligation to oversee the day-to-day operations of the university, but instead is tasked with high-level oversight.

Duty of Loyalty. The second of the fiduciary duties is a "duty of loyalty," which requires board members to exercise their powers in pursuit of the corporation's best interests, not their own interests or any other person's interests. Stated more directly, the duty of loyalty requires a board member to concern himself foremost with the entity of higher education's welfare, even when advancing the entity's needs and interests will be adverse to the director's personal or professional welfare. When faced with a question of whether a board member has fulfilled his duty of loyalty, a court will normally ask whether he acted in the same way that a disinterested person would have acted under the same circumstances.

Judge Freeh's report does not conclude that any of Penn State's trustees violated the duty of loyalty, but questions about the duty of loyalty often arise in subtle ways during times of crisis. Conflicts of interest exist not only when a board member stands to realize a financial gain from a particular decision, but also when a board member has personal loyalties that might affect the ability to exercise independent judgment. When a board member is asked to review the conduct of a university official with whom he or she has a personal relationship or may even have played a role in hiring, the board member must remain cognizant of whatever impulses might affect his or her ability to exercise independent judgment on behalf of the university. Certainly, it is reasonable to assume that one reason why the Penn State Board of Trustees was so deferential to Spanier was because of the relationship that he developed with board members during his 16-year tenure.

Duty of Obedience. The third of the fiduciary duties is a "duty of obedience," which is an emerging duty that has not yet been universally recognized. Where it has been recognized, this duty requires directors to perform their duties consistently with the corporation's purposes, governing documents, and applicable statutes. In some ways, the duty of obedience combines aspects of the duty of care and the duty of loyalty. It requires directors to not only be familiar with the corporation's purposes and governing documents, but also to act consistently with them. The Freeh Report raises the specter of the duty of obedience, given that the governing documents required the Board of Trustees to "receive and consider thorough and forthright reports on the affairs of the university by the president" and charged the board with a "continuing obligation to require information or answers on any university matter with which it is concerned" (pp. 98–99). Although Penn State had implemented these principles on paper, it had not implemented them in practice.

Other Sources of Obligations

Beyond the common-law fiduciary duties, many states have statutes that define the duties of board members of nonprofit corporations. Reviewing these statutes is beyond the scope of this discussion, but there is an additional source of obligations that takes front and center when organizations face an ethical or leadership crisis—the 2013 *U.S. Sentencing Commission (USSC) Guidelines Manual* (hereafter federal sentencing guidelines).

In 1991, the U.S. Sentencing Commission published federal sentencing guidelines to guide judges in imposing sentences upon those who engage in criminal conduct. One unique aspect of the federal sentencing guidelines is that they apply not only to individuals who engage in criminal conduct, but also to organizations. One only has to look to the major corporate scandals of the past decades—Enron, Arthur Andersen, and Bear Stearns come to mind—to realize that the conduct of corporate entities has the potential to inflict catastrophic harm upon individuals and societies. To discourage corporate wrongdoing, the federal sentencing guidelines are "designed so that the sanctions imposed upon organizations and their agents, taken together, will provide just punishment, adequate deterrence, and incentives for organizations to maintain internal mechanisms for preventing, detecting, and reporting criminal conduct" (U.S. Sentencing Commission, 2013 p. 489).

The first question often raised when dealing with the federal sentencing guidelines is whether a particular entity is subject to them. The guidelines take a broad perspective and define an *organization* as "a person other than an individual," which is broad enough to capture all of the various forms that an institution of higher education might take, including "unincorporated organizations, governments and political subdivisions therefore, and nonprofit organizations" (U.S. Sentencing Commission, 2013, p. 490). Consequently, all governing boards should become aware of the guidelines.

The federal sentencing guidelines provide a mechanism for calculating the sanctions that a court can levy against an organization that engages in criminal conduct. For the purposes of this discussion, the most crucial aspects of the guidelines are the provisions that mitigate sanctions when the organization has an "effective compliance and ethics program" (U.S. Sentencing Commission, 2013, p. 497). To avail themselves of these provisions, the organization must exercise due diligence to prevent and detect criminal conduct and promote an organizational culture that encourages ethical conduct and a commitment to compliance with the law. Although the Freeh Report did not explicitly mention the guidelines, the report's recommendations are certainly geared toward "promot[ing] an organizational culture that encourages ethical conduct and a commitment to compliance with the law," including a recommendation to "establish values and ethics-based decision making and adherence to the Penn State Principles as the standard for all university faculty, staff and students" (p. 129).

At a minimum, the guidelines require that "the organization's governing authority be knowledgeable about the content and operation of the compliance and ethics program and shall exercise reasonable oversight" to ensure that the program operates effectively. Although the guidelines don't specify the contents, "a code of ethical conduct is a centerpiece of a compliance program" that meets the guidelines' intent (Gordon, 2012, p. 41). That code of conduct specifies that the organization expects lawful, ethical, and transparent behavior by employees, including a requirement that employees report unlawful conduct. Obviously, one element of effective oversight is a requirement, not just on paper, that the university's leadership report to the governing board any ethical breaches that represent a significant risk to the institution.

Governance Versus Management

At this point, we know that governing boards have a duty to care that requires the members to be informed and knowledgeable when they make decisions that affect the institution. We also know that standards from the federal sentencing guidelines require the governing board to institute both ethical standards of conduct and a mechanism of oversight. The question then becomes how those elements actually come into play when the institution faces a crisis, particularly one that raises ethical and leadership concerns.

Before going further, it's important to distinguish between management and governance and to define the roles of the administration and the governing board. An effective governing board does not attempt to manage the institution on a day-to-day basis and instead delegates those functions to the president and the executive team. The governing board should not normally play an active role in ordinary decisions, such as human resource disputes, student discipline, and budget management, but instead should rely upon the administration to make those decisions. On the other hand, the governing board's obligation is to make sure that the institution has defined its policies and standards of conduct in a way that the administration can reliably and accurately administer. An effective governing board has to resist the temptation to micromanage, which is generally associated with excessive control or attention to detail that disempowers a person from performing the functions of his employment.

The temptation to micromanage is often most acute in times of crisis, which are stressful moments that have the potential to significantly affect the institution. And, although some crises occur outside of the public eye, many of them occur with a great amount of media attention and scrutiny. When media attention adds to the pressure on the institution, it is crucial that the governing board and administration both understand their roles and responsibilities as they proceed. Otherwise, the institution faces the risk that the governing board and its administration appear to be on different pages, and when that occurs, the apparent dysfunction between them compounds the crisis that the institution already faces. Indeed, Penn State's Board of Trustees was dissatisfied with Spanier's statements to the media and unconditional public support of Curley and Schultz. Given that the underlying facts were not yet known, the Penn State Board of Trustees' dissatisfaction with how Spanier was reacting to the media appears to be one of the primary reasons why the board relieved him of his duties.

Communications to the Governing Board in a Time of Crisis

It's very difficult to anticipate the different circumstances that might give rise to a crisis. Indeed, if you look at the headlines from institutions of higher education in the past several years, you will find topics as diverse as sexual misconduct, abuse of student athletes, violence perpetrated by students or faculty, fiscal misconduct, and other ethical lapses. Rather than attempting to define each of the particular subjects that might give rise to a crisis, the better strategy is for the governing board to define its expectations in broad terms that may be applied to the circumstances. The governing board may define its expectations in thinking about these basic questions:

- What matters should the administration bring to the governing board's attention?
- When should the administration bring matters to the governing board's attention?
- Who should be responsible for the communication?
- How should the communication occur?

What to Report

Before a crisis arises, the governing board must make its expectations clear about what information the administration should communicate to it. Penn State's Board of Trustees got off to a good start by stating that it expected "thorough and forthright reports on the affairs" of the institution, but Penn State's policy does not identify the types of matters upon which the trustees expected reporting (Freeh Sporkin & Sullivan, 2012, pp. 98–99).

There are some areas where the governing board can reduce its expectations to a policy, such as to indicate that the governing board expects the administration to promptly inform it of any known or suspected material violations of university policy or criminal conduct that is reasonably anticipated to have a significant financial, operational, or reputational impact upon the institution. This standard has some degree of flexibility and requires the administration to exercise some discretion in determining which matters require reporting. If the president of the institution is charged with domestic abuse, that charge is likely to have an operational or reputational impact upon the institution, although the same conduct by an employee in facilities maintenance would not have the same impact. By phrasing the expectation broadly and tying it to a significant potential impact upon the institution, the governing board can discharge its oversight responsibilities without unduly interfering in matters that are properly resolved at an administrative level.

At another level, however, there are some instances in which the governing board should be informed, even if the standard of reporting isn't codified into policy. Although some of these instances fall within the range of common sense, there are a number of questions that the administration can use as guideposts in determining whether reporting is necessary or appropriate:

- Does the issue implicate the governing board's obligation to exercise oversight over the institution?
- Does the issue implicate the governing board's obligation to be knowledgeable about known or suspected criminal conduct in the institution?
- Does the issue implicate the governing board's obligation to ensure that the day-to-day leaders of the institution discharge their responsibilities with a high degree of ethics?
- Does the issue implicate the institution's fundamental mission?
- Does the issue implicate the institution's key stakeholders?
- Does the issue naturally attract the attention of the media or the public?
- Does the issue potentially affect the institution's ability to meet its financial obligations?
- Does the issue give rise to questions about the efficacy of either the institution's day-to-day leadership or its governing board?

If the answer to one or more of these questions is "yes," then it is most likely time to provide information to the governing board. Although the administration does not wish to overload the governing board with matters beyond its concern, it's also probably safe to say that most governing boards appreciate being informed of a potential problem, even if it does not materialize into an actual crisis.

When to Report

Once the governing board has defined its expectations about the types of matters that the administration should report, the question inevitably arises about when the reporting should occur. Many administrators do not want to take rumors and unconfirmed information to the governing board, which is understandable, but the window for informing the board is often narrow. In an age when Twitter and Facebook have created the capacity for virtually anyone to transmit a rumor to the public at large, the administration has to be prepared for the possibility that it will be necessary to inform the governing board even before the facts are fully developed. Nothing prevents the administration from reporting that it has received information about a matter of concern, that it will be investigating, and that it will provide additional information as it becomes available. Providing even this amount of communication keeps the governing board from feeling "in the dark" and gives the administration the ability to more fully develop the information that it will bring to the board's attention.

Once a crisis has erupted and the governing board has received an initial briefing, the administration acquires the obligation to provide ongoing updates. Again, it's difficult to underestimate the governing board's need for information during a time of crisis, but many institutions run into difficulty because the administration believes that it is doing a better job of keeping the board informed than it actually is. Particularly when the media is active and will be publishing stories, even stories of little consequence, maintaining steady communication with the governing board works to the administration's advantage. During a recent high-profile crisis at the University of Colorado, in which a former student perpetrated a mass shooting, I updated our Board of Regents daily over the initial weeks of the crisis, sometimes just reporting on the developments of the day, because these updates allowed the governing board to remain on top of the situation. As the media attention receded, I was able to reduce the number of communications, and now, even though the former student's criminal trial will not be resolved for at least another year, I need only to update the Board of Regents as significant events occur. Because of the frequency of our initial efforts to provide information to the governing board as the crisis unfolded, I believe that the administration built a foundation of trust that allowed the governing board to discharge its oversight obligations without becoming involved in the day-to-day decisions.

Who Should Report

After the administration has reached the conclusion that it is the appropriate time to inform the governing board of a potential or pending crisis, the next question is who should make the communication. Absent extraordinary circumstances, there are normally two logical choices for such communications: the president of the institution or the general counsel. Often the choice between these two alternatives is driven by whether the crisis will generate potential liabilities to the institution. For example, if the crisis is a wildfire near campus that has prompted the evacuation of student housing facilities, there may not be significant liability concerns, and the president would be charged with informing the governing board about the institution's response to the wildfire. On the other hand, if the crisis is that a university official is being investigated for sexual misconduct with a student, that issue definitely raises significant liability concerns, and the communication would probably best occur through the general counsel.

In assessing the question of who should make the communication, the issue is essentially whether there is an institutional need for the communication to be subject to a legal privilege. Courts in every state, as well as the courts in the federal system, recognize the existence of the attorney-client privilege. The attorney-client privilege exists to encourage institutions to seek legal advice by protecting the communications between its officials and its attorney with confidentiality. When a communication is privileged, the institution generally has a valid justification for withholding that communication from third parties, and the communication normally would not be admissible in a civil or criminal trial. Communications made by the university's administration (other than the general counsel) are often not privileged (unless there is an independent legal basis for withholding the communication, for example, that it raises a student privacy issue under the Family Educational Rights and Privacy Act) and would be discoverable during litigation.

Unfortunately, many institutions misinterpret the scope of the attorney-client privilege and assume that communications are privileged merely because an attorney had some role in the communication between the members of the governing board and the administration. But those assumptions are inaccurate because the attorney-client privilege exists only when (a) communication is occurring between the client and the attorney; (b) the purpose of the communication is either for the client to seek or for the attorney to provide legal advice; (c) the communication is made in a manner that is confidential; and (d) the attorney-client privilege cannot be used as a mechanism to prevent discovery of purely factual information in the institution's possession. Stated another way, the attorney-client privilege does not serve as a shield for communicating information to the governing board if the communication does not raise any legal issues or does not provide any legal advice.

How to Report

Crises, by their very nature, do not schedule themselves to occur at the most accommodating times, such as during an already-scheduled meeting of the governing board. Consequently, the administration often has to decide not only when to communicate with the governing board, but also how those communications should occur. Often this decision will be governed not only by the exigencies of the situation, but also by any formal requirements upon the board's ability to convene.

For public institutions in particular, the governing board may be subject to open meeting laws that require advance notice before meetings. For example, in my home state of Colorado, the law states that "all meetings of two or more members of any state public body at which any public business is to be discussed are declared to be public meetings open to the public at all times" (Colorado Sunshine Law, 1972, (2)(a)). This requirement exists whether the meeting occurs in person, by teleconference, or by other electronic means. For any such meeting where a quorum of the governing board is in attendance, the institution is required to give "full and timely notice to the public" before the meeting occurs (Colorado Sunshine Law, 1972, (2)(c)). Obviously, even if the subject matter of this meeting is confidential and can be held in an executive session that the public cannot attend, these requirements can affect how the administration provides information to the governing board.

Beyond any legal limitations upon the governing board's ability to meet as a whole, one of the first decisions the administration must make is whether to convene the board as a whole or to provide information to board members through individual communications. In most cases, I believe the best strategy for approaching this decision is for the administration to first notify the chairperson of the governing board of the situation, explain the circumstances, and jointly determine the best course of action for informing the other members of the governing board. In some instances when the communication is purely informational, it may be feasible to communicate with individual board members, but there are two drawbacks to this type of approach. One is the possibility that different board members will ask different questions and consequently receive different information when communicating with administrators. The other is that it leaves the board members in a vacuum in determining what they should do in response to the information they've received. Often these individual communications are valuable as an initial medium to inform members of the governing board of a developing situation, but they should be considered a precursor to a more nuanced conversation involving the board as a whole.

Another consideration is whether communications with the board should take the form of oral or written transmissions. In an era of modern communication, we often have the inclination to communicate with groups of people through "blast" e-mails, but it's equally true that e-mail and other electronic forms of communication are imperfect. Notwithstanding the ease by which e-mail can be used to communicate with a large number of people, e-mail communications often do not provide sufficient context for meaningful communication, do not give an opportunity for people to respond to the information being provided to them (at least not without a flurry of additional e-mails), and can be inadvertently (or intentionally) forwarded to others who do not have a need for the information.

Additionally, for public institutions in many states, e-mail communications may fall within the requirements of open records laws that allow interested parties to request copies of any written communications. During a period of crisis, a governing board may not wish for its communications with the administration to be subject to open records requests, particularly as it determines how it will respond to a rapidly evolving situation. Moreover, even if the attorney-client privilege may protect an initial e-mail communication from the institution's general counsel from an open records request, subsequent communications between board members by e-mail may not retain the same privileged status. For these reasons, e-mail should be used only as a temporary means of providing information to the governing board in the interim until the board can be assembled, either in person or by electronic means, to discuss the situation. In any such e-mail communications, the administration should remind the board member of any open records requirements that might apply to their communications and advise them of their fiduciary obligation to hold privileged information confidentially.

The Governing Board's Response

Up until now, our discussion has focused primarily upon the administration's role in initiating communications with the governing board in a time of crisis. In some cases, the governing board may only need information and not take any response, but in other cases a response may be necessary. This need for the governing board to respond is particularly high when the crisis involves the possibility that the institution's leadership has engaged in criminal conduct, has acted unethically, or is unable to provide competent leadership.

Because "an effective board appreciates the limits of its proper role and delegates management of the institution to the president and senior administrators," the governing board's obligation may be supporting the administration (Association of Governing Boards of Universities and Colleges, 2010, p. 37). As the Association of Governing Boards of Universities and Colleges (AGB) has recognized, "The president needs to know that when faced with taking controversial or unpopular actions, he or she can rely upon backing from the board," at least in those situations where the governing board does not have substantial disagreement with those decisions (p. 37).

Whether or not the governing board is called upon to respond independently of the administration is often driven by its fiduciary and legal duties. Consider a situation in which the president of the institution is accused of having embezzled funds. Under those circumstances, from a duty of care perspective, would a reasonable and prudent governing board acting in the best interests of the institution remove the president's financial oversight pending the outcome of an investigation? Under the federal sentencing guidelines, would a governing board charged with promoting an organizational culture that encourages ethical conduct and a commitment to compliance with the law ask the Department of Internal Audit to investigate and report its findings to the governing board? In every crisis involving the university's leadership, the key question is, "Did the governing board take the actions reasonably necessary to protect the institution's constituents, resources, and reputation?"

Although it would be optimal if there were a decision tree that allowed the governing board to reach the "right" decision in response to an institutional crisis, that resource does not currently exist, and likely never will. Each governing board must be guided by its own conscience in formulating a response, but few boards will feel comfortable responding without guidance from legal counsel. There are times when the institution's legal counsel is perfectly competent to provide this advice. In other cases, the governing board may wish to seek independent legal counsel. I would generally advise a governing board to seek independent legal counsel when the general counsel has been accused of any misconduct, when the general counsel has advised an administrator on the subjects giving rise to the crisis, or when the general counsel has firsthand participation in the events giving rise to the crisis. Each of these situations arguably falls within the ambit of the American Bar Association's *Model Rules of Professional Conduct* (2013) for an attorney, which prohibit an attorney from providing services when "there is a significant risk that the representation of one or more clients will be materially limited by the lawyer's responsibilities to another client, a former client or a third person, or by a personal interest of the lawyer" (rule 1.7). Stated another way, the governing board might feel the need to seek independent legal counsel in any situation when it reasonably believes that the general counsel has a conflict that would potentially impair his/her ability to provide the board with objective legal advice.

"If serious lapses occur at the highest levels of the institution's governance, confidence on and off campus in institutional oversight and integrity will inevitably suffer" (Association of Governing Boards of Universities and Colleges, 2010, p. 30). Although this is no doubt true, even the specter of such a serious lapse can cripple an institution unless it affirmatively responds to the allegations. In contrast to many lawyers who "unfortunately still regard public communication as a risk that is never really worth taking," I find the data compelling that many people presume entities to be guilty simply because they were accused, and "no comment" is perceived as, "They've got something to hide" (Levick & Smith, 2007, p. xviii).

Because "judgment is nearly instantaneous, often unforgiving, and increasingly permanent, sometimes with consequences in the criminal as well as civil justice system" (Levick & Smith, 2007, p. xviii), the institution cannot allow the media to formulate the narrative without its perspective. At best, silence will be received as a message that the institution is out of touch, and at worst, the public will draw the conclusion that the institution is unethical or corrupt. From a governing board's perspective, none of these messages is in the institution's best interests, so the question then becomes, "What message will the governing board send?"

The governing board must first determine the target audiences of its message. In a public institution of higher education, the communities that will receive the message can include students, parents, faculty, alumni, donors, regulators, politicians, and the media. Sometimes a press release will convey the messages that the governing board wishes to send to each of these communities, but there can be value in separate communications. If the president of the university is accused of embezzlement, donors may be concerned about the sources of the embezzled funds, whereas politicians might be more concerned about whether the institutions has implemented controls to prevent wrongdoing. If the governing board chooses separate communications to different stakeholders it should anticipate that those messages will not remain isolated and, therefore, ensure that each of them is factually and thematically consistent.

The governing board must next determine the content of its messages. Because of the nature of a crisis, the governing board may not have complete information, and it would naturally fear making statements that are later proven to be wrong. Fear of the unknown, however, is not a good enough reason to refrain from any comment. At a minimum, the institution can reinforce its commitment to its core values—honesty, ethical conduct, and transparency—even while stating that it is currently investigating the issues in a manner that will allow the governing board to uphold its fiduciary obligations. If the institution is committed to doing the right thing, and the public believes that its leadership will ensure the proper resolution of a crisis, that confidence gives the governing board the flexibility to determine the right approach. As we saw with the Penn State scandal, it is when the public lacks confidence in the leadership's ability to respond that the governing board's actions appear rushed and ineffectual. Because Spanier miscalculated and immediately made statements expressing unconditional support for administrators who had been accused of serious crimes, the governing board was left with the task of trying to mitigate the public outrage and was forced to relieve Spanier of his duties four days later.

As a general proposition, a governing board should structure its communications in a manner that does not blur its role with the administration. The president "ordinarily speaks for the institution," and when it is necessary for the governing board to speak, it's important to remember that the board is a collective entity, and none of the individual board members has the authority to act on its behalf (Ingram, 1995, p. 30). It is also true, as a general principle, that board members must be "willing to support decisions and policies approved by the board's majority," even if an individual board member disagrees with them (Ingram, 2003, p. 15). Times of crisis can test a governing board's adherence to these tenets.

When possible, it is best for a governing board to uphold the principle that "only the board chair speaks for the board and ordinarily is presumed to be delegated the responsibility to address controversial issues or board decisions with the media" (Ingram, 2003, p. 15). When it is not possible, and a board member feels the need to speak in disagreement with the actions of the governing board, that board member should make clear that he is voicing his personal opinion and is not speaking on behalf of the institution. The goal of these principles is not to quell dissent or any individual board member's ability to speak, but instead to ensure that the governing board does not send mixed messages about where it stands.

Planning for a Crisis

One thing is certain: Every institution will likely face a crisis. Accepting that reality, and not knowing in advance from which corner of the institution the crisis will arise, the question then becomes, "Is there something that I can do now to prepare?" Yes, there are steps, and some of them are reflected in the Freeh Report:

- Every governing board member should receive an orientation upon joining the board.
- Every governing board should receive education on the fiduciary duties that it owes the institution, including the duty of care, duty of loyalty, and duty of obedience.
- Every governing board should develop a conflict of interest policy for board members.
- Every governing board should receive education on the federal sentencing guidelines and its role in promoting "organizational culture that encourages ethical conduct and a commitment to compliance with the law."
- Every governing board should promulgate, in consultation with the administration and faculty, a code of institutional ethics that sets the governing board's expectations.
- Every governing board should approve a compliance and ethics program and exercise reasonable oversight to ensure that the program operates effectively.

- Every governing board should communicate to university leadership that it expects candid and timely reports of unlawful or unethical conduct.
- Every governing board should annually evaluate the president on his or her efforts to promote a culture of ethics and compliance.
- Every governing board should have an audit committee that exercises oversight over regulatory and ethical compliance, including an assessment of whether the institution has appropriated sufficient budget for compliance functions.
- Every governing board should receive education on its obligations under open meetings and open records laws to ensure that it understands how its communications should occur in times of crisis.
- Every governing board should receive education on the requirements of the attorney-client privilege and other applicable privileges so that it does not misapprehend whether certain communications will be protected from disclosure.
- Every governing board should develop a crisis communication plan that allows members of the administration to communicate with board members during times of crisis.
- Every governing board should consider and adopt protocols describing its role in public communications.

Each of these recommendations is targeted at setting effective and efficient structures that will allow the institution and its governing board to react appropriately when a crisis occurs. It is only by developing firm foundations that undergird the institution that a governing board can perform its duties.

References

American Bar Association. (2013). *Model rules of professional conduct.* Retrieved from http://www.americanbar.org/groups/professional_responsibility/publications/model_rules_of_professional_conduct/model_rules_of_professional_conduct_table_of_contents.html

Association of Governing Boards of Universities and Colleges. (2010). *Effective governing boards: A guide for members of governing boards of independent colleges and universities.* Washington, DC: AGB Press.

Colorado Sunshine Law, *Colo. Rev. Stat. §24-6-402.* (1972, rev. 1996, comp. 2013). Retrieved from http://www.lexisnexis.com/hottopics/colorado?app=00075&view=full&interface=1&docinfo=off&searchtype=get&search=C.R.S.+24-6-402

Freeh Sporkin & Sullivan, LLP. (2012, July 12). *Report of the Special Investigative Counsel regarding the actions of the Pennsylvania State University related to the child sexual abuse committed by Gerald A. Sandusky.* Retrieved from http://progress.psu.edu/assets/content/REPORT_FINAL_071212.pdf

Gordon, S. D. (2012). Implementation of effective compliance and ethics programs and the federal sentencing guidelines. In C. A. Myers & K. T. Williford (Eds.), *Corporate compliance answer book 2012–13,* Vol. 1 (pp. 33–63). New York: Practicing Law Institute.

Ingram, R. T. (1995). *Effective trusteeship: A guide for board members of independent colleges and universities.* Washington, DC: AGB Press.

Ingram, R. T. (2003). *New trustee orientation: A guide for public colleges and universities.* Washington, DC: AGB Press.

Levick, R. S., & Smith, L. (2007). *Stop the presses: The crisis and litigation PR desk reference* (2nd ed.). Washington, DC: Watershed Press.

U.S. Sentencing Commission. (2013). *USSC guidelines manual.* Retrieved from http://www.ussc.gov/Guidelines/2013_Guidelines/index.cfm

II

TOOLS TO REBUILD AFTER A CRISIS

Janice M. Abraham

A crisis on campus can result from a natural disaster or human action, and it can occur suddenly and unexpectedly or arise from a long-simmering issue. Hurricanes, fires, active shooters, virulent flu, Medicaid fraud, wide-scale cheating, scientific misconduct, and sexual molestation are among the recent crises that have plagued higher education institutions. Creating and developing a team that can respond to any crisis requires the same leadership skills and foresight as leading a complex organization: trust, candor, and communication. A crisis highlights and exaggerates a team's inefficiencies and gaps that may be less apparent under normal circumstances. Any dysfunctions a president senses in the leadership team prior to a crisis will inevitably magnify during an emergency. An effective crisis response team will always display trust and candor forged in shared crisis management experiences—even if the crisis is manufactured in a tabletop drill.

A well-functioning team that exhibits trust and a shared vision can lead an institution through a crisis and help rebuild it afterward. But even a highly functioning team can flounder during a crisis without a well-rehearsed plan. The following eight steps provide a map for equipping the team with the tools to recover from and, ultimately, thrive after a crisis.

Set the Tone at the Top

Crisis response preparations must begin with support from the top; otherwise, no one else will take them seriously. Leadership must accept that bad things may happen and may leave the leadership team and the entire campus straining under the weight of response, recovery, and rebuilding. The leader's role is to minimize the strain and speed the recovery with critical building blocks: teamwork, shared values, and preparation. Leadership must also establish communication channels; clear information to those who need to know can prevent or minimize a crisis or hasten recovery. Fostering a culture that focuses on candor and trust among members of the senior team and governing board and throughout the institution will hasten the flow of vital information. Leadership is also responsible for prohibiting a "blame game" in the midst of a crisis. There will be ample time later to dissect lessons learned and modify the campus crisis response plan.

Provide Resources and Establish Roles and Responsibilities

Crisis management is preparing to know what to do if a fire breaks out and which emergency personnel need to be involved. But once the firefighters leave, business continuity is what happens next. Establishing a clear description of individual roles and responsibilities and providing appropriate training is essential when asking individuals to lead an institution through a crisis. An effective crisis response requires several teams to appropriately plan for their role in responding to a crisis. The senior leadership team establishes institutional priorities and policies and, during a crisis, remains focused on maintaining operations. A small working group of managers and directors, sometimes called the crisis response team, implements policies, provides training, schedules drills, and performs specific functions during an actual crisis. A crisis communications team, described later, communicates with the media and internal and external constituents. A business continuity plan team takes over after the initial crisis to keep the institution open and functioning. There will be overlap among the teams—for example, the president will direct the senior leadership team and serve on the crisis communications team—so clear descriptions of team roles and responsibilities will minimize gaps in the immediate response.

Rollins College, in responding to a trustee request to improve its crisis response protocols, learned the following lessons from its emergency management response initiative:

- Downsize to maximize efficiency. A small group worked best to review and revise crisis response policies. The group called on experts throughout the college to consult in the review.
- Train positions, not people. Assign specific crisis response duties to a position, provide ongoing training to staff in the position, and have backup resources available.

- Smaller institutions can adapt large institution policies. Large universities often have well-developed crisis response plans that small colleges can review and scale to meet their needs (e.g., refer to www.rollins.edu/marketing-communications/emergency).

Increasingly, large universities are creating specific positions to provide full-time coordination of all crisis response plans. Whether the institution has a dedicated crisis response position or relies on a team of managers to implement the plan, senior leadership should provide financial support for drills and appropriate training to ensure the campus is ready to respond and recover when the crisis strikes.

Identify Potential Crises

Although crises may be inevitable over the history of an institution, they are not predictable. However, with leadership's endorsement and encouragement, the institution can identify potential emergencies as groundwork for a flexible plan that the team can practice and improve. The crisis identification process is a campus-specific exercise involving senior leadership, managers of schools or departments, and the crisis response team. An institution's location, ties to the community, and mission all factor into identifying potential crises. Weather, geography, size, and national and international locations contribute to the type and scale of a crisis. Unfortunately the daily news provides myriad examples of crises that could occur at an institution.

Care teams or behavioral assessment teams, put in place on many campuses after the tragedy at Virginia Tech, are examples of shared responsibility for crisis identification and mitigation. Staff and faculty across an institution, gathering to identify at-risk students and crafting an intervention plan before a crisis occurs can be a model for other cross-functional teams to identify and defuse potential crises. The crisis identification process also enables the institution to question sacred cows, asking how it would respond if a crisis focused on these esteemed people, programs, activities, or traditions. There are many examples of institutions failing to challenge revered individuals, traditions, and programs or assess them through a risk or crisis prism, leaving the university vulnerable and unprepared when a crisis struck. Experience reveals that sacred cows are questioned only if senior leadership invites and fosters such candid discussions.

Develop a Crisis Response Plan

Identifying potential crises is an ongoing process that does not generate a definitive or comprehensive list. Beginning with a broad list of possible disasters, learning from others, and focusing on the institution's unique characteristics guides campus leaders and the crisis response working group in construction of a plan. It's impossible to predict when and where a crisis will occur, but addressing the most prominent programs is a good starting point. For example, institutions with large athletic programs, extensive research activities, or campuses in other countries should be prepared to respond to a potential basketball program scandal, an allegation of scientific misconduct, or a terrorist event at the branch campus, respectively. Residential campuses should include alternative long-term housing and dining plans and well-tested family communication protocols. In all cases, a crisis response plan should reflect the institution's values and mission, calling on core beliefs as decisions are made.

A crisis response plan should address care of vulnerable populations (people with disabilities, minors, elderly, etc.), interaction with the local community (including utilities and other institutions), training for first responders, and unique aspects of the campus (athletic venues, child care facilities, clinical practices, research labs, etc.). Identifying outside experts the institution can call upon as needed should be part of building a crisis response team. No campus communications team is prepared to respond on its own to a crisis the size of the Duke lacrosse or Penn State molestation scandals. It's too late to interview public relations/crisis communications firms after a crisis. During the planning process, the team should interview and select outside experts who will become part of the team and update them at least annually on the campus plans. The team should also identify sufficient licensed counselors to help the community deal with grief in the immediate aftermath of a shooting or other tragedy.

The National Incident Management System (NIMS) and the Incident Command System (ICS) provide guidance in preparing for and mitigating sudden crises, such as inclement weather or violent crimes. Using the NIMS protocols, the U.S. Department of Education's 2010 *Action Guide for Emergency Management at Institutions of Higher Education* provides a thorough outline for emergency preparations.

Practice and Improve the Plan

Crisis plans that gather dust and outdated staff contact information are more dangerous than helpful. Institutions should regularly practice and improve the plan and update essential contact information. The institution should be able to implement a crisis response plan any time, when the president is out of the country, in the summer, or over a holiday break. Teams can improve with practice, such as conducting extensive tabletop drills, stepping through the individual and collective responses to a potential crisis, sometimes using a recent event at another institution. Debriefing and reviewing the plan after the tabletop exercise is essential, and the institution should test any improvements and changes formally incorporated into the plan at the next drill or real event.

During a major flood, the crisis response team of a residential campus learned three important things that it incorporated into its plan: (a) The maintenance crew needed to make sure their own families were safe and secure before they could devote their energy to helping the campus recover; (b) improved communications with the town water department and advanced contracts with local portable toilet providers would mitigate the crisis when water was abruptly turned off; (c) backup plans for processing payroll are critical because staff and faculty needed immediate access to cash after power outages disrupted bimonthly payrolls.

An important part of team practice and continuous improvement is identifying and implementing the training needed for various campus constituents. Common training topics for crisis response include Clery Act reporting, the Family Educational Rights and Privacy Act, mandatory reporting for sexual molestation, shelter-in-place and evacuation procedures, and alert/communications notifications. Training for senior leadership may include responding to the media and other advanced communication techniques.

Communicate the Plan to the Community

Communication and preparedness are companions in team building for crisis response and recovery. Faculty, staff, students, governing board members, families, and community members have a role in responding and rebuilding after a crisis and deserve to know that the institution is prepared, where and how they can expect to receive information, and their role, if any, in the response. Sharing the appropriate level of information about the plan with each constituent in advance builds confidence in the leadership's ability to guide the institution and defines the important roles each group or individual performs in the recovery.

Communication During the Crisis

A strong crisis response plan articulates how the leadership will keep the community informed. The communications plan should do the following:

- Include objectives of the communications plan
- Ensure timely release of accurate information

- Communicate verified facts rather than speculative information
- Protect the welfare of involved personnel and their families
- Retain all constituents' confidence in the institution
- Use the crisis, when appropriate, to educate the community on the institution's values and future crisis prevention efforts
- List the audiences to receive communication: students, families, faculty and staff, board, prospective students, alumni, boards, donors, government officials, and the broader community

The crisis communications team should include the director of communications/public affairs, head of campus law enforcement, president or chancellor, dean of students/campus life, vice president of information technology, and general counsel or outside legal counsel. The plan should identify external experts to call upon when the crisis reaches a level and scope beyond the expertise of the campus crisis communications team. Partnering with crisis response experts who are familiar with the institution before the crisis occurs is a best practice.

After the Crisis: Rebuilding the Team

Campus leaders who have weathered a crisis will face a long personal healing and recovery process. A damaged building can be reopened, but emotional and mental stresses take longer to heal and should not be neglected. A leader is responsible for not only surviving the immediate crisis but also supporting the team's mental and emotional health and recovery. Providing professional counseling for the crisis team and entire campus community is essential. A crisis response plan should identify auxiliary counseling support, either through an employee assistance program, a reciprocal sharing agreement with another local institution, or outside firm equipped to provide immediate support. The president will be "griever-in-chief" and the public face of the institution, carrying a huge burden. Taking care of the leadership team through exercise, healthy meals, adequate sleep, and counseling is paramount during and after a crisis.

Highlights of an effective team and crisis response include the following:

- Use news reports of crises at other institutions to practice and improve the institution's crisis response plans.
- Question and examine the institution's sacred cows to uncover potential threats and lurking crises.
- Practice the crisis response plan regularly, using various scenarios and involving outside groups, including the local first responders.
- Have a backup for every position assigned responsibility in the plan.

- Communicate the plan to governing board members and inform them of their role in the recovery.
- Establish clear communication channels with senior leadership to reduce the possibility of surprises.
- Emphasize that everyone is part of the solution and finger-pointing and blaming are not conducive to rebuilding.
- During the crisis and recovery, open all communication channels within the team and with outside constituents. Good ideas can come from anywhere.
- Ask for advice and help from leaders at other campuses who have been through similar scenarios.
- Show compassion for crisis victims and their families while demonstrating professionalism to strengthen an institution's incident management. This "Cool Head, Warm Heart™" approach will become your most effective crisis response tool.

Reference

U.S. Department of Education. (2010). *Action guide for emergency management at institutions of higher education.* Retrieved from http://rems.ed.gov/docs/REMS_ActionGuide.pdf

12

COURAGE, COMPASSION, COMMUNICATION

Connie J. Gores

Crises occur when you least expect them and without warning. A crisis can be anything that disrupts normal conditions and threatens personal safety, financial operations, institutional reputation, or the integrity of the entire institution (Zdziarski, 2006). There are environmental crises (flood, tornado); facilities and/or technology-related crises (fire, data breach); crises that involve human lives (death of student, faculty, staff); and personnel or governance issues (theft, embezzlement, harassment). Regardless of the nature of the crisis, someone and/or some group has to respond to the situation and deal with the aftermath.

When tragedy strikes, the campus community, stakeholders, and the local community look to leadership for direction and guidance. How leaders respond in the first several hours and in the days that follow offers tremendous opportunity to bring a campus together or put the campus at risk. It is not possible to predict or control a crisis, but it is possible to control the response and the way in which the institution reacts to it.

Preparation and campus readiness are critical to responding effectively to a crisis. It is important to recognize the novelty of each situation and acknowledge that no two crises are the same. Equally important is building an effective team that responds appropriately and compassionately to the situation and that is supported throughout the crisis and beyond.

What follows is a firsthand account of an incident involving the near-drowning of an international student participating in an English language program at Winona State University (WSU). After several days in intensive care, the student passed away. From the moment they learned of the incident, campus leaders worked closely with the student's family, the U.S. Embassy, members of the student's university in China, and others to respond to the situation. Great care was taken in building a cohesive campus team that not only responded effectively, but did so with care, compassion, and ongoing communication.

Nestled alongside the Mississippi River, Winona State University, in Winona, Minnesota, is an idyllic place to spend a summer. With its warm weather and cool breezes, it is the perfect time of year to bring international students to campus to study English and learn about American culture in the English Language Center (ELC) program. In July 2009, 24 students joined the ELC program from Hebei University of Technology, a sister school in China. As part of their planned social activities several days after their arrival, the students went on a swimming excursion at a local lake. There was an unfortunate swimming accident and an ELC student nearly drowned. Fortunately, a group of local first responders happened to be involved in a practice drill nearby, and seconds after the student was pulled from the lake, he was treated by these paramedics. He had taken in so much water, however, that he was rushed to a local hospital and airlifted to a regional medical center 30 miles away.

At the time this was unfolding, in my role as vice president for student life and development, I was giving closing remarks at a dinner celebrating the accomplishments of a summer program for underrepresented youth. As I walked to my office feeling great pride and a sense of satisfaction from the uplifting dinner event, I glanced at my phone and retrieved a voice mail from a security officer telling me of the tragedy at the lake.

I sprang into action and called others to campus. Within 30 minutes of hearing the initial phone message, a team of 10 people was assembled in my office. Gathered were a campus security officer, the director of the ELC program, a member of the campus communications office staff, a residence hall staff member and summer programs assistant, a faculty member, a staff member from the International Services office, and a mental health counselor. Also present were several of the graduate student supervisors who had accompanied the ELC students on the excursion—the graduate students who had witnessed the near-drowning, one of whom pulled the student out of the lake.

Things happened quickly, and soon the medical doctor treating the student in the intensive care unit of the regional medical center was on the phone asking to speak with a member of the student's family. One of the graduate students (whose first language was Chinese) reached a family member of the student in China, and there was a four-way conversation among the medical doctor, the grad student, a family member, and me.

During that call, the medical doctor asked me to ask the graduate student to tell the family member that "survival is unlikely." The graduate student looked plaintively at me and asked, "Do I really have to say that?" I reassured him that he was strong and we had confidence that he could do this; I also reminded him that everyone in the room was there to support him. The graduate student spoke to the family in Chinese, and the English speakers in the room (as well as the medical doctor on the phone) trusted that the graduate student shared the specific information with the family.

This was the first time that I had met the graduate student; I didn't know him, and I had no sense of his abilities or the level of his maturity. When I told him that I was confident that he could convey the very delicate information to the family, I said so with an air of certainty that I really did not feel; truth be told, I had no idea if he was going to be able to handle the situation or not. I didn't share my concerns with anyone, but I secretly whispered a prayer to the universe asking for guidance and support with what we were experiencing. The standard protocol involving the health and safety of a domestic student is that a staff member contacts the student's family or emergency contact. Because this student had no family in the United States, I determined that the university was going to act as his family until a family member could travel from China to Minnesota. I decided to assign 24-hour bedside coverage at the hospital so the student was never alone. Six-hour shifts were organized, and university officials were assigned to rotating slots in the four daily shifts. In each shift, there was an administrator or a person who could represent the university and an interpreter who would serve as a translator for communication and messages between the hospital staff, the family, the university, and any others. Cell phone numbers, e-mail addresses, and other contact information were collected and a contact sheet was prepared and shared with all members of the response team. I made a decision not to assign myself a time slot at the hospital; instead, I would remain at the "command center" on campus.

The first couple of days, the graduate students in the ELC program served as translators at the hospital and in my office when a family member called me from China. Once the family arrived later in the week, faculty members whose first language was Chinese served as translators at the hospital and with the family.

Before the team disbanded for the first evening, we determined that we would meet twice daily for briefings and to touch base with one another. Times were arranged and a location was identified. After the others departed, the international services staff member and I remained on campus and began making calls to the family in China, the U.S. Embassy in China to facilitate the visa application for the family, and the partner university in China. With a 12-hour time difference between Beijing, China, and Winona, Minnesota, it meant that when the workday was winding down in Minnesota, others were waking up and starting their workday in China. This made for very long days for the International Services staff member and me.

During the twice-daily meetings, we updated the team on the status of the student and apprised the group of actions taken by the university and other officials. The team membership changed (it grew depending on the day and the availability of other vice presidents or the university president). Team makeup depends upon the culture of the institution and the expertise of its members. In this instance, some members served on the crisis response team because of their functional role on campus, and other team members were included because of their unique strengths or talents. At several points, we included members of the system office and of the state risk management team in phone meetings and/or conversations.

The incident commander must be comfortable giving direction up, down, and sideways. At several points, I gave directives to the president, my immediate supervisor—I told her what I needed her to do (be present when the family cleaned out the student's residence hall room), and I reminded her of the importance of conveying sadness and compassion to the family. I regularly gave directions to my peers serving on the shifts at the hospital, and I also delegated tasks and gave explicit instructions to those who served in other roles following the incident. Ongoing and regular communication is key to effective response, and there was a need to keep the communication flowing at all levels of the response team (Bataille, Billings, & Nellum, 2012).

In terms of what was conveyed to the campus community, we tried to strike a balance between sharing essential information and not sharing too much information too often or in too much detail; we attempted to strike a balance between the need to inform and include others, but not to overwhelm them with unnecessary details.

On the morning of the second day during a team meeting, a senior official of the university made a comment that the university had to be careful not to get sued, that we needed to consider every step we took in light of possible litigation. I quickly responded by stating that there was time to talk about legal issues later and reminded everyone that the most important thing to consider was the health and safety of the student involved in the accident. I made a conscious choice not to discuss the legal question with the entire team; instead I asked a smaller group of senior officials to stay after the team meeting to discuss the legal implications of the situation. My thought process was really quite simple: I felt there was no useful purpose served in discussing the topic with individuals who were not typically involved in university-wide issues with legal implications; I felt that sharing this kind of information with them would only serve to frighten them and may distract these team members from doing the right thing when it came to assisting the student. Fortunately, the senior official who mentioned the legal implications did not raise such questions again in front of anyone but a group of vice presidents.

For most of the ELC students, it was the first time they had traveled away from home; they were still in their teens, and nearly every one of them was an only child. As would be expected, they were frightened and uncertain. The international services staff member and I met with the ELC students twice a day to keep them apprised of the situation and to keep the communication flowing. Many of the students wanted to visit their friend in the hospital, but I decided that that would not be advisable given the student's medical condition: He was not improving.

Each day during the meeting with the ELC students, I gave an update on the student's medical condition. Knowing that it was highly likely that the student would not survive, each day I gave progressively more detailed accounts of the student's condition. I was careful not to intentionally frighten the students, but I felt that it was important that the students understood the gravity of the situation. On the first day after the accident, we asked the ELC students to write messages to their friend that the translator in the hospital would read to him. The students were happy to prepare the messages and appeared relieved that they were able to do something tangible for their friend. During this time, students continued with their English language program, and the ELC staff tried to keep the daily routine as normal as possible.

On the second full day after the accident, when meeting with the ELC students, I suggested the students make paper cranes to be placed by the hospital bed of the student—the ELC students willingly and actively made the cranes for their friend.

When it was certain that the mother and a family member of the student were en route to Minnesota, I asked the students to write messages to the mother, so she would have something to read and hold when she arrived in the United States. Again the students were happy to comply and quickly composed messages to their friend's mother. In hindsight, this was one of the most important steps we took in assisting the family.

Sadly, the student did not regain consciousness, and he passed away. After the student passed away, we involved the ELC students in planning a memorial service for their friend. They did a remarkable job of celebrating him and honoring their short time together on campus. They prepared a multimedia presentation at the memorial service on campus, including video, photographs, and music. This process helped the students process the death of their friend and brought them closer together as a group. As surprising as it may sound, not one student left the ELC program as a result of the tragedy; every student stayed and completed the program.

Although the other ELC students from China were either Christian or agnostic, the student who was involved in the swimming accident was Muslim. We had no idea how devout he was in his faith or how active. We did, however, engage the services of a Muslim cleric, who was an adjunct faculty member of the university and very active in the Winona community. He was instrumental in helping us understand customs and rituals associated with Islamic tradition.

When the family finally arrived from China on the third day after the tragedy, we made sure to have halal food available for them. We arranged for a local restaurant to take special orders from the family and provide food upon request to them. Our security officers (and others) drove the family to the restaurant and other places in town to ensure they did not have to incur the expense or hassle of a taxi.

Similarly, we worked directly with the Muslim cleric on the protocol and rituals associated with the final moments of a life on Earth. He instructed us on religious tradition, and we worked with the hospital to ensure that he could perform the religious rituals in accordance with the faith tradition. Fortunately, he was at the student's bedside when the student passed away. The student's cousin had also arrived from China several hours before he died, so a family member was with him at that time.

No one is ever totally prepared for serving as an incident commander in an ongoing crisis situation. No one can predict what will occur or how others will react. After several days of serving on shifts at the hospital, it was clear that some of the individuals assigned to the hospital were exhausted and the assignment was taking an emotional toll on everyone who served in the rotation of the hospital shifts. One particular case was quite telling.

One of my colleagues—a fellow vice president—had extensive experience in the military serving in very high-ranking roles on several military bases. He had seen more than his share of death, and he had dealt with many extremely challenging situations. After serving several shifts at the hospital over several days and watching this young person's condition deteriorate, it became too much for him to handle. On the third day after the drowning accident, the student's body began shutting down, and it was clear that the student was very close to death. My fellow vice president called me and expressed how difficult it was to be at the hospital and see this young person's life slipping away. Although I had worked closely with my colleague and we had dealt with more than our share of "challenges" together (town/gown issues, budget challenges), I had never seen him so affected by a student situation. It was then when I realized that not only does the incident commander have to be a cheerleader to the team and a coach to all who are involved in responding to the situation, it is also important to serve as a counselor for those who are most directly affected by the loss—especially the loss of someone so young and so far away from home.

If at all possible, make counseling services available to the response team, whether through the institution's counselor services or through the employee assistance program. Even the members who do not verbalize their need for personal assistance will be affected by the tragedy and will need support. Everyone grieves differently, and all team members need to be supported. There is no fixed process to follow, and grief often comes and goes.

On the afternoon of the first full day after the accident, the response team was told that we were not to discuss anything with the media nor were we to provide any financial assistance to the family. In both cases, it was too late. When I learned of these instructions, I was on my way to meet with a television crew and immediately following that engagement, I was scheduled to have an interview with the local newspaper.

Fortunately, each of the vice presidents had undergone media training earlier in the year. I made the decision to participate in the interviews with the media. I knew that I could not discuss the near-drowning incident (there was a police investigation under way), and I could not discuss the condition of the student (he was in the hospital, and that information was private), but I could (and did) discuss the steps that the university was taking to support the 23 other students from China and communicate with the family in China.

Disregarding the instructions not to talk with the media was not done in protest, nor was it done as an act of resistance; instead, talking to the media and putting a human face on the tragedy was the right thing to do. It was the right thing on behalf of the student, and it was the right thing to do on behalf of the university. In a small town of 30,000 people, the university is an integral part of the community, and what happens at the university is news. In talking with the media, we helped frame the situation in terms of the university's response and the actions we took rather than focus on the incident itself; in essence, we changed the narrative by doing the right thing. As Teresa Valerio Parrot states, "Sincerity serves as the ultimate litmus test for your response" (Parrot, 2012, p. 18). We were able to manage policy and operational concerns effectively.

Similarly, the president, another vice president, and I made a decision to fund the family's travel to Minnesota from China. We assumed that the family did not have significant financial resources. We knew that they were not well traveled, and this would be their first time outside their home country. We helped facilitate the visa application by working directly with the U.S

Embassy in Shanghai, and we paid for round-trip travel to the United States. We understood the inherent risks in paying for the travel (we may not get the money back from the family or there might be a perception of complicity in our funding this activity). Nevertheless, we chose to assist the family in this way because we felt it was the right thing to do. As it turned out, no legal steps were taken against the university and the family has many times expressed their appreciation for everything that was done to assist them during this difficult time.

Just as it was important that vice presidents and key campus leaders had undergone media training so they knew what could be said to the media, it was also important that the entire response team understood their role in responding to the situation. Fortunately, members of the campus were prepared when the tragedy occurred because most of them had undergone a simulation training exercise the previous August that involved Winona County, the City of Winona, the university, and other entities. As part of that simulation exercise, most of the team had also received certification in National Incident Management System training. They were familiar with Incident Command System language and the suggested framework for an incident command team.

At each step of the response and recovery process, we were intentional with the questions we asked and the points we considered. At each step, we asked the response team to consider carefully the steps we would take, who would be involved, and what we might be overlooking. We considered the following questions: What should we consider? What steps should we take? Whom should we contact? Who should be involved? What questions should we be asking? What have we missed?

Arnold Howitt and Herman Leonard of Harvard University are often called in to consult on large-scale crises such as hurricanes and earthquakes. They are quick to point out that each crisis is unique, and campus leaders should not assume that because they have dealt with one type of crisis scenario they are going to be ready to deal with another crisis, even if similar in nature. Although there might be similar components to crises, each situation and crisis is novel (Howitt & Leonard, 2009).

From the first meeting of the response team, it was clear that people were processing information differently. In some cases, team members talked about every detail and asked a lot of questions at each step. In other cases, team members only wanted to know what they considered the most important facts, and they felt that sharing too much information was unnecessary or superfluous. It was a challenge balancing the communication needs of all the crisis response team members.

As the chair of meetings and the person in charge of the team, I was ever mindful of different styles of communication. In every team meeting, for example, I stated the objectives of our meeting and reminded the team why we were gathered together. I was intentional about thanking people for their good work and regularly asked if anyone had questions. To engage the introverts, I often asked them specifically to share their insights and opinions; I regularly asked them if they had questions. Although being asked direct questions in a group meeting may have been uncomfortable for some people, it gave them an opportunity to give voice to their thoughts and share their concerns.

No crisis lasts forever; at some point, things settle down. It is in the best interests of all to build resiliency and resourcefulness in the crisis response team. Just as it is important to respond carefully to the immediate crisis, it is also important to learn from the situation in order to apply that knowledge to future planning and preparation. Undoubtedly, team members will decompress differently, so it will be necessary to provide more than one avenue to debrief what has occurred.

We held several meetings in which we walked through the steps we took in responding to the crisis and the ensuing days. At each step, we identified what went well, we highlighted our positive actions, and we acknowledged where we could have been more effective. We discussed changes that were necessary to our protocols and procedures, and we celebrated our effectiveness.

Several days after the weeklong crisis was over, we held a social gathering outside in a lovely home setting. We shared food and socialized in a relaxed environment. Even though team members had spent a lot of time together and may have initially preferred to spend time alone, being together in a different setting was helpful. The social gathering helped to create new memories for the team and to keep the dialogue going.

It is important to recognize that the quality of the response to a campus crisis will have a lasting impact on the culture of the campus and community. Long after the crisis has subsided, memories of how the campus responded will prevail. If the response has been thoughtful, thorough, and human-centered, the crisis narrative will be more positive and the community will be enriched.

References

Bataille, G. M., Billings, M. S., & Nellum, C. J. (2012). *Leadership in times of crisis: "Cool head, warm heart."* Washington, DC: American Council on Education.

Howitt, A. M., & Leonard, H. B. (Eds.). (2009). *Managing crises: Responses to large-scale emergencies*. Washington, DC: CQ Press.

Parrot, T. V. (2012). Communicating in times of crisis. *The Presidency, 15*(3), 16–18.

Zdziarski, E. L., II. (2006). Crisis in the context of higher education. In K. S. Harper, B. G. Paterson, & E. L. Zdziarski II (Eds.), *Crisis management: Responding from the heart* (pp. 3–24). Washington, DC: National Association of Student Personnel Administrators.

PART FOUR

DEALING WITH THE MEDIA

Who to Tell What and When

Most campuses have well-established plans for dealing with the media, but all of that changes in a crisis situation. Day-to-day relationships are usually with the education reporter for the local paper or key contacts in national sites, but when a particular crisis hits, there are new players in the media as well—local, national, and even international. These reporters may not know the campus leadership and may seek stories from the least likely sources, making it imperative that the whole campus is aware of the protocols for dealing with media.

Holding an annual "media tour" or "media day" is a useful strategy for establishing and building relationships with local, regional, and national media outlets before a crisis strikes. Media days can provide campus leaders the opportunity to use both off-the-record and on-the-record meetings to ensure that when the need arises, the president and reporters are known to one another and understand each other's perspective. Having well-established relationships with the media can pay off when a campus is faced with a potential crisis situation that could easily spiral out of control if a high level of trust hasn't been built over time with local newspaper reporters through regularly scheduled meetings and conversations.

One certainty campus leaders can expect during a time of crisis is that the media—local, national, international, and social—will broadcast a narrative about the campus that will remain in the public domain long after the tenure of a campus leader. Sometimes the media will not be fair and will deliver messages that are untrue or ill conceived; other times, campus-based legal counsel may present apparent barriers to the leader's ability to communicate effectively. Either way, there are multiple constituencies (e.g., students, faculty, community members, and media) that require different information at different times. Communication to each of those groups must not involve changing facts, but must reflect an understanding of what each needs to know. Before a crisis occurs is the time to consider media relations training for the leadership team and to begin nurturing relationships with media outlets, in particular local education reporters and other stakeholders. Media training information is available from many external sources, including United Educators (www.ue.org).

Senior leadership must also take the necessary steps in order to effectively manage an outsized media response, such as the one experienced by the Virginia Polytechnic Institute and State University (Virginia Tech) as a result of a shooting incident. Lawrence G. Hincker discusses how the senior leadership team handled the massive media presence over a long period of time and distills lessons learned from the tragedy. At the height of the crisis, the media response and global interest generated by the events that unfolded on the campus severely tested the institution's communications infrastructure. Although crises such as the one experienced by Virginia Tech are thankfully rare, the need to have protocols and systems in place to be able to quickly handle such demands, even during the course of less serious incidents, is ever-present.

The role of legal counsel can present some challenges for campus leaders interested in interacting effectively with the media. It is, of course, the responsibility of legal counsel to safeguard the institution from a legal standpoint, but striking a balance between the need to protect the university and the need to inform the public isn't always easy. Whatever else happens, the story will often be written with or without a statement from the institution, and it is the president's responsibility to determine who will write the story and what story is told.

In the era of Twitter, Facebook, texting, and blogging, no one waits to read about an incident in the morning paper anymore. Hiring a social media specialist may be critical in some situations, particularly if posts on Twitter, Facebook, and other social media outlets drift too far from the truth. It is critical to monitor social media and then respond with factual information using those same outlets as well as the university website. Thanks to thorough preparation and conscientious relationship building, campus leaders are able to prevent crises from becoming unmanageable (or, in some cases, from happening in the first place). However, more often than not, crises strike without warning and, therefore, demand a swift response or explanation. It is crucial that the senior leadership team understand the core set of facts about the situation and communicate effectively with not only the media, but with the various groups having a stake in the institution. Despite a natural sense of urgency to respond, campus leaders need to "take a step back" in order to assess the situation and to consider the various approaches to (re)engage the media.

Because credibility as an institutional leader depends in large part on the ability to get out in front of the story, it is important to engage the campus-based communications team (including social media specialists or consultants), legal counsel, and well-established media contacts prior to making a statement. Relationships build over time, and forging those relationships may buy more time if the media view the president as someone who is truthful and honest before the crisis. Whether or not the president has developed relationships with these individuals in the past, it is important to make contact with them immediately to determine what facts can and should be communicated and to ensure the media and other constituents that information will be available as soon as possible. Establishing a central web location (e.g., university site, Twitter, Facebook) with relevant information is an efficient method to provide media outlets and the campus community with information about what happened or is happening.

At some point, the leadership team will decide that it is time to make a statement, and a critical first step is determining who the appropriate spokesperson is. As Teresa Valerio Parrot advises, under many circumstances, including a major crisis, the president needs to be in front rather than another senior administrator or the chair of the institution's board of trustees. The president must be proactive and must tell the truth. Reporters and the general public are often quite forgiving when it comes to honest mistakes and omissions but are typically staunchly unforgiving when it comes to lying or selective truth telling. When the decision is made to respond to the media, it is important to be transparent with reporters, think carefully about what their needs are with respect to their profession, and articulate an understanding of their desire to understand the facts.

In the end, the story will be told and the memories will linger on far beyond the incident. As the authors in this section emphasize, the role of the leadership team is critical, and the relationships that have been forged with various media representatives will make a difference in how the institution and its leaders are portrayed. As with advice given elsewhere in this book, the honesty and forthrightness of the messages can make the difference in how the final story is slanted, and evasion and dishonesty will leave a mark forever on an institution's reputation.

13

CRISIS COMMUNICATIONS

Lessons Learned From the Virginia Tech Tragedy

Lawrence G. Hincker

Traditional news cycles are dead. Modern communications are instantaneous and global. News coverage is immediate and incessant. Are you prepared to respond to an emergency or crisis? Universities and most colleges are essentially small cities. Just about any out-of-the-ordinary event can morph into a crisis demanding high intensity and rapid media interactions. Moreover, there are high expectations for quick response among the many college or university constituencies.

Unexpected or natural events, like hurricanes, earthquakes, fires, chemical explosions, or, heaven forbid, a mass shooting such as my university experienced in 2007, demand immediate and sometimes massive media relations response. Media scrutiny surely follows internal strife, too—trustees acting badly, students acting like students, faculty no-confidence votes, campus land-use controversies, town-gown friction, racial unrest—all can explode into a full-blown crisis in a heartbeat.

The higher education news office must be prepared for an outsized media response. We use many monikers for institutional communications in higher education—news office, public affairs, university relations, university communications, media relations. I use them all to refer to the chief communications office responsible for managing institutional communications and responding to media inquiries.

Like most large universities, Virginia Tech had seen its share of crisis events, such as monster snow and ice storms, tornadoes, hurricanes, student suicide, campus protests, presidential controversy, but nothing like the mass tragedy that struck on the cold blustery morning of April 16, 2007. One angry young man with easy access to powerful killing weapons created carnage like never before—49 people shot and 30 dead in 9 minutes. The media response and world interest tested our capabilities and infrastructure. About 1,000 journalists or staffers descended on our campus in the mountains of western Virginia, some decamping their normal lairs for two weeks or more to our small town. Almost 16,000 unique news stories were filed around the world in the first 2 weeks after the event. Our electronic communications infrastructure was severely tested by massive demand for information.

Although Virginia Tech–like experiences are thankfully rare, the need for protocols and processes to quickly respond to even simple events has become the norm. The instantaneous and ubiquitous nature of modern electronic communications demands multilayered response and capability of any university relations office, both during and after a crisis event. We'll explore some of the techniques and tools later in this chapter, but first a review of my version of Crisis Communications 101.

The basics of crisis communications are as follows:

- Have a plan
- Keep the CEO visible and out front
- Ensure a designated spokesperson, but use experts where necessary
- Have a communications command center
- Communicate as much as possible, and as often as possible, to all your constituencies
- Stay on message

It All Begins With Planning

There are myriad formats for crisis communication plans with various levels of sophistication. At a minimum, the plan should identify the key institutional leadership, senior communicators, their roles, contact information, whether you need an "on-call" structure, and how you'll staff it. You may or may not elect to have key-player contact information in this document (likely not, if it's a public document), but be sure that someone in the communications office (or another office, like the president or emergency planning) keeps a list, keeps it up-to-date, and distributes it regularly.

The plan should identify facility locations for news conferences and a communications command/work center. If part of a public body, the latter would be the Joint Information Center (JIC), where public information officers (PIOs) from many agencies assemble to share information. The JIC jargon stems from the National Incident Management System (NIMS) and various earlier protocols to coordinate emergency preparedness and incident management or response among the public and private sectors.

Although not necessary for successful crisis communications, a NIMS-trained university leadership is likely better prepared to handle an event. The concomitant training not only exposes weaknesses in your system that can be fixed before a crisis but also familiarizes various players, inside and outside the university. Already knowing the players, when blood pressures rise, helps immensely. Indeed, one important aspect of NIMS training is the emergency preparedness mind-set that ensues.

Whether or not NIMS is adopted, frequent emergency response exercises are akin to physical exercise—they build intellectual and institutional muscles you will use when you least expect it. When I have found myself in crisis events, I'm reminded of General Dwight Eisenhower's admonition (admittedly, clumsily paraphrased), "In war, planning is everything; in battle, plans go out the window." You can't follow any plan to the letter. But frequent planning and various exercises afford you the mind-set to react quickly, and when necessary, toss the plans out the proverbial window when events dictate another path.

The Chief Executive Is the Face of the University

The public expects the president to be in charge during a crisis. In our visual world, the president at the podium in front of the cameras underscores his or her leadership role. It sends a strong message not only to external constituencies, but internally as well. Students and employees will draw their strength from those images. University leadership sets the tone for recovery, and the messages they send, overt or subliminal, feed organizational resilience. Ensure that the president is media trained long before a crisis hits. Standing before dozens of cameras is not the time to explain the need for short answers, staying on message, refraining from speculation, or keeping one's cool.

During our time of crisis, Virginia Tech's president, Charles Steger, gave live national interviews the night of the shootings, the next morning, and the next afternoon. Although he was busy managing the crisis after that and the university spokesperson became the face of the school, his immediate appearance and willingness to face tough questions set the tone for the institutional response.

The Designated Spokesperson

I cut my public relations (PR) teeth working for a nuclear utility. We were grounded in the notion that there is one spokesperson for a crisis. That can be anyone appropriate for the event—but continuity is important for many reasons—clearance of facts, consistent voice, preventing confusing positions, and so on. However, universities operate not in tightly controlled corporate environments, but in loose confederations of free spirits. As the university spokesperson, I maintained that role, but used other experts during news conferences when appropriate. During a quickly unfolding event, the chief communicator simply doesn't have the time to become "expert" on every facet of the crisis and needs experts quickly to be in front of the cameras.

Faculty and students may elect to engage the media. We can't and shouldn't attempt to control that, but we can provide guidance. For example, several times during our crisis, I provided via a blast e-mail to campus, "guidelines for engaging the media." It began with a cautionary freedom—"You don't need to conduct an interview if you don't want to." I am often surprised how friendly people are on college campuses. Many of our students and faculty, at first, felt obliged to succumb to the bushwhack camera. They were thankful when I relieved them of that notion. The e-mail went on to offer advice on how students and faculty should conduct themselves and what they might address, if they agreed to be interviewed. In my mental map, the designated spokesperson also manages news media information needs. Knowing what's been said and released or what's been asked at press conferences or other inquires, enables the senior communications executive to deploy resources appropriately and identify experts.

Communicate Often; Do Not Fear Repeat

Reputation management starts on day one. Openness and transparency go a long way in building media trust. You will not know all the answers early in the crisis, but for the big events, you must engage the media quickly. They will find answers from someone whether you talk or not. It is a frightful experience facing the cameras and interviewers who are tossing probing or hurtful questions when you don't have answers. Senior communicators must gauge the trade-offs of not engaging the media, but be advised—they will descend on your campus, whether invited or not.

Your constituencies need to hear key facts again and again. Where do we go if our dorm is burned out? How do I find the status of my loved one? When will classes start again after the tornado? Are the buses running? Who do I call for . . . ? The questions are endless.

There are myriad tools for constituency or public communications. Make sure that you've flexed and used them before a crisis. Your website likely is your most valuable and high-profile tool (more on that later). Twitter and Facebook are a close second. Don't forget to use the parents' e-mail newsletter, send blast e-mail to the university community, and contact the governing board, advisory groups, and alumni. News conferences are mandatory for many crises.

During our crisis, we were inundated with media interview requests—more than 350 on the first day alone. Faced with such outsized demand, the news conference format was the only viable method of interaction. Moreover, it ensured consistent answers to emotion-laden questions. We conducted 11 news conferences in 8 days. From a practical standpoint, the news conference affords an opportunity to take the pulse of the media via questions asked. The senior media relations managers can use that understanding to find other experts or third-party advocates.

Don't forget about local media. The demands of national media are insatiable. But their interest is often transient, and they move on. College media relations pros know that they must deal with local journalists again and again. To the degree possible, help the locals get the stories they need.

The Communications Command Center

Your plan should have an identified location where you will brief the media. Identify where you might park a few dozen media satellite trucks. More than 125 such behemoths suddenly appeared at Virginia Tech within hours of our tragedy. If you plan on using a command center different from your normal office, is it outfitted with phones and computers? Do you have TVs, and can you monitor the major networks? Have you addressed if and how the normal media relations phone lines would be transferred to the command center? What about providing media access to campus networks? Cell phones and air cards have minimized the need for usage of the network, but many still want it.

Staying on Message

Staying on message means different things to different people. For me, it means simply focusing on the most important aspects of the crisis at the time. For example, when responding to a fire or weather event that displaces students from dormitories, it's best to focus on their immediate needs and not peripheral issues. Recognize also that universities are not tightly controlled operations. Your faculty or students might opine before a camera, ratcheting up the angst factor in the university news office. Don't try to control, but do share media interview techniques and key messages. Trying to help rather than stifle those voices will add to institutional credibility over the long run.

As we departed the "acute" phase of crisis communications and began the long slide into the "chronic" phase, knowing when to engage the media became problematic. The Virginia Tech campus and extended community were traumatized. For weeks and weeks, it had been analyzed, scrutinized, criticized, and emblazoned across world media. Many on campus needed a little space and a little peace from the media's prying eyes. The university news office retreated from its natural inclination to respond to each reporter's inquiry. Campus experts were tired and, frankly, needed to concentrate on their own work demands. When confronted with such massive media inspection, each campus news office must make choices about which interviews to accept.

The Special Case of the Web and Social Media

The university website might be passé in the minds of new-media mavens, but, in my opinion, it's still the bedrock of a university's communication network. It is the first place people go to for news updates during an emergency. And your college or university homepage is the first place parents, reporters, students, and others will go to for current information. Do you have the capacity to feed information quickly to www.youruniversity.edu?

What is the relationship between the information technology (IT) and public affairs offices? Can the school upgrade file-server capacity on a moment's notice? Is your campus prepared for web traffic increases of 10 times? 100 times? 1,000 times? Who on the communications staff has access to the homepage? Can university communicators post updates from home or other remote locations? These questions need answers long before the crisis hits.

Do you have a "light page" designed and ready to post? University homepages tend to be laden with "heavy" graphic content of large electronic files. Such sites load slowly and may crash when punished by extra demand. Within 30 minutes of the 2007 shootings, we removed the normal homepage and posted our light page (pre-designed and sitting in storage), stripped of all but essential navigation and a window for news updates. Many will use a blog-like format, pushing the most recent post to the top. Some schools automatically post emergency alerts. Whatever you do, the homepage should feature a "slim" design, without the usual pretty pictures and fancy graphic elements in order to ensure rapid loading.

The Virginia Tech homepage experienced a 15-fold increase in traffic within hours of the shootings. Web hosting changed from two to four and ultimately to five servers to handle traffic. When we experienced another shooting almost 5 years later in December 2011, we mounted eight computer servers. Without the light page and the additional file servers, our website would have crashed and compromised our ability to quickly report on the status of events.

Using social media for emergency notification or various forms of news releases greatly magnifies your active constituency base. But this action also drives traffic to the university sites. Most likely, your messages will include active links to your website, driving even more traffic. By December 2011, we had fully employed Facebook and Twitter for emergency notification and for posting news updates. As a result, visitor traffic to www.vt.edu during the December 2011 event increased by 85 times our normal load!

The "IT wars" between campus communicators and information technology staffers seem to be a thing of the past. But I still find instances in which public relations staff cannot post information to their school's homepage or the PR types have not a clue about who's responsible for hosting the campus file servers. The IT and PR staff need to be on a first-name basis long before an emergency strikes. The website is not only a broadcast medium for news updates, it is a file box for storing every shred of information related to the emergency.

Emergency Notification Systems

Although this chapter is focused on preparing for and responding to media during a crisis, a word about emergency notifications systems (ENSs) is warranted. Such systems were almost unheard of prior to April 2007. Few schools had the ability to quickly touch campus community members, particularly if they were on the go. Blast e-mail, if one had access, was the standard communications channel. Mass text notification was just coming onto the scene during that time frame. As a result of the Virginia Tech shootings, an entirely new cottage industry was born for higher education. Even the federal campus crime notification law, the Clery Act, was modified in response to the Virginia Tech tragedy.

Most colleges and universities deploy ENSs with multiple communication channels. No one channel will serve all constituents equally. Users have different preferences. And most important, during a crisis one or more channels might become inoperative. Cell phone coverage, the backbone of text messaging, likely will be the first to fail. What's the first thing students do when faced with a problem? They probably call a friend or call home on a cell phone. After the August 2011 East Coast earthquake, cellular networks up and down the Atlantic Coast region quickly degraded. Our campus cell networks were essentially useless for more than 24 hours after the April 2007 shootings. And what about your campus network if you have power outages?

Thus, any ENS ought to have multiple distribution channels such as blast e-mail, text or phone messages to reach mobile devices (normally rendered through an outside service), computer pop-up messaging, loudspeakers, recorded hotlines, special campus signage, and social media. Virginia Tech is currently investigating using each building's fire suppression system network as a backbone for ENS loudspeakers. Whatever service or scheme is adopted, never rely on one channel, one system, or one vendor for campus emergency notification.

Protocols

Technology is great, but when should it be used? Indeed, having instant communications capability creates expectations of, well, *instant* communications. Who has the authority and ability to send an emergency notification? If relying on text messaging, can it be said in 140 characters or fewer?

Over the years, most campuswide notifications have been the province of the central communications office. But in the new era of high expectations, timeliness is paramount. The U.S. federal law, the Clery Act, originally required institutions to give timely warnings of crimes that represent a threat to the safety of students or employees within the generally accepted practice of 24–48 hours.[1] Congress amended the Clery Act[2] in the wake of the Virginia Tech shootings to require institutions to "immediately" notify the campus community upon the identification of a threat to the health or safety of students and staff. Today, campuses must have many people authorized to send notifications and many more with the technical know-how to compose and distribute ENS messages. In addition to professional communicators, police and other emergency responders and senior administrators should be trained.

And what about the messages themselves? Anyone who has composed notifications during the stress of an emergency knows of the difficulty in getting it right, particularly when confronted with the length limitations of text messaging. Every word and character counts. Nuances count. After one emergency, we discovered that few on our campus knew north from south, which had been embedded in an evacuation notice. Who knew?

Most campuses now deploy their ENSs with prewritten templates for various scenarios. Virginia Tech's ENS contains 20 such templates, ranging from "active shooter" to "tornado" to "bomb threat" to "snow emergency."

Emergency notices should be as specific as possible. Issue a secure-in-place alert if faced with an ambiguous situation, continue with updates to fill uncertainty, and issue a close-out notice when the event is over. Follow up with traditional communications.

Conclusion

Transparency early in the process and a commitment to assisting reporters, even amid controversy, goes a long way in establishing credibility. A commitment to transparency opens a window into your university culture. Reputation management begins with the start of a crisis and the organization's credibility will either bolster or undermine its reputation.

Every crisis event has its own life and characteristics. Campuses have different cultures and expectations. Technical capabilities differ. However, a major event will draw reporters, either electronically or in person, to your campus in a flash (as well as gawkers, sightseers, crackpots, and do-gooders). Prior planning of some sort is essential. Be on a first-name basis with key emergency response players inside and outside the institution. Ensure the communications staff is trained. Understand your campus's needs and its leadership's skills and desires. Have the technical capabilities to quickly respond.

Sadly, emergency planning is seldom near the top of a communicator's priority list and is hard work, too. Few in the profession gravitate to emergency planning. Little of what you do in this regard promotes the university or builds your brand . . . until you need it. But if you do need it, the world is watching. Through the power of modern communications and media megaphones, your brand is transparently on display.

Notes

1. There were no implementing regulations defining *timely*. Rather, the *Department of Education Handbook for Campus Crime Reporting*, the guidance document for Clery compliance, published in 2005, states, "The issuing of a timely warning must be decided on a case-by-case basis in light of all the facts surrounding a crime, including factors such as the nature of the crime, the continuing danger to the campus community and the possible risk of compromising law enforcement efforts" (see chapter 5, page 62). In fact, one timely warning example in the handbook is of a warning given 48 hours after the incident.

2. See the Higher Education Opportunity Act of 2008 (Pub. L. No. 110-315, 122 Stat. 3078 [August 14, 2008]). This specific amendment is codified at 20 U.S.C. § 1092(f)(1)(J). The amendment requires schools to "immediately notify the campus community upon the confirmation of a significant emergency or dangerous situation involving an immediate threat to the health or safety of students or staff occurring on the campus."

14

WORKING EFFECTIVELY WITH THE MEDIA

Advice From the Front Line

Teresa Valerio Parrot

Pick up any local newspaper or log on to any higher education trade publication, and higher education crises are likely to be included among the top headlines. Based on the successes and failures of academe's previous responses, campus leaders are being held to higher and higher standards for their communications with the audiences they need to reach. In addition, they are judged on their level of participation in the media and the successes of these efforts. The days of presidents receiving a pass from the media and general public for their response to a crisis are over.

When asked, presidents most often raise grand-scale tragedies such as active shooters and acts of terrorism as the situations they most fear. Although those types of situations should be planned for in advance, they are statistically less likely to occur than the more mundane but just as impactful scenarios—all of which necessitate the development of proactive communications strategies.

Frequently occurring scenarios less often mentioned include misappropriation of funds; data breaches; violations of National Collegiate Athletic Association (NCAA) guidelines; natural disasters; campus deaths; lapses in professional judgment by presidents and boards, their administration, or any member of the campus community; high-profile personnel actions; and sexual misconduct by those in positions of trust.

How then should a president respond to the media, and how can an administrator's participation help to shape the resultant media coverage?

First, any communication or action must be made with the institution's best short- and long-term interests in mind. Any other priorities must be reviewed by the president and cabinet for their rationale and underlying intentions. This perspective should be the foundation for the institution's crisis communications plan.

Second, you can never go wrong by telling the truth. That's not to suggest there won't be some pain when addressing a crisis and its nuances, but leaders who have confessed their mistakes or those by members of their campus community have a better chance of lessening the impact of the situation and are more likely to retain their jobs or land a leadership position on another campus.

Few see or write on the topic of collegiate crises more than Doug Lederman, coeditor of *Inside Higher Ed*. He stated, "I can say that in a crisis, one should be honest and forthright. Don't ever try to hide the truth because if the media believe you are covering up the truth, or if it is found that there were truths being covered up, there is a good chance that will be worse than the actual crisis itself" (Doug Lederman, personal communication, April 15, 2013).

Similarly, there was a time when institutional leaders could use plausible deniability as a defense publicly and with the media. But the days of saying, "I didn't know" or "nobody told me" are over if you are in a position to know what questions a leader should ask and where your institution's vulnerabilities lie. Saying you were in the dark doesn't affirm presidential behavior and suggests you haven't been doing your job.

Finally, ensure that your crisis communications talking points include language that summarizes the current state of events and provides direction for the future. Your faculty, staff, students, and community will want to see leadership in action, and you can provide assurance that the institution is stronger than any one event, circumstance, or moment in time.

How Can You Differentiate Between a Crisis and a Problem?

Before initiating any response, differentiate between a problem and a crisis in advance of diagnosing your situation. The unit of measure I apply is a very basic definition of a *crisis*: any event that can jeopardize your institution's short- or long-term image, reputation, or financial stability. Any situation that does not meet that threshold should be viewed as a problem. A problem can escalate into a crisis if not addressed head-on, handled well, or communicated clearly and carefully.

With this definition in mind, truthfully sharing an institution's story is the only way its leadership can hope to shape coverage and build support for their response. Telling the truth is a proactive response—it means your media relations staff have been brought into the situation early so they can make the most of their relationships with the media to communicate the institution's position. Those responsible for representing the institution in the media must be available and prepared to respond to the most obvious and dreaded questions a reporter might ask.

Your media relations staff and cabinet should be well versed in what Family Educational Rights and Privacy Act (FERPA) does and doesn't cover so that they can give you sound advice on its applicability to the situation at hand. Often, institutions hide behind federal guidelines or campus policies to avoid answering tough questions. Hiding isn't presidential, and it never serves an institution well. Expect more from yourself, your leadership team, and the institution's communications professionals.

"There's a big difference between a crisis of their own making [a scandal], or one externally imposed, like a natural disaster or the equivalent," stated Lederman. "Places get a lot of latitude in the latter, much less so in the former. But in all cases, transparency is key—reporters generally understand that there is going to be information that can't be shared at certain times (because of privacy concerns, legal issues, etc.), but will sniff out when they're being BS'd, and will come back with increased intensity when that happens" (Doug Lederman, personal communication, April 15, 2013).

There are times, however, when FERPA and personnel policies do prevent institutions from responding to media requests. That's understandable. But, rather than giving an emotionless or legal-sounding response, consider explaining to the reporter why you can't respond, when you might be able to respond, and the context for your silence. Then, point the reporter in the direction of the policy you are citing and let him or her know related topics that you can address.

"I know there are times when institutional leaders feel that they can't respond to something—because they will seem to be bullying (or violating the privacy of) employees or students, or dropping to the level of critics," stated Lederman. "But I tend to think that university leaders are more often too timid than too aggressive" (Doug Lederman, personal communication, April 15, 2013).

What Is the Leadership Role for a President With the Media?

The president of an institution is responsible for setting the stage for a leadership response and ensuring communications flow to the audiences that want or need an update. The appropriate role for a president includes leading change, providing future direction, beginning the healing process, or discussing what must be done differently. Every crisis can make the industry and its leaders stronger—take advantage of those opportunities and learn from others' effective and ineffective actions.

Crisis responses provide opportunities for presidents to step up and be presidential, earn their pay, and personify the title they hold. Initial messaging must lead with the truth and share next steps. In effective media relations, the direction is established by the president and reaffirmed by the board. The specific words that will be used, however, should be carefully drafted by media relations and approved by the president.

"I think presidents (or other top officials) set the tone," stated Lederman. "You can certainly have individuals within an institution who have their own way of doing things—positively or negatively—but my sense is that the leader sets the tone, and that those who want their institutions to be transparent, forthcoming, etc., tend to set that tone for their workers" (Doug Lederman, personal communication, April 15, 2013).

Conversations between the president and cabinet should focus on how the media can be used to reach the audiences most interested in the story, and all messaging should be rooted in truth. Any member of the cabinet or board who suggests "spin" as an option should be redirected toward transparency and reminded of the expectations to uphold the best interests of the institution.

Telling the truth can be scary because every crisis unearths vulnerabilities for an institution and its leaders. The key is to rise to the challenge, tell the truth, and use even the darkest of moments to build support for your institution. Difficult moments are often communicated best to the media through one-on-one interactions, allowing compassion and leadership to be conveyed, misinformation to be addressed, and specific questions to be answered.

This level of personalization isn't always possible. Press conferences and written statements can be used to broadcast messages to large groups of people and are especially effective if there is a threat to campus safety, the situation is moving so fast that immediate updates are necessary, or the media interest is so strong that there is no time to personalize the message. Having said that, return to one-on-one communication as soon as possible so that the institution's leadership can personalize and humanize its media approach. This means making the president available for interviews with local television, radio, and newspaper outlets and picking up the phone and proactively reaching out to national trade media, such as the *Chronicle of Higher Education* or *Inside Higher Ed*.

Remember to use members of the president's cabinet and content experts from across campus to provide specific context for situations and affirm campus expertise. Their perspectives can be used to share details on campus processes or policies; explain audit, review, and adjudication procedures; or share examples of excellence or parallel successes. Allowing them to represent their professions shows the campus has management depth and authorities who, at the direction of the board and president, can participate in the leadership necessary to rebuild an institution.

What Should an Institution Do When Working With the Media?

Make sure that your responses to reporters' questions are paired with offers for access to resources and provide them with the information and sources they need. Not only do you have high-definition photographs and videos, data sets, policies, and campus experts to share, you can provide an introduction to association leadership and national thought leaders who can provide a landscape viewpoint for higher education issues. Their perspective can help to provide context for situations you face or examples of how you aren't alone in facing controversial issues. You pay association dues for many reasons—one of them is for the support association leadership can provide during times of crisis.

"In crisis situations the American Council on Education (ACE) can help by providing the media with much-needed context on both the crisis at hand and the long-term resilience of institutions," stated Timothy McDonough, vice president for communications and marketing for the American Council on Education. "Whatever the incident and its perceived uniqueness, the chances are something similar has happened before at another institution that was able to overcome it and, in time, emerge in a much stronger position. Faculty no-confidence votes, executive or staff malfeasance—even major accidents with multiple deaths or injuries—have all occurred at one time or another and institutions have responded and survived. Providing that long-term view in a 24-hour news cycle is extremely important—it's the one thing campuses really seem to appreciate most" (Timothy McDonough, personal communication, April 24, 2013).

Write in words that the "average person" will understand and avoid industry jargon. We work in a complex industry, and most people outside of academia don't understand how we govern and operate our institutions. Avoid the use of industry acronyms in your statements, quotes, and media responses at all costs. Explain concepts like tenure, shared governance, and academic freedom by providing analogies to everyday concepts. Even if you are talking to reporters who cover higher education exclusively, remember that their audiences may or may not work within our industry and the online availability of their pieces is global.

Share information that tells your story and then stop talking. There is a fine line between telling your institution's story and oversharing so that weaknesses are exposed. As an example, share your thoughts as a leader, not your opinions as an individual. Not keeping your emotions under control or opinions at bay are weaknesses for your institution.

When a student's murder brought media critique and community attention to the increased diversity of the Frostburg State University student body, President Jonathan Gibralter quickly found himself on the wrong side of that line. Dr. Gibralter stated, "My natural reaction was to defend the campus and our actions and, in several instances I found myself being defensive and communicating too much, sometimes not at a presidential level. In other words, I didn't let my media people handle the details, while I managed the university-wide public statements" (Jonathan Gibralter, personal communication, February 27, 2013).

Remember that your job is to be presidential. The easiest way to do so is to allow your staff to do their jobs—including reminding you of your own professional and personal vulnerabilities.

Ensure statements that bear your name sound like words you would say. Media statements should reflect the situation as well as the personality and role of campus leadership. Written quotes for the board, president, or cabinet should be done by the staff who know and can reflect the individual voice of each. Test the personalization of statements by removing the name associated and then read the quote to trusted advisors. If they can match the words with the speaker, then the personality is reflected. If not, start over. Statements written by consensus or committee rarely say anything of substance—which doesn't help the institution—or sound academic rather than empathetic.

Similarly, media and public statements written by legal counsel usually sound like legal counsel wrote them. Have those responsible for representing the institution in the court of public opinion draft public statements, and have those responsible for the institution in the court of law review them. Respect the expertise all bring to the table and allow them to do their respective jobs.

Texas Christian University received positive feedback for its strong response to drug-related arrests of students, including student athletes, because they addressed the situation directly and allowed the chancellor, athletic director, and football coach to share their thoughts in their own words. Each was able to share their emotions, including disappointment, and then pivot to strong leadership positions that left no questions about enforcement of the university's zero-tolerance policy or how seriously they took their respective campus responsibilities. Those with media responsibilities recorded statements in each leader's own words, legal counsel reviewed them, and then they were distributed in a timely manner. That approach resonated with their internal and external audiences, in part because individual leadership and communications styles were reflected in the responses.

Watch and learn from others as they navigate through crises. It is rare that a response to a higher education crisis could not have been informed and messaging improved by reviewing the experiences of our peers. Have staff perform relevant key word searches on sites such as *Inside Higher Ed* and the *Chronicle of Higher Education* and blogs similar to those on the *New York Times*, *Washington Post*, and *Huffington Post* to provide insights on how well messages and actions have been received by internal and external audiences. Learn which crises benefited from aggressive approaches and which situations were best treated like problems and did not escalate to full-blown crises.

What Should an Institution Not Do When Working With the Media?

Don't "spin." Remember the initial advice in this section: All communications and actions must be made with the institution's best short- and long-term interests in mind. Not telling the truth, or the whole truth, should never be viewed as a possible response to media inquiry. Reporters and the public can forgive mistakes, but they rarely forgive lying or selective truth telling. Often, the final nail in the coffin for an institution's leadership is hammered home when the truth surfaces and it doesn't match the institution's telling of the story. And the truth always surfaces.

"The [institutions] that fare least well are generally those that are eventually proven not to have been forthright originally," stated Lederman. "I'm a big believer in the view that the cover-up is worse than the crime, and while I think we have a very forgiving public, in general, we are far less forgiving when there's evidence that information was withheld, obfuscated, or otherwise misrepresented" (Doug Lederman, personal communication, April 15, 2013).

And those reporters who have trusted an institution's leadership and feel as if they've been led astray will focus their efforts on exposing the lying or mistruths they've been told. Lies mask vulnerabilities for your institution and/or your leadership. Once those lies are exposed you will have made an enemy of those who could have helped you to tell the truth and positively shape sentiment.

"I believe [presidents] get in the most trouble when they cross reporters," stated Lederman. "Reporters are human, rumors to the contrary, and when they believe they are wronged, stonewalled, lied to, etc. they can be ruthless" (Doug Lederman, personal communication, April 15, 2013).

Don't use "no comment" as a response. Even if you aren't able to address the situation head-on, you still should have your media relations staff get back to inquiring reporters in a timely manner and provide an alternative perspective. "No comment" often suggests that a reporter should dig deeper on the topic or that he or she may be on the right track for a story. "Too many stories get a 'no comment' when, at least on background, they could be getting their side of the story out there," suggests Lederman (Doug Lederman, personal communication, April 15, 2013).

Don't go off the record. Ever. You get paid to be a leader, so make sure your leadership occurs on the record. And, if you are worried about getting a specific question right, you can always have your staff provide background information or fact sheets.

Don't take too long to respond to the media's questions. There is a direct relationship between the speed with which you respond to a reporter's request and the resultant time spent responding to the thoughts of others and correcting misinformation. Get to them early and you can shape the direction of the story. Wait to return their calls, often so that a committee response to communications can occur, and you will find yourself answering more questions about other people's thoughts on the situation. Any time spent responding to the opinions of others is time you don't have to advance your story, expertise, or knowledge.

Don't make a reporter resort to Freedom of Information Act requests to obtain information. The only hope you have of influencing coverage is to tell the truth and be of assistance to the media. If a reporter asks for information, share it or explain why you legitimately can't. And don't be afraid to offer resources or information beyond their initial request. Talk to them about what they are covering and think through how you might be of assistance.

Don't respond when you are exhausted. You are human, and you will be asked to put in very long days when a crisis hits. That's understandable. What isn't understandable is granting an interview when you aren't at the top of your game.

Even if you miss one reporter's deadline, wait until you have a clear head and are able to craft messaging that benefits your institution and speaks directly to your key audiences. Weariness is an indicator that you may need additional assistance with the media, and fatigue leads to misinterpreting media requests or shaping language in ways that harm the institution.

"Looking back, the only thing I would have done differently [during crisis] would have been to bring in external media consultants to assist earlier," stated President Gibralter. "I found that our own people who were exhausted and working 24/7 to monitor communications were not always able to take a view as if they were an outsider. They were too close to the crises. Bringing in external consultants helped us tremendously in managing through these events" (Jonathan Gibralter, personal communication, February 27, 2013).

Don't take public responses personally, period. A crisis is not the time for board members, the president, or members of the institution to take media coverage or community backlash personally. Once a response is taken personally, then future communications are shifted to focus on protecting the emotions of the hurt party and positioning the best interests of the institution. These two goals are not always congruent, and when push comes to shove, the personal perspective usually overtakes the needs of the institution. In my mind, this is when a crisis begins to escalate even further and often results in a resignation or firing of a member of the core leadership team—even the president.

Allowing emotion to take hold and lead further communications often taints ensuing interactions with the media. For example, once a president or administrator believes the media is out to get him or her, responses become shorter or snippier, and shifting blame for the spiraling situation will often underpin all responses.

"What I learned was that you have to stop and listen to your people when you feel most emotional," stated President Gibralter. "You can write a response to something someone says that troubles you deeply and might even take personally, but do not hit 'send' on that e-mail until your emotions have subsided and you can reconsider the content" (Jonathan Gibralter, personal communication, February 27, 2013).

Don't "wing it." Allow yourself the time you need to be successful. You would never wing important milestones in your career, including your dissertation, research findings, or presentations to your board. And you should never make light of any media encounter. Treat the reporter, your institution, and your career with the respect each deserves.

Don't try to do the reporters' job for them. I work with a president who previously served as a provost and still teaches students. He reverts to his experience in the classroom when responding to questions from reporters—he answers the question asked and then answers what he thinks is the logical follow-up question. He usually guesses the next question correctly in a classroom setting, but in an interview, he often, unintentionally, steers the interview in directions that are less advantageous for the institution. I make a point of reminding him before each interview that his job in the interview is to communicate the institution's strength, and it is the reporter's job to ask the questions. Let reporters do their job.

Final Thoughts

Trepidation for working with the media is understandable, but fear should never delay the issuance of a response or participation in an interview. Presidents must model the highest levels of leadership possible by proactively sharing their institution's story—a story that must be rooted in truth and framed with engaging language—and providing a plan for future direction. Once incident and communications strategies have been developed, then their deployment must be swift. One indicator of success is engagement of the media to reach the institution's most important audiences. Institutions and their presidents can survive crises. The key is to have the courage to step up to the challenge and the microphone.

PART FIVE

REMEMBRANCE AND HEALING

On every campus, a considerable amount of time is spent putting out many fires, some larger than others. However, it is important not to assume that others have moved on from an issue, just because the leadership team has moved on. After a crisis, many presidents agree to interviews only if a particular issue is avoided (e.g., the recent crisis). However, taking the interview and highlighting several issues, including positive aspects of the recovery, may be a better approach because the issue may still be alive for many community members and ignoring it may do more harm than good. On campus, an assessment of new needs after the crisis is necessary. It may be necessary to hire more admissions counselors if enrollment will be affected in future years. Similarly, new protocols are sometimes warranted, such as instituting new policies to update contact information for students as well as their families. And once the crisis is past, the recovery period is a critical element in the chain of events. The repercussions likely will endure. Even when a large number of students, faculty, administrators, and staff seem to have weathered the crisis well, some may still be in pain or suffering emotionally. Recovery may take years. Some say Kent State University didn't recover from the death of their students during the Vietnam War protests until President Carol A. Cartwright decided to draw attention to the history with alternative programming.

In her chapter, Cartwright takes readers back to May 4, 1970, and the death of four students shot by National Guardsmen. The *Newsweek* cover is etched in the minds of those old enough to remember that time, and a large reproduction of the cover hangs in the Washington, DC, Newseum as a reminder of that fateful day. As Cartwright recounts, the healing process has taken several decades.

Harold Lee Martin Sr. had been chancellor at North Carolina A&T for barely a year when a young man died during an unofficial football tryout. Prompted by deaths of athletes at Rice University and Western Carolina

University, the National Collegiate Athletic Association (NCAA) had mandated the sickle cell solubility test for all athletes in Division I and II sports just a week before the death occurred. It wasn't until 2013 that the NCAA voted to mandate the Sickle Cell Solubility test for all athletes. Because North Carolina A&T was an HBCU (historically Black college or university), the campus athletic staff should have been aware of this new requirement, but the test had not been given to the incoming athletes. The student death from complications of the sickle cell trait was a tragedy for the family and the campus, but Martin and his colleagues recognized that the lack of campus preparation for the media attention was a crisis in the making. Fortunately, the campus came together to address the human loss, and in an honest appraisal of what the campus did in the middle of a crisis, in chapter 16, Martin and his colleagues demonstrate to readers the importance of campus preparedness.

Kevin M. Ross's chapter is both sad and hopeful, as the title ironically suggests. It is sad for a campus to lose two faculty members and four students, all of whom were participating in humanitarian support for a country in need, in a single incident. They all perished in the Haiti earthquake, one of the world's worst natural disasters. But what Lynn University did to celebrate the lives of these six gives hope that the university and particularly future students can learn from these deaths. The recognition of this event year after year has changed the lives of students who continue to come to the campus and participate in commemorative events.

The thoughtfully designed memorial at Lynn University remains a tribute to those who perished and a beacon for those who come later. The song "Lean on Me" that was sung at the candlelight vigil is a reminder to all who live and work at colleges and universities that it is through mutual support that crises can be survived; it is our commitment to one another that makes a difference in the end.

Student deaths are crises no president wants, and the responses must honor the memories of those who are gone while respecting the wishes of the families. Whether that response includes memorials or revised policies, closure will only come with honest assessment of how the events have affected the campus. These three chapters focus on the worst nightmares that a president imagines and give hope that in remembering comes healing.

15

THE DUTY TO REMEMBER

The Privilege to Inspire Change

Carol A. Cartwright

On January 17, 1991, the conflict known as Operation Desert Storm began with air strikes to expel Iraqi troops from Kuwait. Within days, reporters descended on Kent State University, expecting to find students protesting the war as some were in 1970, when the campus was catapulted into the international spotlight after four students lost their lives. I had been appointed as Kent State's president in December 1990 and was at the University of California, Davis, preparing for the transition to Ohio when the calls came from Kent State about students' reactions to the war and the crush of media attention. The student newspaper, the *Daily Kent Stater*, published an editorial on January 24, 1991, describing the mood on campus: "Becoming annoyed at this latest barrage of media attention is easy. No, this isn't Vietnam. No, this isn't the 1960's. No, Kent State University isn't a hotbed of radicalism and it never has been" (p. 2). The editorial also pointed out that intense coverage is an opportunity: "We can show the nation and the world that at Kent State, we now know that honest communication must take place between all sides in an emotional debate. . . . We can show we have learned a positive lesson from May 4" (p. 2). I was interested in these

This chapter is based on personal reflections and experiences, but others provided important assistance. I wish to acknowledge the wise counsel of Professors Jerry M. Lewis and Laura Davis, eyewitnesses in 1970 and May 4 scholars, who commented on drafts and provided many valuable perspectives. Dr. Sally Kandel directed the cultural self-study and was most helpful in commenting on drafts and locating documents from the culture project.

views and wondered how widely they were shared. I would soon learn much more about the mixed emotions regarding the events and the aftermath of May 4, 1970 (known throughout the university as "May 4"). I would come to understand at a much deeper level the lasting impact of that date on the entire university, and about my leadership role in helping the community gain perspective, achieve closure, and move forward. As important as it is to listen and learn about defining moments in institutional history, there is no substitute for personal experience. An understanding of institutional culture and how it affects decision making is also essential.

Kent State University in 1970

On May 4, 1970, at Kent State University, Ohio National Guardsmen fired shots at unarmed students. After 13 seconds of gunfire, 4 students lay dead and 9 were wounded, 1 permanently paralyzed. The world looked on in horror. The university was closed, and in the immediate aftermath, there were no opportunities for the community to come together and grieve. Initial reports were that students had killed Guardsmen, which served to escalate tensions and add to the turmoil. This context is essential to understanding the deep feelings about May 4 that are still palpable today. "In an emotional sense, the facts never did catch up with the falsity of those first reports" (Hildebrand, Keller, & Herington, 1993, p. 183).

Many misunderstandings and incorrect perceptions surround the events leading up to May 4, 1970, and the tragic events of that day itself. In *This We Know* (2012), Kent State faculty members Carole Barbato, Laura Davis, and Mark Seeman provide a chronology of the shootings as well as a caution: "While many know generally what happened, they are often surprised by the details. It is not a story in which what you think happened necessarily is what did happen. Common sense and logic do not fully explain the sequence" (p. ix). There were protests at Kent State, like there were on hundreds of other campuses, over the invasion of Cambodia and the escalation of the war in Vietnam, but no one would have guessed that Kent State would be the place for a violent ending.

A common misunderstanding is that the Ohio National Guard was specifically mobilized to deal with protests at Kent State. That was not the case. The Guard was already in the area because of a wildcat strike by the Teamsters in nearby Akron. The Guard's presence because of labor strife, not student protests, reminds us of the turbulence of the 1960s in many areas: labor relations, civil rights, student activism, sexual liberation, the draft and its role in the Vietnam War, to name several. These issues of social justice, and the chasms between the generations about them, are an essential part of the story of May 4, 1970.

Kent State faculty members Jerry M. Lewis and Thomas Hensley provided a comprehensive summary about the events in a search for historical accuracy. They argued that the May 4 shootings need to be remembered: "[T]he shootings have come to symbolize a great American tragedy which occurred at the height of the Vietnam War era, a period in which the nation found itself deeply divided both politically and culturally." They also pointed out that the need for healing continues: "Healing will not occur if events are either forgotten or distorted, and hence it is important to continue to search for the truth" (Lewis & Hensley, 1998, p. 18). Twenty years of attempts at healing occurred before I arrived in early 1991, but I soon discovered there was still much work to be done.

Dedication of the May 4 Memorial in 1990

During Kent State's presidential search, I learned about the dedication of a May 4 memorial on the 20th anniversary of the shootings. The tone of the conversations was about the healing power of creating the memorial. Governor Richard Celeste participated in the dedication ceremonies and shocked those gathered when he offered a formal apology to the slain students and their families and friends. Many believed that this provided a sense of closure and a platform for moving beyond the emotions surrounding May 4.

My predecessor, Michael Schwartz, led the process of building the memorial—a process filled with false starts and controversy. He saw it as a way for the university to signal that it was not trying to hide from May 4 and that it was acknowledging the historical events of 1970. He notes in his contribution to the May 4 Oral History Project (www.library.kent.edu/page/11247) that through the creation of the memorial, "we can get at least the beginning of an ending. An ending in the sense of the anger and bitterness." Dr. Schwartz arrived at Kent State in 1976 and became president in 1982. He personally experienced the deep emotions and the controversies associated with how—or even whether—to remember May 4. He would agree that not only do we need to remember, we have a responsibility to share what we have learned. The theme of the memorial is "Inquire, Learn, Reflect"—the words engraved on the stone threshold at the site of the memorial. The physical space, with abstract components symbolizing the four who died, invites contemplation and personal reflection. A nearby hillside is planted with 58,175 daffodils in honor of those who died in service to their country in Vietnam.

The theme of "Inquire, Learn, Reflect" builds on prior initiatives to remember and memorialize the four dead students, the nine who were wounded, and the two students killed at Jackson State on May 14, 1970. In the years immediately following the shootings, the university sponsored a candlelight march and vigil organized by faculty and students who recognized the need for coming together to grieve and remember. In 1976, the university discontinued its sponsorship of these events. They were subsequently led by the May 4 Task Force, a registered student organization, which continues to organize the march and vigil. The Center for Peaceful Change (now the Center for Applied Conflict Management) was established in 1971 as a living memorial. Scholarships were established in honor of the four dead students, and other forms of remembrance have been developed over the years (Hildebrand, 2009).

Professor Jerry M. Lewis, an eyewitness to the shootings, describes the years after May 4, 1970, as generally dysfunctional. He stated, "It is generally assumed that the social remembering of an important cultural event is a good thing. This is particularly true when the remembering concerns events that have caused serious personal and public trauma. Social remembering is considered a positive way to honor the people and institutions associated with tragic events." However, he noted, "almost every major step in the social remembering process associated with the May 4, 1970, shootings has been characterized by controversy and debate" (Lewis, 2012, p. 176). May 4 continued to elicit strong positions and reactions decades later. I came to understand that cultural forces put in motion by May 4 remained relevant when I joined Kent State, and still echo today.

A Research Study of Organizational Culture

The decade of the 1990s was one of tumultuous change in higher education. Kent State and other Ohio universities were deeply engaged in confronting changes on many fronts—some imposed by the Ohio Board of Regents and the legislature and others that each university identified as essential for its future. At Kent State, we understood the human tendency to resist change as well as the complexity of the change agenda. With these considerations in mind, I engaged the senior leadership team, and we decided to learn more about our organizational culture. Our goals had nothing to do with May 4, 1970, and everything to do with improving our understanding about the barriers to change that might exist in our institutional culture. We wanted to know what levers for change we might discover beneath the surface of everyday life at Kent State.

We contracted with Cultural Research, Inc. (www.culturalresearch.com), to advise us about a research project to accomplish our goals. For nearly 30 years, Cultural Research, Inc., had developed and tested a comprehensive approach to assessing the culture and subcultures of organizations, and the impact of culture on organizational outcomes. They designed unique software to analyze large sets of quantitative and qualitative information and built a massive database that provides a way to map open-ended comments onto validated beliefs that exist in organizational cultures. The iterative research process begins with interviews to identify key issues, followed by the development of questionnaires designed to reveal belief systems.

In the fall of 1997, questionnaires were mailed to all employees to gain perspectives about institutional culture and uncover beliefs of faculty, staff, and administrators about various change issues at Kent State and in the broader domain of higher education. The university received quantitative and qualitative results organized by issues and across the three groups, but nothing that would reveal anyone's identity. The report included analysis and recommendations to support effective culture-based decisions and the success of organizational initiatives. We received the final results in the summer of 1998 and asked a broad-based university advisory committee to review them and make recommendations for action.

The impact on Kent State of May 4, 1970, was revealed through the process and incorporated into the final stages of the research. The results were extremely informative. They led directly to actions that proved to extend healing and place Kent State in a more positive position regarding the legacy of May 4. Once we knew we needed to delve deeper into the shootings, questions were developed to probe the extent of the impact and explore possible solutions. Asked if there was still an impact from May 4, 56 percent replied that there was and 29 percent said there was no current impact. When asked about the type of impact, most responses were highly negative and focused on areas such as enrollment, community relations, fund-raising, and state support. This statement is representative of the negative comments: "There is an intangible, almost indefinable 'gray cloud' hanging over many departments. . . . I believe this stems directly from May 4, 1970" (Carol Cartwright, personal files, 1998). Another said, "Negative aspects of the event will haunt us forever" (Carol Cartwright, personal files, 1998). Others urged us to leave May 4 behind, noting that we were spending too much time on it.

Another group of responses was that May 4 is "what we are known for" and provides "instant name recognition"—often accompanied by statements that these were positive attributes. Some respondents focused on May 4 as an important part of history. An example of this view is the following response: "May 4, 1970, was a historic moment for the entire country. The University should embrace this history—not deny it or hide from it" (Carol Cartwright, personal files, 1998). A significant minority saw the lessons learned from May 4 as a positive force, serving to make Kent State a better institution. Another group of respondents argued for the powerful role of lessons learned and reflections on the past to inform the future. Overall, the results revealed divergent beliefs, but the majority were negative.

We asked if further action should be taken. The result was "no" from 58 percent and "yes" from 20 percent, which created a serious dilemma about next steps. The beliefs about May 4 were not only mixed, they were very emotional. The researchers remarked that they had not seen such an outpouring of feelings in previous research. People wrote in the margins and on the back of survey forms—they shared their deeply felt thoughts in great detail.

If we had taken the easy route and followed the majority, we would have missed a major opportunity for further healing. Cultural Research, Inc., advised that as much as we were being urged to let go of May 4, as an organization, we did not have that option because "it is virtually impossible for an organization to simply let go of events as significant as those of May 4, 1970, no matter how much people may wish to do so. Instead, a symbol of this power can usually be let go of by creating an equally powerful new symbol" (Carol Cartwright, personal files, 1998).

The 30th Commemoration and the Democracy Symposium

Reflecting on the findings of the culture research project, several opportunities and ideas began to converge. Foremost in my mind was the need to follow the advice about developing a powerful "symbol project" to counter the angst and ambivalence about May 4. We were also aware of another finding from the research that documented the very positive attitudes of faculty, staff, and administrators toward the office of the president. In their interpretation of the findings, the advisory group stated, "The President is seen as a powerful source for change" (Carol Cartwright, personal files, 1998). Clearly, whatever we did would need to be seen as a very high priority coming from the office of the president. Making this personal, I knew that I would need to be the champion of the ideas and activities to develop our symbol project and that I would need to be directly involved at all stages.

Fortunately, we had an experience in 1995 that modeled the type of project we were seeking. During the milestone 25th commemoration, the university sponsored a two-day academic symposium on "Legacies of Protest" to examine the many forms that protest had taken over that time period. In the opening remarks for the symposium, I recalled, "May 4 has been called the 'watershed' event of a generation. It was a time that defined and clarified the thoughts of our country" (Carol Cartwright, personal files, 1998). I acknowledged that our identity was linked forever to the events of May 4, 1970, and that we had become a university with "a heightened awareness of the rights and responsibilities of free speech and of the need to resolve conflicts peacefully" (Carol Cartwright, personal files, 1998). We also included special events to honor Vietnam veterans during the 25th commemoration.

During the same time as the culture study, we embarked on an ambitious project of envisioning the long-term future of the university. We needed to build stronger external relationships and begin the important work of fund-raising after years of being more internally focused. Never before had Kent State convened such a large-scale volunteer initiative to seek constructive criticism and to review our strengths and opportunities for the future. We formed the Centennial Commission comprising 160 members (88 were alumni). There was considerable risk in asking such a diverse group to advise us about issues that were so far into the future. I was convinced that the volunteers would be captivated by the idea that children going to kindergarten during the year they were engaged on the commission would be in their first year of college as Kent State celebrated its centennial in 2010. That was an intriguing idea that took hold and invigorated the deliberations.

Business and community leaders joined representatives of our faculty, staff, and students to examine the university through the eyes of an external audience. They identified broad issues that would need attention in the decades to come and made recommendations about priorities for the future. One of the five task groups focused on "Values, Identity, and Communications" and concluded that we should recognize and promote the unique history of May 4: "[I]t is time to move forward from this tragic moment in the University's history—not to forget the lessons of May 4, but to embrace the opportunities they provide to inquire, to learn, and to reflect, and for serious study of democratic values" (Carol Cartwright, personal files, 1998). With this validation, we were at the threshold of a new approach.

A long-standing issue was resolved in 1999, with the dedication of markers in the parking lot where the students had died. As I understand the history, the parents of the slain students initially rejected the idea of permanent markers because they did not want the site altered. Over time, concerns were expressed about preserving the historical integrity of the site, and there was an ongoing interest in marking the spaces. A group from the May 4 Task Force approached me at the vigil in 1999 and told me that permanent markers were now desired. With a deep sense of respect for their loss, I took time to gain assurance that the families were ready. They were, and we moved forward. We chose to dedicate the parking lot markers at a time other than May 4 because we wanted to keep the events family oriented and more personal, which the families appreciated.

Finally, we understood the significance of the turn of the century as a pivot point for new beginnings, and the signal of the passage of 30 years as a changing of generations. All these components convinced me that Kent State was ready to be bold about its ownership of the events of May 4, 1970. We resolved to use the 30th commemoration to present ourselves differently—confident about our role in history and forward looking in our mission and role as a learning organization. I decided that the entire spring semester of 2000 would be devoted to commemoration and established a large committee of faculty, staff, students, alumni, and community representatives to plan events around the theme "Experiencing Democracy: Inquire, Learn, Reflect." Everyone was invited to participate, and funds were provided to support a variety of events—poetry, lectures, musical performances, student service projects, and more—all designed to broaden the commemoration to include the study of democratic values. The events concluded in July 2000 with the premiere of "Song in Sorrow" by Augusta Read Thomas, commissioned by the university and the Cleveland Orchestra. Ms. Thomas took the theme of the memorial—"Inquire, Learn, Reflect"—for the three movements in her music, which was a fitting conclusion to six months of activities addressing democratic values, while also honoring the memories of Allison Krause, Jeffrey Miller, Sandra Scheuer, and William Schroeder, who died on May 4, 1970.

The scholarly centerpiece of the 30th commemoration was the inauguration of a new annual academic symposium to explore the issue of rights, responsibilities, and challenges of living in a democracy. I believed we had a duty to share our experiences, especially within the context of our academic mission. In response to a question—"Enough of May 4"—posed by the *Akron Beacon Journal*, I wrote in an op-ed that the real question was not whether to commemorate, but how to make what we did meaningful. My view was that we could not just remember the dead, but that we had to celebrate their lives by teaching about civility and tolerance: "At Kent State, we realize that, amid the tragedy, something historic happened here almost 30 years ago—an event that changed the way America looks at its own rights and values. Because of Kent State's unique past, we can look ahead with a special perspective on some of the nation's most troubling current issues: violence in society, the boundaries of free expression or simply how best to live and work in an increasingly diverse society" (Cartwright, 1999, p. A9). I was determined that we must not miss the opportunity to turn from looking back on bloodshed and violence toward a more inclusive view of our academic responsibilities to teach about the democratic values that are the foundation of American society.

The idea of an academic symposium on democracy was suggested, and it gained support quickly, especially from faculty who told me they were motivated by my personal support as well the provision of financial resources, which made it clear that I wanted them to produce a first-rate symposium. We had found the symbol project recommended by the culture study, and it was firmly based in decades of research, reflection, and learning. The first symposium, "The Boundaries of Freedom of Expression and Order in American Democracy," focused attention on this delicate and difficult balance. Professor Thomas Hensley, chair of the Symposium Subcommittee, described the importance of the topic: "Freedom of expression and order are both important values that are deeply cherished in the United States. They are values embedded in our constitutional structure, and they are absolutely essential to a stable and free society" (Hensley, 2001, p. xi). He also pointed to the problems when these values are in conflict, as they were on May 4, 1970. The students who gathered to protest the war and the presence of the National Guard on campus believed they were expressing their rights to free speech, and the National Guard, believing that assemblies had been banned, viewed their role as keeping order. "The confrontation between two groups supporting two fundamental but clashing societal values ended tragically" (Hensley, 2001, p. xi).

The symposium was an unqualified success. Three truly distinguished First Amendment experts and authors participated as keynote speakers: Kathleen Sullivan, dean of Stanford University Law School; Anthony Lewis, Pulitzer Prize–winning columnist of the *New York Times*; and Cass Sunstein, professor at the University of Chicago Law School. Nine other speakers were selected from 110 submissions, resulting from a national call for papers. The depth and breadth of the scholarly presentations during the symposium were very impressive and were preserved for further study in an edited book (Hensley, 2001).

The inaugural symposium provided a template for future symposia and established a new tradition—an academically oriented, future-focused way of commemorating May 4. Each year since 2000, the university has sponsored a democracy symposium with diverse themes, such as the media, religion, globalization, homeland security, and the arts, but always with the fundamental core principle of exploring democratic values in civil society (www.kent.edu/democracy/symposium_archive.cfm).

The 40th Commemoration of May 4

The 40th commemoration, four years after my retirement, included several milestone events that are clear indications that Kent State University is not just acknowledging, but is fully embracing, its role in history (www.kent.edu/about/history/may4/newsroom). The continued momentum is important because healing is an ongoing process. The passage of time is helpful because it allows for the development of more perspective about the meaningfulness of the events. The simple passing of the years is not adequate, however, and university leaders must be intentional and ensure that events and activities over time are used wisely. A good example is the tenth Democracy Symposium, "Re-Membering: Framing, Embracing, Revising History." The symposium was used as part of the process of creating a May 4 Visitors Center through a discussion of how societies remember and document their history. The new center opened in October 2012 and provides a superb museum-style experience for visitors as they are reminded of the context of the 1960s and the legal, political, and social struggles that followed the shootings. Also during the 40th commemoration, the university dedicated a plaque documenting that the site of the shootings is now on the National Register of Historic Places. A May 4 Walking Tour, which features a marked trail and a documentary narrated by civil rights activist Julian Bond, was also formally dedicated on May 4, 2010.

Inquire, Learn, Reflect

Over more than 40 years, many have stepped forward to become part of a long-term process to gain historical perspective and contribute to healing. They have done so in the spirit of the words on the May 4 Memorial and the concepts embedded in the annual commemorations. As a learning community, we have become informed—we have inquired. We have placed significant focus on the academic mission of Kent State and found that learning can come from crisis and tragedy. Finally, we have provided ways to reflect on past events and future opportunities through physical spaces and places as well as intellectual pursuits, creative works, and service projects. Through it all, we have remembered, and over time, we have come to an understanding that we must embrace our role in history.

References

Barbato, C. A., Davis, L. L., & Seeman, M. E. (2012). *This we know*. Kent, OH: Kent State University Press.

Cartwright, C. A. (1999, September 18). KSU has a duty to share May 4 wisdom. *Akron Beacon Journal*, p. A9.

Editorial. (1991, January 24). *Daily Kent Stater.*

Hensley, T. R. (Ed.). (2001). *The boundaries of freedom of expression and order in American democracy*. Kent, OH: Kent State University Press.

Hildebrand, W. H. (2009). *A most noble enterprise: The story of Kent State University, 1910–2010.* Kent, OH: Kent State University Press.

Hildebrand, W. H., Keller, D. H., & Herington, A. D. (1993). *A book of memories: Kent State University 1901–1992.* Kent, OH: Kent State University Press.

Lewis, J. M. (2012). Social remembering and Kent State. In C. A. Barbato & L. L. Davis (Eds.), *Democratic narrative, history & memory* (pp. 176–193). Kent, OH: Kent State University Press.

Lewis, J. M., & Hensley, T. R. (1998). The May 4 shootings at Kent State University: The search for historical accuracy. *OCSS Review, 34*, 9–21.

16

THE BLAME GAME—IT'S A TEAM SPORT

Harold Lee Martin Sr., J. Charles Waldrup, and Nicole M. Pride

In today's society, higher education is faced with unprecedented challenges as organizations struggle to adapt to changing demands and expectations. In the business of higher education, these strategic challenges include a variety of issues and a complex group of constituents, including the student body. Despite the end of in loco parentis in regard to a university's former control over students, families continue to entrust their children's safety, education, and well-being to their respective universities, and it is the responsibility of the administration to uphold that trust. Faculty and staff demand more from the administration than in the past, as do state officials in regard to accountability by public institutions. To meet these changes in expectations, colleges and universities must steer their public image from that of the ivory tower to one of an engaged, transparent, safe, and accessible environment.

With tragedies striking college campuses throughout the United States, it is imperative that colleges and universities develop and maintain a strategic crisis management plan and a team that can execute it effectively when necessary. Without a doubt, this team must include a strong public relations office that has previously established solid partnerships with the media. Although all of these factors seem to be a practical imperative to the maintenance of a large business, North Carolina Agricultural and Technical (NCA&T) State University found itself lacking all of these things during the fall semester of 2010.

On August 19, 2010, NCA&T State University experienced the tragic loss of one of its students during an unauthorized, unofficial track and field tryout. Neither the student nor several other prospective student athletes participating in tryouts that day had a physical examination on file with the athletics department, nor had they undergone testing for sickle cell trait. Approximately one week prior to this death, National Collegiate Athletic Association (NCAA) rules requiring all students to have physical exams—complete with the sickle cell solubility test—before participating in sports, including tryouts, practices, and games, became effective. In addition, the tryout did not appear on the university's schedule of events, nor was a trainer present.

Immediately following the student's death, an investigative committee composed of members from the chancellor's cabinet and public relations team was assembled to look into the circumstances of the student's death. An autopsy later revealed that the student died from complications of sickle cell trait. This tragedy became more complex as the university and the athletics program fell under increased scrutiny because of the loss of another student-athlete just two years prior to this incident. In 2008, a football player had died on the practice field from complications of heat stroke.

Prior to these tragic events, NCA&T made the costly mistake of underestimating the need for a crisis plan and a team to execute it. There were also key staff members in the public relations office that had what could be characterized as an average and sometimes contentious relationship with the media. These factors worked in tandem to make a terrible situation worse. Not only was the A&T family mourning the loss of a student, but it also found itself in the midst of a media frenzy.

In hindsight, it is apparent that a group of university personnel from the chancellor's cabinet should be identified as the crisis team well before a tragedy strikes. The crisis team membership should be adjusted based on the area and type of crisis. This team should be composed of individuals with demonstrated leadership skills, regardless of position or title.

Two vital areas that should be included on all university crisis management teams are legal counsel and public relations representation. Both will offer advice that puts the best interests of the university at the forefront, but the president can expect to hear distinct differences in the advice from these areas. Public relations should focus on maintaining trust, credibility, integrity, and transparency with university constituents and the media. Legal counsel will look to limit the creation of documents during an investigation that could provide discoverable evidence in litigation and to avoid defamation claims attributable to the release of information about employee failures. The key is striking a delicate balance between the two areas. The president or chancellor must find the place that allows the institution to be as transparent as possible with all constituents without breaking the law or needlessly falling on the sword publicly. It is equally important to exclude from the crisis team the leadership of the area that is under investigation because it may taint the investigation. In-house legal counsel should seldom be the lead investigator because this can create a perception of a threatening environment that may hinder the discovery of facts. An external investigator may be worth the expense.

The lead investigator should be the least threatening representative of the crisis team or one who can build rapport, credibility, and ultimately, trust. Be wary of interviewing subordinates in the presence of their supervisors. We found that a lack of belief in the quality of the investigation led to ongoing internal leaks to the media that fed a frenzy of increased public records requests. It was frustrating that our own employees preferred to speak with a news reporter rather than with the internal investigators. We were so busy trying to respond to the media requests that it was a challenge to find time to investigate the underlying matter. The media's requests do not necessarily parallel the course an investigation should take.

The cliché "A chain is only as strong as its weakest link" can be applied to university crisis management as the crisis team is only as strong as its crisis management plan and each member of the team. An adequate plan identifies key players, their roles, and the resources needed to address the crisis in advance. The team's plan can be, and will need to be, altered to fit the specific crisis. Effective plans will also include a command base, effective and timely internal communication, a media staging area, a timeline of events, and a plan of action to release information to university constituents and the media. These elements are activated based on need.

Once the crisis team and plan are in place, effective public relations professionals who have strong relationships with the media are needed to effectively communicate to university constituents. This is a unique dilemma because university constituents span generations and geographic locations, including students, parents, alumni, faculty, and staff, as well as university friends, donors, and the local community. It is best for the public relations team to have its own crisis communications plan in place to ensure timely, accurate, and transparent information is being disseminated. That plan should make effective use of the university's own channels—website, social media, emergency alerts, if necessary—and local media.

The crisis communications plan works best when supported by solid relationships with the media. Those relationships should be in place and cultivated prior to an emergency. It is imperative that the public relations staff be responsive and open to telling the media all the information they can—what they know and what they don't know—before, during, and after the emergency. Don't let the crisis get ahead of you. Consistent follow-up with the media in times of emergency and nonemergency can buy time, and it can support the institution's credibility. It is necessary to get the media the most accurate information available at the time. The absence of follow-up and the withholding of information can make it appear as if the university has something to hide, which in turn can lead to being overwhelmed with public records requests, as we were. These requests may include everything from memorandums to employment contracts to e-mails. If the university is supported by taxpayer dollars, this information is considered to be public record and subject to open records laws. In addition, expectations must be set with the media as to what information may not be released under public records law. In-house legal counsel can advise accordingly and needs to be included throughout the process.

Colleges and universities are tasked with preparing tomorrow's leaders to adapt in times of crisis and instability. As effective and accountable leaders, university administrators have to be able to adapt to those very challenges. One of these challenges includes accepting responsibility for actions and inactions whenever appropriate. Although the university mourned and struggled to rebuild trust and credibility after a blow to its reputation, our deceased student's family, friends, and classmates were forced to cope with his death. It's been three years, and just as his family and friends have had to make adjustments, so has the university.

The university has been working diligently to restore trust and credibility in its athletics department and the university as a whole. New athletics policies have been implemented, and a new athletics director and a compliance officer have been hired. The university also has regular emergency exercises to train university personnel, including public relations staff, on proper protocol for handling a crisis.

Global competition for student scholars demands that higher education institutions adapt to new challenges and expectations in order to succeed. Bold and innovative leadership practices are necessary now more than ever to ensure organizational success. At its core, strong organizational leadership is a critical component to an organization's ability to successfully adapt to internal and external environments. Effective crisis management planning that revolves around an efficient crisis management team and sound, transparent crisis communication are paramount to obtaining the best possible outcomes.

Crises, major and minor, will always unfold on university campuses. The way a university's administration manages those crises will determine the legacy of leadership it leaves. Will our university's administration leave a legacy of ill preparation or of strong, effective leadership? Only time will tell, but at this time, NCA&T is doing all it can to maintain an effective crisis plan with a strong crisis team and stellar public relations professionals who are consistently building relationships with the media. This should be the expectation for every campus.

17

THE JOURNEY OF HOPE

Kevin M. Ross

When a great tragedy occurs, the struggle to understand an incomprehensible outcome is never ending. In the event of a natural disaster, the campus leaders do all that they can, but in the end, there are limitations. However, as those of us at Lynn University found out, how you deal with a crisis afterward is almost as important as how you deal with it at the time.

On January 12, 2010, two Lynn University faculty members and 12 students were in Haiti on a January term humanitarian and experiential learning trip for a course entitled Journey of Hope. The group had arrived at the island nation the day before and had time to visit a home for handicapped children and a school and orphanage for girls. Then the unimaginable occurred. After the group returned to their accommodations at the Hotel Montana, a 7.0-magnitude earthquake struck the area at 4:53 p.m.

At that moment, the world forever changed for people around the globe, including those on our campus in Boca Raton, Florida. Our campus community came together to pray and support one another, and we were blessed with the safe return of eight of our students, who were outside of the hotel writing in their journals at the time of the quake. A number of caring and extremely generous supporters stepped forward, and we were able to get those students back to the States with remarkable speed. Our university will forever be grateful to those individuals, and we took measures to personally thank each of them for their kindness, whether they donated transportation or just called to express their sympathy.

As we waited for news on the other four students and two faculty members, the campus came together each night for candlelight vigils, during which luminarias were lit and the sounds of "Lean on Me" carried throughout the evening. Press conferences were held in front of the university each day, and the spokespeople were charged with avoiding the spread of inaccurate information. The families of those still missing had arrived on our campus and were updated frequently as we received reports from our contracted search team and other sources on the ground in Haiti. However, there were times when information was very slow coming out of Haiti, so we did not always have updates for the families or the media.

The university continued to hold on to hope, but eventually the rescue operations switched over to recovery. At that time, the university's public message became one of support for not giving up operations until all of our students and faculty were recovered and returned home to their families. About a month after the earthquake, this request finally came to fruition, and the families were able to hold funerals for their daughters and fathers.

Although our campus could not take direct action against a natural disaster, we certainly could make sure the six lost members of our university were honored and remembered. Not only did these six leave behind their mothers, fathers, sisters, brothers, sons, and daughters, but they also left behind their close friends, roommates, classmates, professors, advisors, and colleagues. Although we know that we could never experience the level of pain and loss of their loved ones, there was still overwhelming sorrow and a void within our campus community.

After the six individual funerals, which were held in each person's hometown and attended by me or another university representative, it was time for our campus to have its own chance to say good-bye to the lost members of the Journey of Hope.

On March 12, 2010, exactly two months after the devastating event, our university family came together to celebrate the lives of Dr. Richard Bruno and Dr. Patrick Hartwick and students Stephanie Crispinelli, Britney Gengel, Courtney Hayes, and Christine Gianacaci. The families of the six, who our university will forever be bonded with over this tragedy, attended as our campus sought comfort in the wake of this unthinkable event.

However, at the time we knew it was impossible to condense the celebration of their lives into a single service. These six and this event, even though it was our darkest hour, would forever be a part of the university's history, and we knew that we needed to find a permanent place on our campus to remember and share the Journey of Hope story with future generations.

As our campus leaders began to think about how to memorialize the legacy of the six on our campus, we first met with their parents and families. They had only one request: that the story of their daughters and fathers—who they were and what they were doing—be told.

On January 12, 2011, the one-year anniversary of the Haiti earthquake, our university announced plans to construct Remembrance Plaza, a permanent memorial to Dr. Hartwick, Dr. Bruno, Stephanie, Britney, Courtney, and Christine, at the very heart of our campus.

This day was very special for another reason—it was the first annual Knights Unite Day of Caring. On this day, Lynn students, faculty, and staff all come together and go out into the community to make a difference in the world. Since our founding 50 years ago, Lynn University has had a long history of civic engagement, which was carried on by the Journey of Hope, and this day was created to continue the work the six had been doing when their lives ended much too early. We also end this day by remembering the Journey of Hope and those we lost with a moment of silence, followed by the ringing of six chimes, at 4:53 p.m.

Lynn University has now celebrated three Knights Unite Days of Caring, and the work that our campus does in remembrance of the Journey of Hope is remarkable. Most of the students who knew the six we lost have since graduated, but the work of those six continues to inspire incoming students who never even had the opportunity to meet them.

By January 2013, involvement in Knights Unite was so great that the day had evolved into an entire week. Members of the Lynn community participated in a number of projects, including packaging 24,000 meals for orphans in Haiti, collecting 400 pounds of canned foods for a local food bank, and removing 250 pounds of trash from local beaches. Classes and individuals also began creating their own service projects. One class raised money for a school run by a local charity in Nicaragua, and 10 Lynn community members completed a 14-mile run to raise funds for the Haiti Orphan Project.

Although Knights Unite is a symbolic way to remember and honor the lost members of the Journey of Hope, we also needed a place to make their story known at all times. On March 16, 2012, we were finally ready to unveil Remembrance Plaza, the memorial to the six—and all those lost in the Haiti earthquake—at the very heart of our campus.

The dedication day also included a very special academic ceremony, during which the families of the students were presented with posthumous degrees and those of the faculty members with honorary degrees. The parents of the four women never had the chance to see them graduate from Lynn, so this was a very meaningful and emotional moment for everyone.

It was a long path for our university to get to this point, and we consulted the families as we moved forward. First, our campus celebrated their lives at the university's memorial service, and next we celebrated their legacies through Knights Unite. Then, with the dedication of Remembrance Plaza, our university finally came together to permanently memorialize the lives of Dr. Hartwick, Dr. Bruno, Stephanie, Britney, Courtney, and Christine.

Even though the six are no longer with us, it is extremely important that we never forget them. We constructed Remembrance Plaza so that in our moments of pain, which still occur, we can go to that sacred place to find peace and comfort. We built it to inspire all on campus to live lives full of selfless acts and, most important, to remember the legacies of service and sacrifices left behind by the lost members of the Journey of Hope. As long as that memorial stands, their story will never be forgotten.

At the time of the dedication, more than 600 people had stepped forward and donated more than $1 million in cash, pledges, and gifts in kind and of service. Along with our donors, the architects and builders were able to finally bring this project to fruition.

When designing and constructing a project as significant as Remembrance Plaza, we faced the challenge of creating a memorial that truly represented those who were lost, six completely different people who became united through the Journey of Hope. We worked diligently with the architects, builders, and families, and the result was not just a structure of concrete, granite, and glass, but a sanctuary overflowing with beauty and symbolism.

We did not want a place just to remember the six, but a place where we could feel their presence. As visitors approach the entrance to Remembrance Plaza, they will pass six yellow flowering tabebuia trees. The number of trees represents the six we lost, and the yellow of the flowers represents their faith and friendship.

The entrance to the plaza is through a gated entryway, which represents the transition from the everyday world to a sacred place. The memorial is just off the main campus thoroughfare, across from the student center, and the entryway is on axis with the entry to the campus's Landgren Chapel. Directly east of the entryway is a solitary bench suspended over water, where visitors can contemplate with a sense of feeling suspended in space and thought.

The south end of the plaza is dedicated to the Journey of Hope and the island of Haiti. This spot features the story of the Journey of Hope, as well as a single royal palm, the national tree of Haiti.

Just to the north are the most prominent features of the memorial—six glass prisms, each dedicated to one of the six. The prisms of Dr. Hartwick and Dr. Bruno stand at the ends, flanking and guarding over the four students between them. The prisms represent the characters of Dr. Hartwick, Dr. Bruno, Stephanie, Britney, Courtney, and Christine and feature words of remembrance written by their families. These prisms were also built on a scale so that a mother and father could stand side by side and see their reflections on the face of the prism representing their daughter.

The triangular shapes point in the direction of Haiti, and the main faces of the triangles greet visitors upon entry. The prisms also continuously change color, and when they are transparent, they represent a spiritual presence. When they are mirror-like, they are a reflection of the visitor and the ability to see themselves in the six the memorial honors.

At the base of the prisms is a calm and steady flowing pool of water, and the backdrop is a continuous waterfall. These waters flow toward and across six steps before reaching a lake, symbolizing their return to campus. The six steps consist of a larger step at the top and bottom with four smaller steps in between. Once again, this represents the two faculty members flanking the four students because that is how they appeared in recovered photos from the trip.

Additionally, there are six benches in line with the prisms to sit and contemplate the past, present, and future, and a 10-foot-tall granite wall protects this area. At the north end of the plaza, there is also a wall dedicated to remembering other lost members of the university.

The Remembrance Plaza truly represents Dr. Hartwick, Dr. Bruno, Stephanie, Britney, Courtney, and Christine and serves as a place not only to remember the six but also to heal as a community. Remembrance Plaza ensures that their story is never forgotten, and along with Knights Unite, their legacies continue to live and inspire others to carry on their world-changing work.

And although students, faculty, and staff at Lynn have made an impact in communities at home and abroad, even more people are being affected through the spirits of the six. The families of Dr. Hartwick, Dr. Bruno, Stephanie, Britney, Courtney, and Christine have already done a tremendous deal of good in the names of their loved ones, and their remarkable work continues to make a difference in the lives of people around the world.

The Hayes family created the Courtney Hayes Memorial Fund, which has raised thousands of dollars to help pay bills and put food on the table for families in need in her hometown in Georgia. Christine's Hope for Kids, set up by the Gianacaci family, helps local kids in need in the United States have better lives, and the Stephanie Crispinelli Humanitarian Fund supports nonprofit, U.S.-based charities and carries on her passion for helping those in need. The Gengel family returned to Haiti to build an orphanage through their Be Like Brit organization. In January 2013, the family dedicated the structure in Grande Goave, Haiti, in their daughter's honor.

The loss of Lynn's two faculty members and four students in Haiti was truly tragic, and it was a situation from which our university will never fully heal. We have gone through a number of steps of recovery, but we will always have a deep sadness in our hearts for those we lost. However, instead of solely focusing on the sorrow of their loss, we have found strength in their spirits and have chosen to honor their legacies by continuing to make a difference in the world. We will never fully know the impact of the lives of Dr. Hartwick, Dr. Bruno, Stephanie, Britney, Courtney, and Christine, but we know that the world is a better place—and continues to be a better place—through the work that they did and the work that is now being done in their honor.

REFERENCES FOR FURTHER READING

Abraham, J. M. (2013). *Risk management: An accountability guide for university and college boards.* Washington, DC: AGB Press.

A look back: The bonfire tragedy at Texas A&M. (2007). *Strategies and Tactics, Public Relations Society of America.* Retrieved from http://www.prsa.org/SearchResults/view/945/105/A_look_back_The_Bonfire_tragedy_at_Texas_A_M#.UkSDhIasiSo

Arpan, L. M., & Roskos-Ewoldsen, D. R. (2005). Stealing thunder: An analysis of the effects of proactive disclosure of crisis information. *Public Relations Review, 31*(3), 425–433.

Blasts hit 3 New York skyscrapers. (1969, November 11). *Daily Register, 93*(96). Retrieved from http://209.212.22.88/data/rbr/1960-1969/1969/1969.11.11.pdf

Bonfire collapse. (2008). *CBS News.* Retrieved from http://www.youtube.com/watch?v=1g48S1KvzkE

Bornstein, R. (2013, April 29). How a president can rescue, or ruin, a college's reputation. *Chronicle of Higher Education.* Retrieved from http://chronicle.com/article/How-a-President-Can/138855/

Bowen, W., & Chambers, J. (2006, May 4). *The Duke administration's response to lacrosse allegations.* Retrieved from http://today.duke.edu/showcase/mmedia/pdf/Bowen-ChambersReportFinal05-04-06.pdf

Browing, A., Kubicek, K., Rigsby, S., & Roberts, J. (2010). Crisis management: How to stay out of court. *Parameters of Law in Student Affairs and Higher Education* (CNS 670). Paper 7.

Carlson, S. (2010, February 16). For a campus in crisis, the president's voice is key. *Chronicle of Higher Education.* Retrieved from http://chronicle.com/article/For-a-Campus-in-Crisis-the/64220/

Christian Science Monitor Editorial Board. (2012, September 6). Integrity and the Harvard cheating scandal. *Christian Science Monitor.*

Colloff, P. (Ed.). (2009). Bonfire: An oral history. *Texas Monthly*, 92–99 and 171–180.

Coombs, W. T. (1995). Choosing the right words: The development of guidelines for the selection of the "appropriate" crisis response strategies. *Management Communication Quarterly, 8*(4), 447–476.

Coombs, W. T. (2008). Campus crisis management: A comprehensive guide to planning, prevention, response, and recovery. *Journal of Higher Education, 79*(6), 724–726.

Coombs, W. T., & Holladay, S. J. (2005). An exploratory study of stakeholder emotions: Affect and crisis. In N. M. Ashkanasy, W. J. Zerbe, & C. E. J. Hartel (Eds.),

Research on emotion in organizations, Vol. 1: *The effect of affect in organizational settings* (pp. 271–288). New York: Elsevier.

Coombs, W. T., & Holladay, S. J. (Eds.). (2012). *The handbook of crisis communication.* Malden, MA: Wiley-Blackwell.

Cooper, J. C., & Glass, A. (Eds.). (2000). Special bonfire memorial issue. *Texas Aggie.*

Crisis response planning: A guide for conducting tabletop exercises. (2011). *From the UE Toolbox.* Retrieved from https://www.ue.org/learnue/riskmanagementlibrary.aspx

Crisis-sensitive educational planning. (2012, January–June). *IIEP Newsletter, 30*(1).

Deisinger, G., Randazzo, M., O'Neill, D., & Savage, J. (2008). *The handbook for campus threat assessment and management teams.* Stoneham, MA: Applied Risk Management, LLC.

Diamond, L., & Schneider, C. (2012, August 19). Will data deception damage Emory? *Atlanta Journal-Constitution.* Retrieved from http://www.ajc.com/news/news/local/will-data-deception-damage-emory/nRMLP/

Diermeier, D. (2011, January 1). CEOs must lead the way in reputation management. *PR Week.* Retrieved from http://www.prweekus.com/ceos-must-lead-the-way-in-reputation-management/article/193003/

Diermeier, D. (2011). *Reputation rules: Strategies for building your company's most valuable asset.* New York: McGraw-Hill.

Di Meglio, F. (2012, December 12). Amid ranking scandal, George Washington official steps down. *Bloomberg Businessweek.* Retrieved from http://www.businessweek.com/articles/2012-12-12/amid-ranking-scandal-george-washington-official-steps-down

Doorley, J., & Garcia, H. F. (2007). *Reputation management: The key to successful public relations and corporate communication.* New York: Routledge.

Dubois, P. L. (2006). Presidential leadership in times of crisis. In D. G. Brown (Ed.), *University presidents as moral leaders* (pp. 29–53). Westport, CT: ACE/Praeger.

Dufresne, R. L., & Clair, J. A. (2008). Moving beyond media feast and frenzy: Imagining possibilities for hyper-resilience arising from scandalous organizational crisis. *Law & Contemporary Problems, 71*(4), 201–214.

Emory announces findings in data review. (2012, August 23). *Emory News Center.* Retrieved from http://news.emory.edu/stories/2012/08/upress_data_review_statement/

Fearn-Banks, K. (2011a). *Crisis communications: A casebook approach* (4th ed.). New York: Routledge.

Fearn-Banks, K. (2011b). *Student workbook to accompany: Crisis communications: A casebook approach* (4th ed.). New York: Routledge.

Fisher, B. S., Hartman, J. L., Cullen, F. T., & Turner, M. G. (2002). Making campuses safer for students: The Clery Act as a symbolic legal reform. *Stetson Law Review, 32,* 61–89.

Fortunato, J. A. (2008). Restoring a reputation: The Duke University lacrosse scandal. *Public Relations Review, 34*(2), 116–123.

Freni, P. S. (2001). *Angels on the bonfire*. Lincoln, NE: iUniverse.com, Inc.

From crisis response to recovery. (2011). *Reason & Risk, 19*(1). Retrieved from https://www.ue.org/learnue/riskmanagementlibrary.aspx

Geddes, D. (2012). The fall of a lion. *Risk Management, 59*(3), 47–49.

Hemphill, B. O., & LaBanc, B. H. (2010). *Enough is enough: A student affairs perspective on preparedness and response to a campus shooting*. Sterling, VA: Stylus.

Hill, K. (2010, November 19). Can Duke fix its broken reputation? *Forbes*. Retrieved from http://www.forbes.com/sites/kashmirhill/2010/11/19/can-duke-fix-its-broken-reputation-2/

Human, R. J., Palit, M., & Simpson, D. M. (2006). Risk assessment and the disaster resistant university (DRU) program: The University of Louisville approach. *International Journal of Mass Emergencies and Disasters, 24*(2), 191–202.

Jablonski, M., McClellan, G., & Zdziarski, G. (2008). In search of safer communities: Emerging practices for student affairs in addressing campus violence. *New Directions for Student Services, 2008*(S1), 1–38.

Keehan, A. (2009, December). A guide to developing a campus crisis communications plan. *Risk Research Bulletin: Business and Academic Operations*. Retrieved from https://www.ue.org/learnue/riskmanagementlibrary.aspx

Kerlee, J. C. (2001). *A chance to say goodbye: Hope for grieving parents*. Lincoln, NE: iUniverse.com, Inc.

Leeper, K. A., & Leeper, R. V. (2006). Crisis in the college/university relationship with the community. *Journal of Promotion Management, 12*(3), 129–142. doi: 10.1300/J057v12n03_08

Len-Rios, M. E. (2010). Image repair strategies, local news portrayals and crisis stage: A case study of Duke University's lacrosse team crisis. *International Journal of Strategic Communication, 4*(4), 267–287. doi: 10.1080/1553118X.2010.515534

Mann, T. (2007). Strategic and collaborative crisis management: A partnership approach to large-scale crisis. *Planning for Higher Education, 36*(1), 54–64.

Matheson, K. (2013, April 2). Napolitano taps seven colleges for crisis prep programs. *Diverse: Issues in Higher Education*. Retrieved from http://diverseeducation.com/article/52343/

Mitroff, I. I., Diamond, M. A., & Alpaslan, C. M. (2006). *How prepared are America's colleges and universities for major crises? Assessing the state of crisis management*. Ann Arbor, MI: Society for College and University Planning. Retrieved from http://www.scup.org/page/knowledge/crisis-planning/diamond

Palen, L. (2008). Online social media in crisis events. *Educause Quarterly, 31*(3). Retrieved from http://www.educause.edu/ero/article/online-social-media-crisis-events

Pérez-Peña, R. (2012, November 11). Sexual assaults roil Amherst, and college president welcomes controversy. *New York Times*, A19.

Pettigrew, H. (2012). Keeping campus informed and prepared: The Clery Act's timely warning and emergency notification requirements. *Risk Research Bulletin: Student Affairs*. Retrieved from https://www.ue.org/learnue/riskmanagementlibrary.aspx

Rinella, S. D. (2007). *The presidential role in disaster planning and response: Lessons from the front.* Ann Arbor, MI: Society for College and University Planning. Retrieved from http://www.scup.org/asset/48682/scup-heery-lessonsfromthefront.pdf

Remembering bonfire. Retrieved from http://bonfire.tamu.edu/

Scheider, T. (2010). *Mass notification for higher education.* Washington, DC: National Clearinghouse for Educational Facilities. Retrieved from http://www.ncef.org/pubs/notification.pdf

Schwartz, M. P. (2012, January/February). The big risk in not assessing risk. *AGB Trusteeship, 1*(20), 40–41.

Shaw, M. D., & Davis, L. K. (2011, March). Preparing for campus disasters: Best practices and suggested steps. Presentation at the American College Personnel Association Annual Conference, Baltimore, MD.

Simpson, C. (2007). *Weathering the storm: Protecting your brand in the worst of times.* Washington, DC: Council for the Advancement and Support of Education.

Sokolow, B. A., Lewis, W. S., Wolf, C. R., Van Brunt, B., & Byrnes, J. D. (2009). *Threat assessment in the campus setting.* National Behavioral Intervention Team Association (NaBITA) white paper. Retrieved from http://nabita.org/docs/2009NABITAwhitepaper.pdf

Staff Editorial. (2012, December 3). GW must set the record straight. *GW Hatchet.* Retrieved from http://www.gwhatchet.com/2012/12/03/staff-editorial-gw-must-set-the-record-straight/

Strengthen your crisis management plan with regular exercise. (2006, September). *Risk Research Bulletin: Business and Academic Operations.* Retrieved from https://www.ue.org/learnue/riskmanagementlibrary.aspx

Subotnik, D. (2012). The Duke rape case five years later: Lessons for the academy, the media, and the criminal justice system. *Akron Law Review, 45*(4), 883–921.

Towns, G. (2013, April). Weathering the superstorm. *Currents.* Retrieved from http://www.case.org/Publications_and_Products/2013/April_2013/Weathering_the_Superstorm.html

Ulmer, R. R., Sellnow, T. L., & Seeger, M. (Eds.). (2011). *Effective crisis communication: Moving from crisis to opportunity* (2nd ed.). Thousand Oaks, CA: Sage.

Using social media in a crisis: Higher education results. (2012). Washington, DC: CASE/CKSyme.org. Retrieved from http://cksymedotorg.files.wordpress.com/2012/02/case-cksyme-higher-ed-2012-using-social-media-in-a-crisis.pdf

Using your website to inform the campus community in a crisis. (2005, May). *Risk Research Bulletin: Business and Academic Operations.* Retrieved from https://www.ue.org/learnue/riskmanagementlibrary.aspx

Van Brunt, B. (2012). *Ending campus violence: New approaches to prevention.* New York: Routledge.

Wang, J., & Hutchins, H. M. (2010). Crisis management in higher education: What have we learned from Virginia Tech? *Advances in Developing Human Resources, 12*(5), 552–572.

White, L. (2012, January/February). Governing during an institutional crisis: 10 fundamental principles. *AGB Trusteeship, 1*(20), 34–37.

Winston, H. (2013, September 13). Crisis management on campuses in the age of social media. *Chronicle of Higher Education.* Retrieved from http://chronicle.com/blogs/wiredcampus/crisis-management-on-campuses-in-the-age-of-social-media/46567

You asked UE: Risk management questions and answers: Apologies and expressions of empathy. (2012). Chevy Chase, MD: United Educators.

Zaremba, A. J. (2010). *Crisis communication: Theory and practice.* Armonk, NY: M. E. Sharpe, Inc.

Zdziarski, E. L., Dunkel, N. W., & Rollo, J. M. (2007). *Campus crisis management: A comprehensive guide to planning, prevention, response and recovery.* Hoboken, NJ: John Wiley & Sons.

ADDITIONAL RESOURCES

Action Guide for Emergency Management at Institutions of Higher Education. (2010). Washington, DC: Office of Safe and Drug-Free Schools, U.S. Department of Education. http://rems.ed.gov/docs/REMS_ActionGuide.pdf

This report, produced by the U.S. Department of Education, discusses the need for emergency management on college campuses and provides detailed guidance as well as best practices for developing and implementing an effective emergency management plan.

Campus Safety. www.campussafetymagazine.com

Campus Safety (CS) magazine exclusively serves campus police chiefs, security directors, information technology personnel, emergency managers, and executive administrators involved in public safety and security of major hospitals, schools, and universities in the United States. CS is a product of Bobit Business Media, a business-to-business publishing company based in Torrance, CA. The print version is issued nine times per year and is distributed to more than 18,000 campus security professionals nationwide.

Clery Center for Security on Campus. www.securityoncampus.org

The Clery Center for Security on Campus is a nonprofit 501(c)(3) dedicated to preventing violence, substance abuse, and other crimes on college and university campuses across the United States and to compassionately assisting the victims of these crimes. It provides a model for social change built on the fundamental belief that collaboration among key stakeholders will create safer campus communities. It embodies advocacy, education and training, and policy recommendations.

Comprehensive Preparedness Guide 101—Developing and Maintaining Emergency Operations Plans, Version 2. (2010). Washington, DC: Federal Emergency Management Agency. www.fema.gov/media-library/assets/documents/25975.

The Comprehensive Preparedness Guide (CPG) 101 provides guidelines on developing emergency operations plans (EOP). It promotes a common understanding of the fundamentals of risk-informed planning and decision making to help planners examine a hazard or threat and produce integrated, coordinated, and synchronized plans.

Disaster Preparedness and Emergency Response Association. www.disasters.org

The Disaster Preparedness and Emergency Response Association (DERA) is a membership organization founded in 1962 as a nonprofit association linking professionals, volunteers, and organizations active in all phases of disaster preparedness and emergency management. DERA remains an independent, nongovernmental organization with dual missions of professional support and disaster service.

Emergency Alert System. www.fema.gov/emergency-alert-system

The Emergency Alert System (EAS) is used by alerting authorities to send warnings via broadcast, cable, satellite, and wireline communications pathways. Emergency Alert System participants, which consist of broadcast, cable, satellite, and wireline providers, are the stewards of this important public service in close partnership with alerting officials at all levels of government. The EAS is also used when all other means of alerting the public are unavailable, providing an added layer of resiliency to the suite of available emergency communication tools.

Family Educational Rights and Privacy Act. www.ed.gov/policy/gen/guid/fpco/ferpa/index.html

The Family Educational Rights and Privacy Act (FERPA) (20 U.S.C. § 1232g; 34 CFR Part 99) is a federal law that protects the privacy of student education records. The law applies to all schools that receive funds under an applicable program of the U.S. Department of Education. FERPA gives parents certain rights with respect to their children's education records. These rights transfer to the student when he or she reaches the age of 18 or attends a school beyond the high school level.

Federal Emergency Management Agency. www.fema.gov

The Federal Emergency Management Agency (FEMA) is an agency of the U.S. Department of Homeland Security initially created by Presidential Reorganization Plan No. 3 of 1978 and implemented by two Executive Orders on April 1, 1979. The agency's primary purpose is to coordinate the response to a disaster that has occurred in the United States and that overwhelms the resources of local and state authorities. The governor of the state in which the disaster occurs must declare a state of emergency and formally request from the president of the United States that FEMA and the federal government respond to the disaster. Although on-the-ground support of disaster recovery efforts is a major part of FEMA's charter, the agency provides state and local governments with experts in specialized fields and funding for rebuilding efforts. In addition, FEMA provides funds for training of response personnel throughout the United States as part of the agency's preparedness efforts.

The Handbook for Campus Safety and Security Reporting. (2011). Washington, DC: U.S. Department of Education, Office of Postsecondary Education. http://www2.ed.gov/admins/lead/safety/handbook.pdf.

This new version of the handbook is about the amended Clery Act and the new regulations that were added by the Higher Education Opportunity Act. The handbook explains what the regulations mean and what they require of institutions. It also includes new examples and enhanced explanations of many topics based on questions asked of the Campus Safety and Security Help over the past several years. The handbook emphasizes compliance as a whole system of developing policy statements, gathering information from a variety of sources and translating it into the appropriate categories, issuing alerts, disseminating information, and finally, keeping records.

Incident Command System. www.fema.gov/incident-command-system

The Incident Command System (ICS) is a standardized, on-scene, all-hazards incident management approach that allows for the integration of facilities, equipment, personnel, procedures, and communications operating within a common organizational structure; enables a coordinated response among various jurisdictions and functional agencies, both public and private; and establishes common processes for planning and managing resources.

International Association of Campus Law Enforcement Administrators. www.iaclea.org

The International Association of Campus Law Enforcement Administrators (IACLEA) advances public safety for educational institutions by providing educational resources, advocacy, and professional development services. IACLEA is the leading voice for the campus public safety community. It serves as a clearinghouse for information and issues, shared by campus public safety directors, and represents more than 1,200 colleges and universities.

Jeanne Clery Disclosure of Campus Security Policy and Campus Crime Statistics Act (20 USC § 1092(f)). http://clerycenter.org/jeanne-clery-act

This is the landmark federal law, originally known as the Campus Security Act, that requires colleges and universities across the United States to disclose information about crime on and around their campuses. The law is tied to an institution's participation in federal student aid programs, and it applies to most institutions of higher education both public and private. The act is enforced by the U.S. Department of Education. The law was amended in 1992 to add a requirement that schools afford the victims of campus sexual assault certain basic rights and was amended again in 1998 to expand the reporting requirements. The 1998 amendments also formally named the law in memory of Jeanne Clery. Subsequent amendments in 2000 and 2008 added provisions dealing with registered sex offender notification and campus emergency response. The 2008 amendments also added a provision to protect crime victims, whistleblowers, and others from retaliation.

National Clearinghouse for Educational Facilities. www.ncef.org/rl/disaster.cfm

This is an archived site that provides information on building or retrofitting schools to withstand natural disasters and terrorism, developing emergency preparedness plans, and using school buildings to shelter community members during emergencies.

National Incident Management System. www.fema.gov/national-incident-management-system

The Natinal Incident Management System (NIMS) is a comprehensive, national approach to incident management and provides the template for incident management, regardless of cause, size, location, or complexity. NIMS is applicable at all jurisdictional levels and across functional disciplines. NIMS emphasizes a standardized approach to incident management that is scalable and flexible with enhanced cooperation and interoperability among responders. NIMS reflects the best practices and lessons learned.

National Preparedness Directorate. www.training.fema.gov

The National Preparedness Directorate online course catalog provides searchable, integrated information on courses provided or managed by FEMA's Center for Domestic Preparedness, Emergency Management Institute, and National Training and Education Division.

National Transportation Safety Board. www.ntsb.gov

In 1974, Congress reestablished the National Transportation Safety Board (NTSB) as a separate entity, outside of the Department of Transportaion. The NTSB has no authority to regulate, fund, or be directly involved in the operation of any mode of transportation and so conducts investigations and makes recommendations from an objective viewpoint. In 1996, Congress assigned the NTSB the additional responsibility of coordinating federal assistance to families of aviation accident victims. The program has expanded to provide assistance in all modes of transportation on a case-by-case basis.

***Report of the Special Investigative Counsel Regarding the Actions of the Pennsylvania State University Related to the Child Sexual Abuse Committed by Gerald A. Sandusky* (Freeh Report).** (2012, July 12). Philadelphia: Freeh Sporkin & Sullivan, LLP. http://progress.psu.edu/assets/content/REPORT_FINAL_071212.pdf

This is the report of the Special Investigations Task Force that operated on behalf of the Pennsylvania State University Board of Trustees to perform an independent investigation of the alleged failure of university personnel to respond to and report to the appropriate authorities the sexual abuse of children and to make recommendations for policy changes to ensure such actions are not repeated.

Title IX. www.dol.gov/oasam/regs/statutes/titleix.htm

This federal legislation requires that no person in the United States shall, on the basis of sex, be excluded from participation in, be denied the benefits of, or be subjected to discrimination under any education program or activity receiving federal financial assistance. Although there are some exceptions, in general, this legislation requires that there be no gender discrimination in admissions or programs in educational institutions.

United Educators. www.ue.org

United Educators (UE) is a reciprocal risk retention group, a licensed insurance company owned and governed by 1,200 member colleges, universities, independent schools, public school districts, public school insurance pools, and related organizations throughout the United States. UE is committed to helping educational institutions address risk management and claims handling and is backed by a long history of involvement in higher education.

U.S. Environmental Protection Agency. www.epa.gov

The Environmental Protection Agency provides policies, guidance, and support for institutions and communities to ensure safe environments. Topics include human health, water, contaminants, scientific studies, and weather-related incidents.

U.S. Sentencing Commission Guidelines Manual. (2013). Washington, DC: U.S. Sentencing Commission. www.ussc.gov/Guidelines/2013_Guidelines/index.cfm

The U.S. Sentencing Commission is an independent agency in the judicial branch of government. Its principal purposes are (a) to establish sentencing policies and practices for the federal courts, including guidelines to be consulted regarding the appropriate form and severity of punishment for offenders convicted of federal crimes; (b) to advise and assist Congress and the executive branch in the development of effective and efficient crime policy; and (c) to collect, analyze, research, and distribute a broad array of information on federal crime and sentencing issues, serving as an information resource for Congress, the executive branch, the courts, criminal justice practitioners, the academic community, and the public.

EDITORS AND CONTRIBUTORS

Editors

Gretchen M. Bataille is president of GMB Consulting Group and a strategic partner with ROI Consulting Group. She served as the senior vice president for Leadership and Lifelong Learning for the American Council on Education (ACE) from 2011 to 2013, and from 2006 to 2010, she was president of the University of North Texas, a research university with more than 36,000 students and more than 250 degree programs. She was senior vice president of the University of North Carolina system from 2000 to 2006 and served in other administrative roles at Arizona State University; University of California, Santa Barbara; and Washington State University. Bataille has served as a member of the Board of Trustees of the College Board as well as a board member for ACE. She is a member of the Board of Directors for SAGE Publications and serves as a trustee for Drake University. Among her many publications are articles about faculty and administrative experiences, including *Faculty Career Paths: Multiple Routes to Academic Success and Satisfaction.*

Diana I. Cordova is clinical professor of executive education and academic director of the Kellogg Executive Leadership Institute (KELI) at the Kellogg School of Management, Northwestern University. Prior to joining Kellogg in 2013, Cordova served as vice president for Leadership Programs at the American Council on Education (ACE), where she was responsible for all leadership programs and initiatives, including the ACE Institute for New Presidents. From 1994 to 2000, she served on the psychology department faculty at Yale University and was awarded the 1999 Lex Hixon '63 Prize for Teaching Excellence in the Social Sciences. Cordova also served as assistant dean of the Yale Graduate School of Arts and Sciences from 2000 to 2003 and as acting associate commissioner of the National Center for Education Research, U.S. Department of Education. She holds a PhD in social psychology from Stanford University and a BA from Smith College.

Foreword Author

John G. Peters, president emeritus of Northern Illinois University (NIU), served as the 11th president from June 2000 to June 2013. As NIU's chief executive officer, Peters provided strategic direction and oversight for a nationally recognized, comprehensive university serving more than 23,000 students in 120 areas of study at both undergraduate and graduate levels. Under his leadership, NIU expanded and refined its institutional vision to more closely align teaching, research, and outreach efforts with the emerging needs of the northern Illinois region. He is nationally recognized for his leadership in the face of crisis, having led NIU's response and recovery following a tragic February 14, 2008, shooting on campus. In 2009, the Public Relations Society of America (PRSA) honored NIU with the Silver Anvil Award for the university's crisis communications response. Peters holds a bachelor's degree from John Carroll University (Ohio), a master's degree from Ohio University, and a doctorate in political science from the University of Illinois, Urbana-Champaign.

Contributors

Janice M. Abraham joined United Educators Insurance (UE), a reciprocal risk retention group, as president and CEO in 1998. During Abraham's tenure, UE has become known as the premier risk management and liability insurance expert serving educational institutions. Prior to joining UE, Abraham served the higher education community through her work as chief financial officer/treasurer at Whitman College and various senior positions at Cornell University. She serves as a trustee of Whitman College. In 2013, her book, *Risk Management: An Accountability Guide for University and College Boards* was published. Abraham earned an MBA from the Wharton School at the University of Pennsylvania and a bachelor's degree in international service from American University.

Lee E. Bird serves as the vice president for student affairs at Oklahoma State University (OSU), Stillwater, and has worked in some aspect of student affairs for 34 years. Bird has authored and coauthored several book chapters on responding to emergencies. She consults and speaks regularly on topics such as campus threat assessment and crisis management. She chairs the OSU Behavioral Consultation Team and is a FEMA CERT and incident command instructor. She previously served as the vice president of the Colorado chapter of the Association of Threat Assessment Professionals.

Bonita J. Brown serves as the chief of staff and assistant secretary to the board at the University of North Carolina, Greensboro (UNCG). Prior to joining UNCG, she served as chief of staff to the president at the University of North Texas, where she created the University Policy Office and the

University Office of Compliance and shared the supervision of the Emergency Management Division. She is an attorney by trade and has served as general counsel and assistant university counsel at two public universities in the University of North Carolina system. She is a graduate of the Harvard Institutes for Higher Education and has taught a graduate class in higher education law. She received her undergraduate degree in history from Wake Forest University and her juris doctorate from Wake Forest University School of Law.

Carol A. Cartwright served as president of Kent State University from 1991 to 2006. Her appointment in 1991 made history because she was the first female to be selected as president of a public college or university in Ohio. She served a three-year term as president of Bowling Green State University from 2008 to 2011. Prior to her presidency at Kent State, she was vice chancellor for academic affairs at the University of California, Davis, and dean for undergraduate programs and vice provost of the Pennsylvania State University. She earned master's and doctoral degrees from the University of Pittsburgh and her bachelor's degree from the University of Wisconsin, Whitewater.

Judy Genshaft was appointed president of the University of South Florida (USF) system in July 2000. During Dr. Genshaft's presidency, the USF system has been nationally recognized as a top-50 research university among both public and private institutions. The USF system serves more than 47,000 students in more than 232 degree programs. Nationally, President Genshaft has chaired the NCAA Division I Board of Directors and is a past chair of the American Council on Education. She is a member of the Association of Public and Land-grant Universities Board and is a former chair of the American Athletic Conference (formerly Big East) Council of Presidents. President Genshaft is a native of Ohio and earned her baccalaureate degree at the University of Wisconsin, Madison, and both her master's and doctoral degrees from Kent State University.

Connie J. Gores became the ninth president of Southwest Minnesota State University on July 1, 2013, the first woman to hold the position. President Gores earned her PhD from the University of Washington, her master's degree from Colorado State University, and her bachelor's degree from North Dakota State University. She has served at the cabinet level at Winona State University, Randolph Macon Woman's College, and Cornish College of the Arts. She has also held posts at Willamette University College of Law and Portland State University. In collaboration with colleagues at Harvard University, she coauthored a case study on leading during a campus crisis that is used in

Harvard's Crisis Leadership in Higher Education program. President Gores serves on the Women's Network Executive Council of the American Council on Education and presents regularly across the country on leadership topics.

Burns Hargis was named the 18th president of Oklahoma State University (OSU) and the OSU system in December 2007. President Hargis holds degrees in accounting from Oklahoma State University and in law from the University of Oklahoma. Hargis oversees one of the nation's most comprehensive land-grant university systems with more than 37,000 students, 7,400 employees, and campuses located in Stillwater, Tulsa, Oklahoma City, and Okmulgee. Hargis served as vice chairman of the Oklahoma State Election Board and the Oklahoma Constitutional Revision Commission and served as chairman of the Oklahoma Commission for Human Services. He is a former member of the Commission of the North Central Association of Colleges and Schools. Hargis received the state's highest honor when he was inducted into the Oklahoma Hall of Fame in 2009.

Dianne F. Harrison began her appointment as president of California State University, Northridge, in June 2012. Prior to her appointment, she served as president of California State University, Monterey Bay, from 2006 to 2012 and began her academic and higher education leadership career at Florida State University. President Harrison is known for her commitment to students, academic excellence, and comprehensive development and for building strong community partnerships. Her service on boards and committees includes the Steering Committee of the American College and University President's Climate Commitment, the Board of the Association of American Colleges and Universities, and the NCAA Division I Committee on Institutional Performance. She holds a PhD in social work from Washington University in St. Louis and a master's of social work and a bachelor's in American studies from the University of Alabama. Her areas of expertise include HIV prevention and higher education leadership issues.

Lawrence G. Hincker has been head of Virginia Tech University Relations since 1989. Hincker is responsible for all institution-wide communications. He serves as the university spokesperson and senior communications official responsible for marketing, public relations, issues management, and institutional positioning, including the university-wide branding effort, Invent the Future. He was the university spokesperson and public face of Virginia Tech as it dealt with the largest media gathering on any university campus after the murders of April 16, 2007. Before coming to Virginia Tech, Hincker worked for 14 years in various corporate communications positions.

Cynthia Lawson has more than 30 years of public relations and communications experience in higher education and at a Fortune 500 company. She serves as vice president for Public Relations and Communications at DePaul University. She also is a guest speaker at Harvard's Crisis Leadership in Higher Education, provides crisis consultation to university leaders, and has provided numerous webinars on crisis communications. Her handling of crisis communications during the 1999 Texas A&M bonfire collapse brought her praise from reporters at CNN, CBS, NBC, and ABC, who stated that she handled the crisis "as well or better than the Tylenol crisis." Lawson received both her BA Ed and MA Ed degrees from the University of Michigan. She also is a graduate of Harvard University's Institute for Educational Management.

Harold Lee Martin Sr. was elected the 12th chancellor of North Carolina Agricultural and Technical State University and assumed his position on June 8, 2009. Since his arrival, Chancellor Martin has been instrumental in the development of North Carolina A&T's Preeminence 2020 strategic plan and the opening of the Joint School of Nanoscience and Nanoengineering at the Gateway University Research Park (South Campus), and he played a significant role in Opportunity Greensboro, the city's most recent alliance between the seven colleges and universities and the business community. Before becoming chancellor at A&T, Martin served as the senior vice president for academic affairs for the University of North Carolina system, assuming the post in July 2006. Martin also served as chancellor of Winston-Salem State University from January 2000 to July 2006. Martin holds a bachelor's and a master of science degree in electrical engineering from A&T and a doctorate in electrical engineering from Virginia Polytechnic Institute and State University.

Sally Mason became the 20th president of the University of Iowa on August 1, 2007. Trained as a cell developmental biologist, she is a full professor in the Department of Biology of the College of Liberal Arts and Sciences. She served as dean of the College of Liberal Arts and Sciences at the University of Kansas and as provost of Purdue University prior to her presidency. President Mason has published many scientific papers and has obtained research grants from the National Science Foundation, the National Institutes of Health, the Wesley Research Foundation, and the Lilly Endowment. She has served or is currently serving in leadership roles in such organizations as the Council of Colleges of Arts and Sciences, the National Science Foundation Directorate for Education and Human Resources, the Association of Public and Land-grant Universities (APLU), the American Council on Education (ACE), the Universities Research Association, Campus Compact, the Committee on Institutional Cooperation (CIC), the Big Ten Council of Presidents and

Chancellors, the Herbert Hoover Presidential Library Association, the Task Force on National Energy Policy and Midwestern Competitiveness of the Chicago Council on Global Affairs, and the National Medal of Science President's Committee.

Mark D. Nelson is vice president for student affairs and vice provost for academic affairs at the University of Alabama. He is also a professor of communication studies. His area of expertise is in organizational communication and leadership development. He has coauthored two books, and he has designed and provided consulting services for many organizations throughout the United States. In his dual appointment, he works to foster a collaborative relationship between student affairs and academic affairs.

Patrick T. O'Rourke serves as vice president, university counsel, and secretary of the University of Colorado Board of Regents. He has been with the University of Colorado since 2005 and most recently served as managing senior associate university counsel for the University of Colorado's litigation office. During this time, he was responsible for the trials of some of the university's highest-profile cases. Before joining the University of Colorado, O'Rourke was a director of the law firm Montgomery Little & McGrew, P.C., in Englewood, Colorado. He has represented clients in a broad range of lawsuits, including class actions, employment law, civil rights, professional liability, and product liability. O'Rourke received his undergraduate degree from Creighton University and his law degree from the Georgetown University Law Center. He is a frequent lecturer on the subjects of health care law, professional liability, legal ethics, and appellate practice.

Brenda D. Phillips is professor of sociology and associate dean of Ohio University, Chillicothe. Prior to joining Ohio University, Chillicothe, she served as professor of emergency management at Oklahoma State University and as senior researcher with the Center for the Study of Disasters and Extreme Events. Phillips serves as a subject matter expert for the Office of the Federal Coordinator of Meteorology and the Oklahoma Voluntary Organizations Active in Disaster. She has served on the boards of OK-First and the Oklahoma Office of Homeland Security Citizen Corps. She has published extensively from multiple National Science Foundation grants and is the author of *Social Vulnerability to Disasters, Disaster Recovery*, and *Introduction to Emergency Management.*

Nicole M. Pride is the interim vice chancellor for university advancement at North Carolina Agricultural and Technical State University, where she is responsible for the university's fund-raising efforts and for establishing, defining, and protecting the university's image. Prior to joining North Carolina A&T, Pride served as vice president for development and communications for the Child Care Services Association in Chapel Hill, North Carolina. For almost a decade, she also served in numerous capacities at IBM, including marketing program manager, corporate learning division, and manager of corporate community relations and public affairs. Before IBM, she served as an assistant director of alumni relations at Fairleigh Dickinson University. Pride received her BA in business management and BA in economics from North Carolina State University and her MA in corporate and public communications from Seton Hall University.

Kevin M. Ross became the fifth president of Lynn University on July 1, 2006. Under his leadership, the university has made significant strides, including redesigning its core curriculum, the Dialogues of Learning; receiving a *U.S. News & World Report* ranking as one of the top schools in the country for highest percentage of international students; and being selected as the host site for the third and final 2012 presidential debate. The university was also recently recognized as an Apple Distinguished School for its iPad Mini initiative, one of the most extensive tablet-based learning efforts in the country. Ross received his BA in English from Colgate University, MA in liberal arts from St. John's College, and doctorate in higher education leadership and policy from Peabody College of Vanderbilt University.

Dolores Stafford, the president and CEO of D. Stafford & Associates, has been providing consulting services since 1997. D. Stafford & Associates is a professional services firm specializing in safety and security-related issues on college campuses, including a specialization in Clery Act/Higher Education Opportunity Act compliance issues. As an active practitioner for more than 26 years, Stafford assists client institutions in assessing the security, safety, and federal compliance on their campuses. Stafford was in law enforcement at the George Washington (GW) University, Butler University, and Bucknell University for 23 years and served as the chief of police at GW from 1992 to 2010. Stafford has twenty years of experience overseeing a sexual assault crisis response team at GW and Butler Universities that she implemented and managed at both institutions. She has a bachelor's degree in criminal justice from Mansfield University and has a master's of science in education from Bucknell University.

Joseph Urgo is a senior fellow with the Association of American Colleges and Universities in residence as a visiting research professor at the University of

North Carolina, Asheville. He has served as president of St. Mary's College of Maryland (2010–2013), dean of faculty at Hamilton College (2006–2010), and chair of the Department of English at the University of Mississippi (2000–2006). He came through the faculty ranks at Bryant University. Urgo is the author or editor of more than a dozen scholarly books and writes frequently on issues in higher education.

Teresa Valerio Parrot is principal of TVP Communications, where she applies her expertise in higher education media, crisis communications, marketing, and administration to provide data-driven strategy and counsel to clients. Previously, Valerio Parrot served as senior vice president for Widmeyer Communications' higher education practice and vice president of media relations and crisis communications for Simpson Scarborough. Valerio Parrot counts almost 10 years of experience with the University of Colorado system, including an officer-level appointment as assistant secretary of the university. She earned a bachelor's degree from the University of Colorado, Boulder, and a master's degree from the University of Colorado, Denver.

J. Charles Waldrup is general counsel at North Carolina Agricultural and Technical State University. He was previously an associate vice president for legal affairs at the University of North Carolina (UNC) system's General Administration and before that a special deputy attorney general for UNC Hospitals. He earned both his law degree and doctorate in history from the University of North Carolina, Chapel Hill.

INDEX

"This hefty volume consists of short articles about an amazingly wide array of topics in higher education and will be a welcome reference work for professionals in the field as well as trustees and donors. Those who need to know something quickly about an aspect of higher education that is outside their immediate experience will find the succinct treatment and comprehensive approach of great value. Each section also includes a lengthy bibliography for those who wish to learn more."

—Richard Ekman,
President, Council of Independent Colleges

22883 Quicksilver Drive
Sterling, VA 20166-2102

Subscribe to our e-mail alerts: www.Styluspub.com

Also available from Stylus

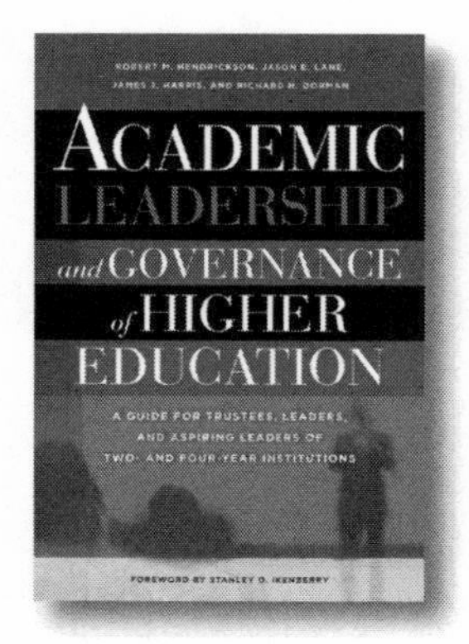

Academic Leadership and Governance of Higher Education

A Guide for Trustees, Leaders, and Aspiring Leaders of Two- and Four-Year Institutions

Robert M. Hendrickson, Jason E. Lane, James T. Harris, and Richard H. Dorman

Foreword by Stanley O. Ikenberry

"The book is content rich for those looking for detailed background information on a wide range of topics. The list is far too long to repeat here, but suffice it to say that this is a comprehensive work that addresses issues related to organizational dynamics, policy frameworks, government interests, academic programs, faculty responsibilities, trusteeship, global education, legal matters, strategic planning, and, of course, student success. If there is one comprehensive text you are prepared to study about higher education, make it this one."

—***The Department Chair***

"Enabling our colleges and universities to reach their highest academic and economic potential requires a commitment to the core values of higher education and to cultivating the partnerships in community, business, and government that allow us to bring those values to scale. *Academic Leadership and Governance of Higher Education* is a mindful handbook that leaders will find themselves referring back to often as the mission of higher education continues to evolve."

—***Nancy L. Zimpher,***
Chancellor, State University of New York

"This encyclopedic compendium of the history and challenges of virtually all aspects of higher education will serve as a handy reference for academic leaders and scholars. It should find a place in all college and university libraries as well as in the personal libraries of presidents. The book's perspective is that, to be successful, academic leaders must be focused on vision, mission, and core values; be able to adapt to a rapidly changing environment; and include key constituents in decision-making. The book is an important contribution to the higher-education literature."

—***Rita Bornstein,***
President Emerita and Cornell Professor of Philanthropy & Leadership Development, Rollins College